INDUSTRIAL
SCHEDULING
TECHNIQUES

DENNIS LOCK

INDUSTRIAL SCHEDULING TECHNIQUES

Gower Press

First published in Britain in 1971 by Gower Press Limited
140 Great Portland Street, London W1N 5TA

© Dennis Lock
ISBN 0 7161 0066 5

Set in 11 on 13 point Times and printed in England by
A. Wheaton & Co., Exeter

CONTENTS

ILLUSTRATIONS

ACKNOWLEDGEMENTS

Acknowledgements are due to the following companies for their advice and material assistance in the preparation of this book:

BARIC Computing Services Limited
CalComp Limited
Herbert-Ingersoll Limited
Industrial Development and Construction Limited
Ingersoll Milling Machine Company (USA)
International Computers Limited
K and H Business Consultants Limited
Time Sharing Limited

I

NEED FOR SCHEDULING

Successful completion of any project can usually be assessed by considering three basic factors. Foremost among these is the functional objective. This, for example, might be a technical specification for a machine, architectural requirements for a new building or the strategic effectiveness of a military defence system. The only likely exception to this rule would be a program set up for pure research, where the outcome is unpredictable and an unexpected result could herald a major scientific discovery.

The second basic factor for success is that the funds set aside for a project must not be overspent. For industrial projects this condition is obvious, because trading profits will be reduced or converted into losses if estimates are exceeded. Most other projects, however, must be governed by strict budgets, either to control the amount of capital invested or to protect public funds.

COMMERCIAL SIGNIFICANCE OF TIMESCALE

Timescale is the third condition for success. Any industrial project finished late will almost certainly result in erosion of planned profits, quite apart from the irreparable damage to customer goodwill. Unexpected delays usually result in unwelcome additions to fixed manufacturing expenses, with space, plant and men committed beyond the economic timespan. These effects will be cumulative, causing disruption to following projects because resources are not released when they are needed.

Many industrial contracts contain penalty clauses, which provide for progressive reductions in price for every day or week by which completion lags behind the agreed date. In any case, final invoicing will be delayed, and this will have the effect of increasing the amount of working capital tied up in work in progress.

As the trend continues for industrial projects to grow more complex, customers are becoming increasingly particular about the capability of contracting firms to meet their promised delivery dates. In some cases, a reliable guarantee of delivery can win an order for a supplier in the face of competition from lower-priced competitors, even where these can demonstrate equal technical competence.

One could imagine, for example, a company wishing to purchase plant necessary for the manufacture of a new product. Such expenditure represents an outlay of capital that must normally be justified by a predetermined level of financial return. The net value of any earnings is dependant to a large extent on the time interval which elapses between spending the money and reaping the reward. The mechanics of such calculations take into account the principle that money available for immediate use is worth more than a sum of the same face value recovered in one or more years' time. This is because of the potential value of interest which money could earn each year, if it were immediately invested. This is, of course, the basis for discounted cash flow calculations (see *Director's Guide to Management Techniques*, Gower Press, 1970).

Timing, therefore, is a highly sensitive factor in launching a new product. Apart from the cash flow considerations, the market itself will probably be very sensitive to the time at which a product is introduced. Seasonal variations, annual trade exhibitions, fashion changes and the efforts of competitors can all dictate the best time for a company to attempt promotion of a new model, or new product range.

Now consider a particular example. In order to achieve his objectives, a manufacturer must have all of his new plant in operation by June 1972. Accordingly, he has invited tenders from several potential suppliers, specifying delivery of the complete plant by 1 May 1972. The situation is illustrated in Figure 1:1, and it is seen that three firms, *A*, *B* and *C* have submitted fixed-price quotations. All competitors claim to be able to meet the delivery requirement.

The purchaser, however, has some knowledge of the actual delivery capabilities of these bidders, based on their reputations and performance in the past. Accordingly, their delivery promises must be questioned, and subjected to some form of appraisal. In this example, the purchaser has been able to make an estimate of the likely actual delivery dates which would result if he placed his order with each bidder. The cost of delaying the start of production has also been calculated, and found to be £25 000 for each full month lost. The basis of such calculations is often complex, and open to debate. For the purposes of illustrating this case, it can be classed as the loss of earnings for the period of delay.

	FIRM A	FIRM B	FIRM C
Last date for tender	1 Jan 71	1 Jan 71	1 Jan 71
Fixed price bids received	£225 000	£250 000	£215 000
Delivery promises received against request for 1 May 1972	1 May 72	1 May 72	1 May 72
Expected actual delivery date, based on previous experience of bidders and their reputations	1 Jul 72	1 May 72	1 Aug 72
Calculated cost of each month's delay in starting up production	£25 000	£25 000	£25 000
Calculated cost of expected delay in starting up new production	£50 000	0	£100 000
Recovery from penalty clause @ £10 000 a month	£20 000	0	£40 000
Estimated cost of lateness	£30 000	0	£60 000
Likely total cost of order	£255 000	£250 000	£275 000

FIGURE 1:1 A PURCHASE DECISION TABLE BASED ON PRICE AND DELIVERY

When a purchaser is choosing new plant, he will consider delivery in addition to price and technical specifications. It is possible to place some value on the cost of delays in delivery, and if these are taken into account they can reverse price differences in the original quotations. Here, for example, Firm *B* submitted the highest price, but because they have a proven record of reliable delivery promises, their quotation is expected to result in the cheapest solution

Set against this loss of earnings will be a recovery from the penalty clause included in the contract drawn up by the purchaser. This provides for a price reduction of £2500 for every week by which delivery is overdue; approximating to £10 000 per month. In the table of Figure 1:1, the buyer has taken all these factors into account in order to assess the probable total cost of purchasing plant from each source. Surprisingly, the most expensive bid appears to offer the least expensive solution. Naturally, technical and functional requirements would have to be considered in practice, but the financial significance of delivery timescale is highlighted.

There are many possible reasons why firm *B* can demonstrate consistent reliability in meeting delivery commitments. The company might simply be able to draw on vast resources, providing adequate reserves in any emergency. Undoubtedly the purchasing department will be effectively managed, and capable of obtaining all necessary materials in time for production needs. Enlightened attitudes to labour relations could be responsible for the avoidance of stoppages and restrictive practices. One indispensable condition is that the company must operate some form of project planning and control system.

CRITERIA FOR SUCCESSFUL PROJECT PLANNING METHODS

Analysis of any proven method of scheduling, ignoring organisational and other external influences, will usually reveal a set of characteristics common to all other successful methods. These characteristics could be described as a formula for success, and in any event they form a useful checklist with which to test the potential worth of any proposed new planning system.

The first essential is that any schedule must be established on the basis of achievable objectives. There can be no point in writing down a set of optimistic target dates without any consideration of the methods to be used in meeting them. If an attempt is made to define the methods, then the resulting list of tasks must be set down in a feasible sequence.

A basic feature of timescale planning is the accuracy to which the durations of individual jobs can be estimated. When resources are being scheduled, these estimates must also indicate the work content of each job, expressed as a rate of resource usage (for example man-hours needed per day). Inability to obtain reliable estimates is a source of concern to many newcomers in project planning, and a commonly used argument by those opposed to any form of planning at all.

In fact, a plan with bad estimates is always far better than no plan at all. Provided that records of actual task costs and durations can be compiled, estimating reliability can be improved in the course of time until it is sufficiently accurate to be completely effective. A start has to be made somewhere, even if initial attempts are little more than wild guesses.

Most plans go astray at some stage, and not many projects can be expected to go right through from start to finish without at least one change in the schedule. When circumstances do alter, plans have to be restructured accordingly. Schedules must be sufficiently flexible to allow even major changes for a minimum amount of time and effort, in order that revised plans can be made available without delay and at least cost. If flexibility is not a feature of the system, there is a danger that rescheduling will be ignored for convenience, because of the amount of work involved. This in turn can lead to the abandonment of the system and collapse of effective control.

Even a feasible plan, based on reliable estimates and logical progression of tasks, will be incomplete unless it is matched to available resources. For some activities resource overloads can be overcome by the employment of subcontractors, although this may not always be economically sound sense. In most companies, however, there are some elements of work that must be carried out on the premises, using special skills or facilities that are not available from any external source.

Resource scheduling has other important objectives in addition to the completion of a single project on time. Foremost among these is the solution of the interaction problem created when several projects compete for a common set of resources. If a comprehensive scheduling system can be devised which integrates all resource requirements, the resulting overall plan can make a very effective contribution to total company strategy and long-range planning. The schedule becomes, in effect, a model of the company's total production commitments.

Whenever there is a choice between different new order opportunities identified by the marketing department, each can be tested in turn against the existing plan to determine the one which is best suited to available capacity. If any one resource appears to be consistently overloaded on the comprehensive plan, short-term arrangements can be made for subcontract capacity reservation, whilst the long-range plans can be adapted to provide a more permanent internal solution.

In apparent contradiction to the comprehensive scope demanded, planning systems have to be kept as simple as possible. Otherwise there would be a danger of building up large planning teams, with their associated inertia and expense. Even for small-scale scheduling problems, simple methods will stand the best chance of acceptance and long-term success. Quite obviously, failure will also result if simplification is carried too far, so that the depth of detail considered is insufficient. Highly skilled judgement is sometimes necessary in order to determine how far to break down a project into individual tasks, or to decide how many resources must be scheduled. Both of these questions will be discussed in later chapters.

In common with most other management information systems, planning and progressing routines must identify and report problem areas in time for corrective action to be possible. The rule of management by exception must be satisfied. Exceptions would include reports of individual activities in danger of falling behind schedule, of forthcoming resource overloads and material shortages. For full project control, reports would also list any instances where the rate of expenditure was higher *or lower* than expected. The risks from excessive spend rates are obvious, but it is necessary to question low rates also, in case the level of working is also less than that planned, in which case it will be necessary for management to inject some pep, and breathe life into the project before it becomes too late.

The characteristics essential to any effective scheduling system are summarised in the checklist of Figure 1:2. Whenever a choice exists between alternative methods for planning and controlling project resources, the checklist can provide a useful aid for decision-making. What is certain is that no plan which fails to meet all of the conditions listed can provide the best answer to a company's scheduling problems.

The most effective schedule will be:

1   Feasible
2   Based on reliable estimates
3   Flexible to change
4   Matched to available resources
5   Viable with plans for other projects which use the same resources
6   Simple as possible
7   Capable of highlighting exceptions

FIGURE 1:2   CHECKLIST FOR AN EFFECTIVE SCHEDULE
Although many external factors, such as organisation, can determine the ultimate success of any control system, the schedule itself must satisfy a basic set of conditions. These provide a useful checklist for assessing the probable value of a plan in advance

2

PROJECT ORGANISATION

No system of scheduling can, by itself, ensure the success of a project. Assuming that the technical feasibility is assured, there may be many hazards along the path to completion and success. If a company employs a strong and capable planning team, ineffective management or a weak organisation structure can render their efforts useless, and good results cannot be expected.

ORGANISATION OF PROJECT MANAGEMENT

Organisational difficulties are most usually associated with the expansion of companies. In the smaller type of firm, the problem may be associated with progression from the manufacture of relatively simple products in batch quantities to lower-volume production of more complex products.

One example is provided by a company which was originally set up for the manufacture and sale of fire extinguishers. This type of product benefits from relatively stable design, so that production can take place from proven drawings. Machine loading and cost data can be found from records, so that production control does not have to rely on inaccurate estimates.

Now suppose that this firm has expanded its interests. In addition to the manufacture of individual pieces of fire-fighting equipment, the company offers the design, supply and installation of complete fire protection systems. The fulfilment of customer orders can no longer be organised between the sales office, stores and production control. Engineering design, installation teams, outside organisations such as the Post Office and local fire brigade services all have to be co-ordinated into one composite plan.

In the first instance, where the company was producing components for stock, or against simple customer orders, all that the organisation demanded for order fulfilment was good line supervision and management, plus related order progress routines. Each department would be working to simple, known commitments. Provided that the procedures for such disciplines as

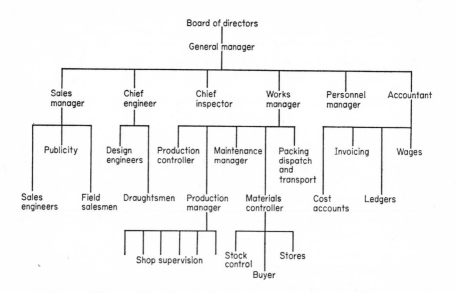

FIGURE 2:1   EXAMPLE OF A TYPICAL LINE ORGANISATION
Many small and medium-sized companies are organised along the lines
of this chart. Departmental responsibilities are defined in precise terms.
When a project is introduced which involves several departments, the
project management responsibility is not so obvious

stock control, invoicing and so on were effective, no special planning
problems need be expected.

Although the fire protection systems represent relatively simple projects,
planning can no longer be left to a distribution of responsibilities throughout
line management and individual departments. There is a need for one
department or individual to take complete charge, in order that the whole
project concept is understood and followed through to a successful conclusion.

These considerations are illustrated by comparing Figures 2:1 and 2:2.
In Figure 2:1, a line management structure is shown which might be found
in any light engineering company engaged in small batch production.
Although there is no ambiguity regarding departmental supervision and
control, no individual stands out who can logically be charged with
responsibility for complete projects.

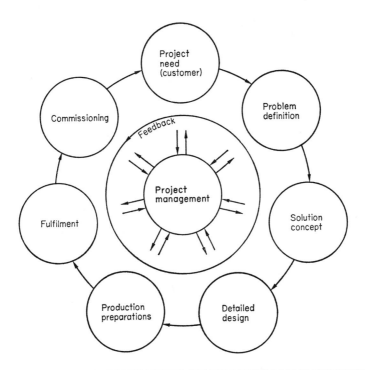

FIGURE 2:2 ORGANISATION OF PROJECT MANAGEMENT
Most industrial and civil projects can be expected to undergo the sequence
of processes shown by the circles around the outside of this diagram.
Project management is seen to be a co-ordinating function responsible
for the progress of the project itself, and not for any particular department

Most industrial and civil projects can be identified with the cyclical
sequence of stages shown in Figure 2:2. A project is usually born when a
customer recognises that he has a need to purchase new plant or some other
capital item. In association with consultants, sales engineers from potential
contractors, or by experts from their own staff, companies must establish
a specification which defines accurately the project requirements. Note that
the study leading up to problem definition can sometimes reveal a project
need which differs from that originally envisaged by the customer.

Once the problem has been identified it is necessary to produce a solution
which can satisfy the customer's needs. It is obviously customary for an
approach to be made to several potential contractors, in order to obtain

competitive tenders, so that the best terms can be secured. (Incidentally, the word "contractor" is used here, and throughout the remainder of this book, in its broadest sense, and not as a specific reference to companies in the construction industry.) Provided that the necessary funds are forthcoming, a contract will be placed with the supplier who can offer the best solution in terms of delivery, price and technical performance. From then on, the project will proceed through the active stages of detailed design, production and commissioning, finally to be handed over to the customer as a completed package.

During the life cycle of a project, the principle centre of activity will undergo a progressive shift, moving through all the departments concerned in the overall fulfilment of the contract. Each department must carry out its commitments under the normal supervision exercised from line management, but it is also necessary to provide overall project control to ensure that all activities are co-ordinated. Timescale and costs will be in danger of overruns if every separate department is allowed to operate as an isolated pocket of activity.

Project control, therefore, is vested outside the formal structure of line management. In very large organisations, project management may have to be entrusted to whole teams of people, using very advanced planning techniques in order to cope with the complexities of big projects with durations extending into many years, and with costs measured in terms of several millions of pounds. At the other end of the scale, a small company may be unable to justify a staff budget which includes even one full-time member as a project manager. The solution for the very small company will probably lie in the use of simple, manual planning techniques, operated on a part-time basis by the same manager who has technical responsibility for projects. What is essential is that the need for this specialised function is recognised and met.

Both large and small projects will generate similar problems, and these must be recognised and overcome before effective control can be established. Planning methods must be chosen that are appropriate to the size and character of the projects being undertaken. Most of the remainder of this book is devoted to explanations and examples of some of the methods available for scheduling resources and costs. But whichever of these methods proves to be the correct choice for any given situation, the most common difficulty in its application will probably be found in setting up efficient communications between active participants and the project management function. No matter how practical and workmanlike the initial planning may be, it cannot be expected to produce the desired results unless it is communicated to those people responsible for carrying it out. By the same token, higher line management will not be able to take any necessary emergency actions to hold work on schedule if they are not kept informed of shortcomings as they occur. The work force, therefore, must be provided with some means of feeding back progress to project management, who can in turn relay any adverse results to management for appropriate action. Project management will not operate in a vacuum.

It is usually convenient to distribute regular reports to every project department which contain an abbreviated version of the overall programme. A typical report might show all the activities scheduled for the following two weeks. Ideally, each department should only receive details of activities in which they must play some part. By this means, departmental managers are given specific information, with irrelevant material cut out to avoid wasting their time. Nothing can be expected to irritate a busy departmental manager more than overloading him with unnecessary paper. This is a danger especially associated with reports generated by computers, because they can produce a demoralising bulk of print-out, if they are not sensibly edited.

The progress achieved by each department must be measured, and gauged against the schedule. For this reason, each department should be expected to answer its project schedule report by a progress summary. Sometimes existing paperwork systems can be arranged to provide some of this information. For example, the completion of mechanical parts, or the receipt of purchased materials can be signalled by having a copy of the stores receipt note sent to the project management office. In most cases, however, much of the responsibility for reporting progress back to the project manager will rest with the departmental managers. Most important of all is the reporting of exceptions—those activities which have not been completed according to program, or which are in progress but threaten to run late.

In Figure 2:3 an example of a project schedule report for one department is shown. This example would be appropriate to a project being controlled by manual methods: that is without the aid of a computer. A corresponding example of a progress return is shown in Figure 2:4. Simple documents like those illustrated in these two examples can be very effective vehicles for conveying schedule information. They are unambiguous, and designed to limit the amount of writing expected from departmental managers.

To_ _ _ _ _ _ _ _ _(department) The following activities are scheduled for your department during the week ending ➞		Schedule		Budget		Period
Cost code	Activity description	Start	Finish	Trade	Hours	Materials

FIGURE 2:3 DEPARTMENTAL ACTIVITY SCHEDULE
Project planning cannot operate in a vacuum. The plan must be communicated to all active departments. Care must be taken to edit the schedule, in order that each departmental manager only receives information relevant to him. Otherwise his time will be wasted needlessly. This form is suitable for small organisations, where a computer is not being used

ROLE OF THE PROJECT MANAGER

The personality of the man chosen to spearhead planning efforts must determine, to a large extent, the ultimate chance of complete success. Communications are not automatic. Even the best systems rely on individual managers and supervisors, who must on the one hand act on routine schedules given to them, and on the other hand report back the corresponding progress achieved. Whilst the procedures for transmitting information should be arranged to minimise the amount of clerical work expected from these individuals, the information will just not flow at all unless there is a project manager at the hub of the project cycle who can demonstrate the personal authority and enthusiasm necessary to provide vitality and momentum.

From_ _ _ _ _ _ _(department) PROGRESS RETURN	For week ending ⟶		Period
Cost code	Activity description	Percentage achieved	Can next activity start? Yes or no

FIGURE 2:4   DEPARTMENTAL PROGRESS RETURN
This form represents the complement of that shown in Figure 2:3. For
every command, an answer must be expected, reporting that the command
has been carried out. Any unexpected setbacks reported in this way can
be used to reschedule the remainder of the project, or to generate other,
more urgent countermeasures. An even simpler way in which progress
returns could be collected would be to design the activity schedules
(Figure 2:3) with reply slips

Although many aspects of project management are little more than the
application of common sense, some of the sophisticated modern techniques
demand that the project manager is provided with specialist training. This
process of education should be regarded as continuous, and not restricted
to a single, one-time short course lasting one or two days. Experience is
gained not only from practical application of planning within one company,
but also by a constant interchange of planning ideas between individuals
employed by different organisations. International meetings, such as those
sponsored by "Internet", provide one forum. But it is not necessary to
await formally arranged meetings; rather each individual should seek
opportunities for himself for exchanging notes with his opposite numbers
in other companies. Training must also be extended to some line supervision,
in order that they can appreciate the aims and methods used to provide

them with their schedules. If they are given a chance to gain some insight into the operation of project planning, their co-operation will be more readily forthcoming.

Technical proficiency is not a prerequisite for a successful project manager, but he will be at a distinct disadvantage without at least some practical experience of his company's particular technology. A pure administrator could probably manage most aspects of program and budgetary control, but a relevant technical background becomes a valuable asset. When, for example, initial workplans and estimates are being discussed, it is relatively easy for a non-technical man to be placated by technical excuses. A situation of this nature can soon build up when one or two unscrupulous engineers recognise a project manager's technical ignorance as his Achilles heel.

It would be unusual for a schedule containing many interdependent tasks to be followed in exact detail right through from start to project completion. Indeed it would be miraculous. Too many variables exist which can produce unforeseen changes. For these reasons there is probably no such thing as a perfect schedule. A project manager who has practical experience in his particular industry is more able to appreciate these difficulties. Too many people in the twin professions of production and project scheduling are striving for perfection, seeking their solutions in terms of mathematically exact quantities, expressed in impressive looking formulae.

Most project planning is a compromise between unattainable perfection and practical reality. "Optimisation of resource usage" is, for example, one ideal that is seldom achieved in practice, although much is written on the subject. In many companies this aim should claim least priority, because the real problems are far more down to earth. Engineering changes, materials shortages, labour disputes, ineffective line management, inaccurate estimates, production errors and organisational shortcomings are some of the factors contributing to an environment hostile to success in terms of exact planning.

In all probability, the methods necessary to achieve the desired objectives will be concentrated on tough progress chasing of missing materials and late jobs. Some attempt to schedule resources must be made, in order to schedule tasks at a rate in general accord with the facilities which can be made available, and to give advance warning of overloads needing special, subcontract effort. But one must never expect these schedules to work out precisely. The power of modern planning techniques lies in their ability to provide a very detailed yardstick, against which achievement can be assessed. When actual work departs from the plan, either it is restored to program by emergency action, or the plan itself is remoulded to produce an alternative solution. This is the climate in which scheduling must usually operate. In these circumstances, a man who can pilot a project through to completion on time, within budgeted costs, and to the satisfaction of the customer has reason to claim success.

For a variety of reasons, project managers must be perceptive individuals. They have, for example, to be able to distinguish between problems which have no real significance and those which merit immediate corrective action. During the planning stages of any project, perception will enable a manager to recognise those individuals most likely to make bad estimates, or to produce ill-considered work plans for their departments. A skilled planner will sense, almost by instinct, whether or not the information given to him for incorporation into an overall plan is feasible or suspect. He will, in consequence, learn to accumulate a series of check questions which he can use to test the validity of his data.

ROLE OF HIGHER MANAGEMENT

Project management is primarily a staff function. Any authority which it can display will be derived from two fundamental sources. One of these is the respect that it can earn by virtue of competence demonstrated by those who are charged with this specialised job. The other main source of authority must come from all levels of line management, who alone have direct disciplinary and executive power over project resources. In common with most specific management techniques, project management cannot by itself cure an inefficient organisation, or counter weak line management. If attempts are made to set up project control in an industrial environment that is not basically capable of carrying out project work in a reasonably orderly and economic way, then the resulting project chaos will defeat the planners, however good their techniques may be.

Even in conditions where a good organisation exists, and the project function is competently staffed, one essential ingredient for success remains. Higher management must give their full backing to project control attempts. This support will include obvious elements, such as the provision of adequate accommodation and facilities, authorisation for the use of computers where appropriate, and opportunities for training. But perhaps the most essential support of all lies in active response to exception reports. A project management team which is on its toes will highlight shortcomings in progress or cost performance as early in the program as possible, in order that there may be time for corrective action to take effect. A lethargic response from management, delaying countermeasures until they are too late, will have adverse consequences for the project, and for the morale and subsequent performance of the project manager.

3 RELATIONSHIP BETWEEN PROJECT SCHEDULES & PRODUCTION CONTROL

In the checklist of Figure 1:2, one feature listed as essential to an effective schedule was that it should be flexible to change. Although this statement is generally true, flexibility is a facility that must be used with caution. Imagine, for example, a factory where the machine shop has workpieces undergoing various processes and machining operations. There may be thousands of separate parts, each group of which has its own drawings and other production documents. In many companies, movement of some heavier parts will involve the use of overhead travelling cranes, and storage of the pieces will have to be very carefully planned on the shop floor itself. Location of the parts, in fact, has to be arranged so that they are convenient to the machines for which they are queueing.

Scheduling of such work will be the responsibility of a production control department. The staff of this department must know, from day to day, exactly where each group of parts is located. They must also know the state of progress needed to meet the company's order commitments, and the actual state of progress achieved against this plan. All of this activity must be undertaken to a very fine degree of detail, so that individual machines can be kept fully working in order that they earn their keep. Forthcoming bottlenecks must be predictable, so that action can be taken in advance to make other capacity available.

In such circumstances, production control departments must rely very heavily upon the commitments presented to them in the form of overall schedules. This is true whatever systems of scheduling are used. And they will be far from pleased whenever some external influence changes the overall schedule, causing a corresponding recalculation of all the detailed production control schedules. Whilst it may be feasible to devise paper systems that can be used to carry out quick rescheduling, perhaps with the aid of a computer, it is not nearly so easy to change the actual situation which exists on the shop floor. It is one thing to take out a pen and cross out a few dates on a sheet of paper, or to push a fresh set of punched cards through the computer. It is quite another to reschedule the hardware itself.

Flexibility in such circumstances is never wholly practicable. At the level where control is actually exercised, the production control clerks will not be pleased if their schedules are constantly being taken away from them to be replaced with fresh ones which do not carry all their handwritten annotations. When this does happen it becomes necessary for them to transfer all their handwritten progress notes from the old schedule sheets to the new. In firms which handle large industrial projects, production control schedules have to be aligned with the needs of projects, and therefore they derive their commitments from the project schedules. It follows that project scheduling, although flexible to unavoidable changes, must not be allowed to become too changeable in itself.

It is worthwhile mentioning here that there are other good reasons for restricting the rescheduling of projects to the barest minimum necessary. If a change in schedule implies an extension to the end date, then it is obviously essential to make some effort to pull the program back into line. If a project runs late, many disadvantages must result for the customer and the contractor. Not least of these is the almost inevitable cost excesses that will occur. Only as a last resort should defeat be accepted, and total rescheduling carried out. On the other hand, if catastrophe does strike and cause some serious and unavoidable delay, then remaining schedules must be adapted and brought into line with the changed situation. Otherwise, the schedules would lose credence, and cease to be accepted as reasonable working documents.

Several chapters in this book will be devoted to descriptions and examples of fairly sophisticated scheduling techniques that are aimed at producing the most practicable and effective project schedules possible. Application of these techniques may be expensive, and will certainly involve training staff and the use of management time. Any project schedule produced with the aid of these methods should represent the most efficient and desirable plan for carrying out the project. It follows generally, although not always, that any subsequent alteration from the original schedule must signal some reduction in planned efficiency. Schedules, although being capable of rescheduling when necessary, should be regarded as a series of fixed targets.

COMPUTERISED PRODUCTION CONTROL

In Chapter 7 the use of a computer for project scheduling will be discussed in some detail. It will not, therefore, be described at length here but it is relevant to list a few considerations that apply to its use in the production control environment. The primary advantages of a computer in this context lie in the ability of the machine to perform a large number of calculations in a very short time, without the introduction of errors, and with the facility to produce the results in nicely tabulated and printed reports. Thus, whenever a change of schedule is needed at very short notice, the computer should prove itself well able to cope with the situation.

In practice there are many difficulties which can intervene. In order to get the computer to turn out reasonable results it has to be fed with reliable information. The time taken to collect that information from the shop floor, have it changed into a set of punched cards, send the cards to the computer, carry out the actual computing, collect and interpret the results, and then issue revised plans can take several days. And after a few days the shop floor situation must have changed considerably, without the benefit of a schedule, or at least without the benefit of the schedule that is wanted by management. The computer is an ideal tool for the provision of long-range forward plans. It is the perfect tool for project scheduling, when all arrangements can be made before work starts. But the computer is a very bad device for short-term shop floor control unless the results can be made available within a few hours of the progress information being collected from the machine shop. Several computer programs exist for production control, but none will work well unless a fast turn-round of information can be achieved. Too many companies are using computers to report back to them historical situations. Instead of asking the computer the question "Where were we two weeks ago?" it is obviously far more effective to ask the question "What jobs should we be doing today, tomorrow and next week?"

LEVELS OF DETAIL

When a project is being planned it is most unlikely that design will be complete, and usually it will not even have been started. It follows that the numbers and descriptions of individual components necessary for incorporation into the final assembly of construction will not be known. Project scheduling, therefore, cannot normally be taken right down to the level of detail where each item is considered rigorously. It cannot be taken down to the level of detail that one should expect to find in the machine shop. Production control, on the other hand, has to consider not only the numbers and designs of parts needed, but also the many operations needed to produce those parts on individual machines. Otherwise machines could not be scheduled efficiently to make full use of their potential capacity.

In order to marry project schedules to production control, a working relationship between the two systems has to be agreed. This is true whether a computer is going to be used for one system, for both systems or for neither system. The key to this solution is found by examining the way in which most industrial projects are handled during the preliminary specification and estimating stages. These are the functions that must be carried out to determine the performance specification, budgets or price, and broad delivery promises that form the company's proposal to the prospective customer or client. If any project is not subjected to this treatment, then it must start life without adequate definition. And a project that has not been defined is a project that cannot be reliably scheduled. Assuming that a correct project specification has been prepared, the arrangement of equipment, components and parts necessary to build the complete project is usually depicted by a "family tree" diagram. At the top of the diagram will be one or more of the main assemblies or structures. Below that level come the subassemblies. This argument can be carried right down to the level that shows each individual nut and bolt, but at the planning stage, the subassembly level probably represents the practical limits to which the project can be defined.

The engineers know what must be produced in general terms. They cannot list all the parts at this early stage, but they should have a sound idea of the size and complexity of each subassembly. These factors become important when cost estimates are being made. Project planning, can often be taken down to the level of separate sub assemblies fairly sensibly. Experience of previous projects helps the planners to assess the likely work content and overall production time needed for subassemblies that are broadly similar to corresponding subassemblies for earlier projects. If the planners can estimate the required start and finish times for groups of components needed for each subassembly, then production control can be given their commitments. Within these groups of parts, the production control team must carry out detailed scheduling of all the parts. This, of course, must await the preparation of production drawings. Meanwhile, the project planners can use their estimates of the work content in each subassembly group to check that shop capacity will be able to cope with the overall volume of work expected.

The picture that emerges, therefore, is of a central project planning team which attempts to fit projects into a company's available capacity. They arrange for each project to be programmed to the level of detail where each subassembly can be given recommended starting and finishing dates in the machine shop. Loading estimates will be taken into account to ensure a smooth work load. These load calculations will be made on a broad basis, probably expressed in terms of men or man-hours needed. Indeed, project planners generally tend to think in terms of man-hours or man-weeks, where the production controllers are more likely to be concerned with individual machines. When the production control team receive their lists of subassembly dates, provided the drawings are produced on time they should be able to plan their machine loads sensibly because the overall load position has already been assessed for them. Work is being supplied to the machine shop at a rate which is consistent with capacity.

When the project planners cannot fit all project work into the machine shop, at least they can signal warning of forthcoming overloads. Production control can be given several months prior notice. Spare capacity, probably in outside firms' machine shops, can then be reserved in the necessary quantity and against the period when the problem hits. Production control experts who read this argument may feel that this is an oversimplification of their problem, because it is always necessary to reserve capacity not only at the right time and the correct amount, but also it must be suitable capacity. There would be considerable embarrassment, for example, if 1000 hours of milling capacity was reserved for March, when in fact the real need was found to be for 500 hours of turning in July and 500 hours of drilling in February. The actual details of capacity needs must always depend upon an examination of the production drawings, and they have not been drawn at the project planning stage. However, in general the argument for long-term planning holds good. A company should always be aware of the kind of balance to be expected between light and heavy machining, and between the different machining processes and operations, for its own particular type of business.

One other problem must be considered. If a machine shop is carrying out work for more than one project, then some priorities have to be decided between the parts for the different projects. These priorities must obviously be arranged so that each individual project can be delivered on time. But when each project has its own project manager, and each manager clamours for his own work to get top priority, then orderly working breaks down and no project will be finished on time, except that for the project manager with the loudest vocal capacity. Most production control systems incorporate some method for allocating priorities to batches of parts. It is recommended here that the planning team for projects should have the authority to plan all projects together, in one combined exercise, and compare the needs against total company resources. This may sound difficult, and certainly it needs the application of some specialised techniques. But it avoids the well known panic situations where all projects jostle each other for priority, and fire-fighting actions are the normal practice to rectify shortages that should have been foreseen long before they became serious. The later chapters in this books are devoted to examples of techniques that can be used to make multiproject scheduling a practical reality.

4

CHARTING METHODS OF SCHEDULING

Any single planning decision depends upon efficient communication before it can be translated into a command. In its simplest form, a spoken request might be quite sufficient to ensure that the decision is implemented. The control of projects, however, always involves the making of many advance decisions, based on the intentions of project management regarding the project timescale, the sequence in which tasks are to be performed, the disposition of project resources and the rate of expenditure. In these circumstances, verbal commands are not enough, and the plan must be recorded by some means in order that it can be used as a control reference during the progress of actual work.

The most obvious and usual method of recording any set of decisions is to write them down on a sheet of paper. Figure 4:1 shows a very straightforward example of a project schedule recorded in this way. Each department is provided with a date by which its part of the project work must be finished in order to contribute to completion on the due date for delivery to customer. The original decisions were made by a senior manager, based on his long experience of similar projects conducted in the past.

ITEM	DEPARTMENT	START	FINISH
Engineering design	Design office	1 Jan 71	31 Mar 71
Part lists	Design office	1 Apr 71	15 Apr 71
Materials	Buying office	15 Apr 71	30 June 71
Piece parts	Production control	15 Apr 71	30 June 71
Assembly	Assembly	1 July 71	31 July 71
Ship to customer	Dispatch	—	1 Aug 71

FIGURE 4:1   A SIMPLE FORM OF PLANNING NOTATION
Any project plan is basically a set of decisions. Some form of notation is necessary if these decisions are to be communicated to all project participants. This type of table represents the simplest method

Plans developed along such painless lines are still used by some companies. They fall into a class of control known as "Management by the seat of the pants." Whilst they may have some use in the planning of small projects where resources are no problem, they are unlikely to be effective in a modern industrial environment.

Probability of success for any planning system depends partly on how the basic method measures up to the requirements given in the checklist of Chapter 1. In the example of Figure 4:1, the main weaknesses are that there was insufficient attention to detail and no attempt to schedule the resources required. There are no intermediate events listed against which performance can be checked as the project proceeds. If the drawings are going to be late, this fact will be discovered on the day they are due for issue, and not before. Then it will be too late to take corrective action.

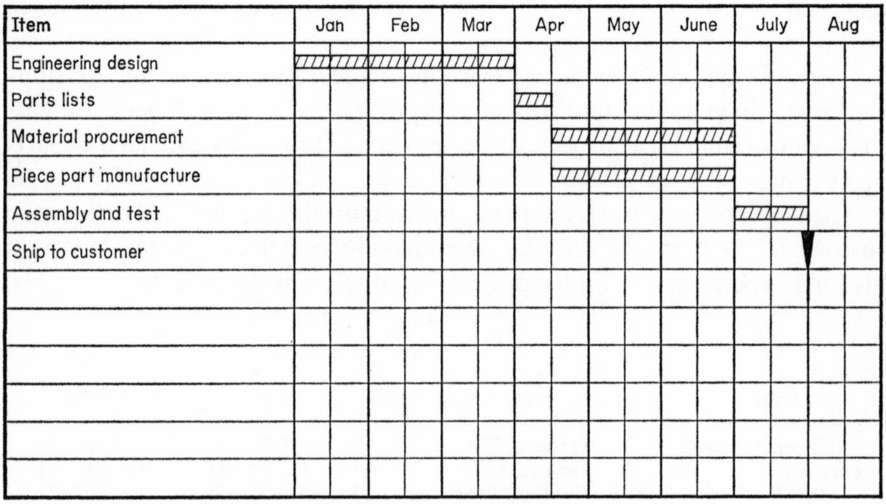

Item	Jan	Feb	Mar	Apr	May	June	July	Aug
Engineering design	/////	/////	/////					
Parts lists				////				
Material procurement				/////	/////	/////		
Piece part manufacture				/////	/////	/////		
Assembly and test							/////	
Ship to customer							▼	

FIGURE 4:2 A SIMPLE BAR CHART EXAMPLE

This chart displays the same information as that shown in the example of Figure 4:1. The visual impact is improved, and there is a sense of proportion because the tasks are drawn along a scale which is proportioned according to time. As a planning tool, however, it is just as ineffective as Figure 4:1, because the basic information contained is invalid

BAR CHARTS

If it is necessary to consider a plan in greater depth of detail, simple listing of project tasks is liable to become tedious, and the result lacking in clear visual presentation. Most realistic attempts at planning are centred around some form of diagram or chart. What the planner is really seeking is an improved method of notation, in order that his decisions can be expressed on paper and adequately communicated.

Figure 4:2 shows a bar chart. The data which it displays is the same as that included in the list of Figure 4:1. The presentation is slightly more effective, because the whole chart is drawn to scale. Use of colour can indicate the responsibilities of individuals or of departments. In this particular case the plan is still likely to prove ineffective. The same lack of detail and seat of the pants decisions have been used in its formulation.

In small, very young companies, planning based on intuitive decisions can achieve limited success in the short term. The whole planning system will be entirely dependent, however, on the skill, experience and memory of one man. Sooner or later, with company growth, the system must break

Item	Week number																																		
	1	2	3	4	5	6	7	8	9	10	11	12	13	14	15	16	17	18	19	20	21	22	23	24	25	26	27	28	29	30	31	32	33	34	35
Write specification	▨																																		
System concept		▨	▨																																
Detail design				▨	▨	▨	▨	▨	▨	▨	▨																								
General assembly												▨	▨	▨																					
Parts lists															▨	▨																			
Order raw materials															▨	▨																			
Order components																		▨	▨																
Await raw materials																	▨	▨	▨																
Await components																			▨	▨	▨	▨	▨	▨	▨	▨									
Make piece parts																		▨	▨	▨	▨	▨	▨	▨	▨										
Subassemblies																											▨								
Main assembly																												▨	▨	▨					
Inspect and test																																▨	▨		
Dispatch																																		▨	

FIGURE 4:3 BAR CHART WITH MORE DETAIL
This bar chart displays the same plan as that shown in Figure 4:2. However, because this version includes a greater amount of detail, it is a slightly more effective planning tool. There are more occasions highlighted on which actual progress can be checked and compared against the plan

down. Either the individual will depart, taking his special skill and memory with him, or the volume of work will extend beyond his mental capacity.

In Figure 4:3 the same bar chart has been rendered more effective by the inclusion of greater detail. Any individual assigned to the progressing of this project now has a series of "milestones" against which he can check departmental achievement from day to day. Late jobs can be picked up in time for corrective action to be effective for the remainder of the project.

One use of bar charts, therefore, is to aid timescale planning and the sequencing of project tasks. The system can be ideal for small projects, especially where there is no need to take complex relationships between different activities into account. Taking a very simple case, suppose that only one man could be made available to carry out an entire project. He would have to finish each job before he could start the next, and one would not show any two jobs in progress at the same time. The sequence would be a simple series, without complex restrictions on the starts and finishes of any activities. Another, more credible example would be a project with a large range of totally unconnected activities, depending, for example on the delivery of materials, and able to draw on virtually unlimited resources because of the small scale of the project in relation to total capacity available.

Several project managers have been successful at using bar charts in circumstances where a more complex interdependence between project tasks must be recognised. Figure 4:4 shows a chart in which restrictions have been imposed on several jobs that cannot be started before others have been finished. These restrictions are shown by vertical strips, which might be given a vivid colour in practice. Should rescheduling prove necessary at any time, the vertical strips can be used as mechanical aids to prevent accidental overlapping of related activities. The planned restraints are retained in the schedule, and the logical sequence of events essential to project completion is kept.

There is a practical limit to the size of projects which can be planned in this way, but the principle is not far removed from some of the more advanced techniques to be described later. Indeed, charts of this type can be used to display the results obtained from network analysis (Chapter 5 *et seq*). For pure visual impact they have the advantage of being drawn to a timescale.

Any charting method will fail for larger projects, where the sequence of activities has to be controlled from a complex arrangement of inter-dependencies. The notation will be too weak to show all connecting links,

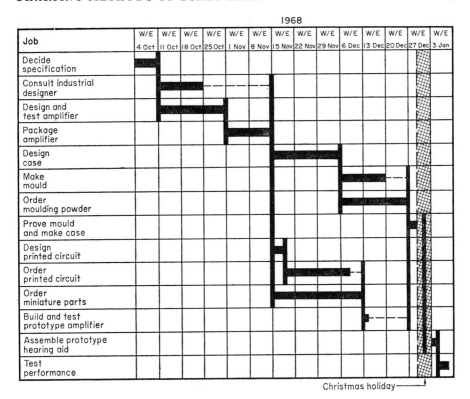

FIGURE 4:4 BAR CHART SHOWING ACTIVITY START
RESTRICTIONS

In this diagram, vertical bars have been added which serve to indicate
simple interrelationships between the various activities. For example,
"Consult industrial designer" and "Design and test amplifier" cannot
start until the activity denoted by the first bar "Decide specification" has
been finished. Although this method represents an effective way of
displaying activity interdependencies, the scope is limited to simple
projects

and in any case there would be far too much detail for any planner to
schedule by hand. It is sometimes possible to set up very large plans by
hand, but it is time consuming, and too inflexible to allow rapid rescheduling
whenever project conditions change.

There is one powerful advantage possessed by bar charts over all other
methods of planning notation. They can be used directly to indicate and
control the deployment of project resources. This principle is widely known
and used, and illustrated in the example of Figure 4:5. By using a method

of coding for each job according to the type of resource required, the resources needed in any period can be found by adding up the number of appropriately coded strips in each period column. Provided that each strip represents the same rate of resource usage, such as one man per job, the calculations are straightforward and simple. Coding is often done by using colour. Care must be taken not to be over ambitious in the number of colours used, because the method is dependent upon simplicity for flexibility and dramatic presentation.

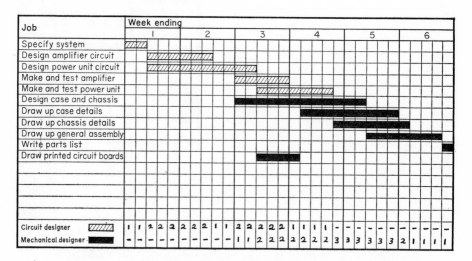

FIGURE 4:5   RESOURCE LOADING WITH A BAR CHART
In this bar chart, project load requirements are displayed. This has been achieved by coding each activity strip according to the type of resource needed. In this particular example, very simple resources are shown. Only one man is needed for each activity. Day by day requirements are found by adding up the occurrence of strips of the appropriate colour in the daily columns. This has been done here, and the results are seen in the table at the foot of the chart

Usually, of course, project tasks will all demand resources at different rates of usage. Whilst one job might need one man for a week, another could be planned to use four men for two days. The simple method of using colour coding to identify the type of resource must now be extended to indicate the rate of usage. In the example of Figure 4:6 this has been done by the addition of numbers to each strip. Each figure denotes the number of men needed to carry out each task. In order to find the expected resource usage for the whole project in any period it is now necessary to add up the figures appearing on all strips of the same colour, in the appropriate column of the chart.

Job	Week number 1				2				3				4				5				6			
Assemble frame	4	4	4	4																				
Fit lights													2	2	2									
Fit wall panels						4	4	4	4	4														
Fit doors and motors									2	2														
Fit ceiling boards									2	2	2	2	2	2										
Fit emergency lights														1	1	1								
Fit roof covers																					2	2		
Fit trims													2	2	2	2	2							
Fit operating lamp															1									
Fit wall mounted units									2	2	2	2												
Wire all lights																1	1	1	1	1	1			
Wire emergency lights															1	1								
Wire wall units											1	1	1	1										
Wire control panel												1	1											
Wire door motors										1	1													
Test all electrics																		2	2	2				
Fitters	4	4	4	4	4	4	4	4	6	6	4	4	2	2	5	5	5	2	2	–	–	–	–	–	–	2	2	–	–
Electricians	–	–	–	–	–	–	–	–	–	1	1	2	2	2	2	1	2	1	1	1	2	2	2	–	–	–

FIGURE 4:6   RESOURCE LOADING WITH A BAR CHART—
MULTIPLE RESOURCES
Compare this chart with that shown in Figure 4:5. The principle is the same, but the effectiveness of the method has been slightly extended by allowing each activity to be coded to show not only the type of resource, but also the quantity. If more than one type of resource happened to be required for any activity, this too could be incorporated in the chart by the simple expedient of using more than one strip for each activity

Production control departments all over the world still use these simple methods for the loading of small departments. Machine loading charts, similar to that shown in Figure 4:7, are a useful variation on the same theme, with perhaps an even more widespread use. Charts which employ this principle for the loading of machines are sometimes called Gantt charts, after their originator, Henry Gantt. Their simplicity and flexibility offer a very effective solution to the problems associated with scheduling small machine shops, provided that the work content of each different job has been estimated with some accuracy. For larger machine shops, computer controlled methods are now being used. When very flexible project scheduling methods are being applied to control overall project resources, the production control schedules must be made equally flexible. In these circumstances charting will fail.

Machine	Hour beginning							
	08 00	09 00	10 00	11 00	12 30	13 30	14 30	15 30
Capstan lathe	1053	1053	1053	1154	1154	1154	1154	1154
Herbert lathe	1186	1186	1186	1186	1186	1701	1701	1701
Holbrook lathe	1188	1188	1188	1188	1188	1188	1790	1790
Jig borer	REPAIR AND MAINTENANCE							
Universal miller	IDLE	IDLE	IDLE	IDLE	1185	1185	1185	1185
Horizontal miller	1081	1081	1081	1081	904	904	904	1225
Automatic—1	1300	1300	1300	1300	1300	1300	IDLE	IDLE
Automatic—2	IDLE	IDLE	IDLE	IDLE	IDLE	IDLE	IDLE	IDLE

FIGURE 4:7 A DAILY MACHINE LOADING CHART
Charts similar to that shown here are widely used to plan the day by day
loading of machines in small workshops. They are usually blackboard
and chalk affairs. The capacity of each machine is allocated to waiting
jobs by writing in the job order numbers in some given order of priority.
Each square represents one hour of machine time in this case. This is a
very simple method, but will be effective provided that the workshop is
small and the job estimates are accurate

Should it be necessary to extend the significance of a display even further,
other coding methods are available. These include the use of differently
shaped symbols, in addition to colour coding. Some charting methods allow
for the horizontal strips to be extendable not only in length, but also in
height. They can be built upwards, out from the board, in three-dimensional
fashion. This is achieved by fixing strips on top of each other with the aid
of a proprietary method. A situation where such a chart might be needed
would be a project which used more than one type of resource for each job.

If all of these methods are used indiscriminately there is a very real danger of any chart becoming cluttered with too much detail. This destroys the visual impact, and makes the information displayed difficult to see at a glance. The more detail a chart attempts to show, the more difficult it will be to reschedule when project conditions change. For the same reasons of clarity and flexibility, it is wise not to attempt scheduling of projects with over approximately one hundred different activities on charts, but to use instead one of the more powerful techniques described in following chapters.

An important extension of the use of bar charts for resource planning is realised when the arrangement is set up on an adjustable panel which allows the relative position of all the strips to be changed at will. Shuffling the activities around in this way provides a means for smoothing out unwanted peak loads, although by doing this a delay might be caused in the overall completion of a project. Figure 4:8 illustrates the principle involved. When the chart is manipulated, it is necessary to make certain that no impossible working sequences are introduced, which could happen for example if one task were to be delayed without allowing for a corresponding delay in all following tasks.

PLANNING DEPARTMENTAL LOADS BY BAR CHART

Sometimes, when a departmental manager is attempting to relate jobs to his manpower resources, it is difficult for the planner to choose between two basic methods of presentation. Either one lists all the jobs, and writes people's names against them across a chart, or he lists the people and allocates the jobs. The two possible alternatives are illustrated in Figure 4:9.

There is, in fact, a solution to this problem which is both logical and straightforward. This combines both of the alternative arrangements shown in Figure 4:9. First, all forthcoming jobs in the department are listed down the left-hand side of one chart. These jobs might be activities from one or more projects, or they could be a set of completely unrelated tasks, such as the processing of separate sales inquiries by sales engineers.

For each job, some plan of action will be known, whether this results from a project schedule or a date by which a prospective customer expects his quotation. The key events from this action plan must be shown on the chart for every job, according to a timescale. The total length of time shown on the chart will be a matter of choice, and must depend also on the type of activity. Typically, three to six months will be found convenient. When all

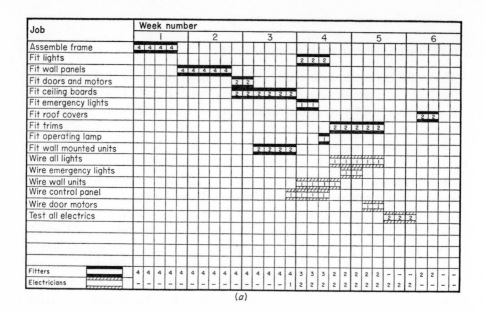

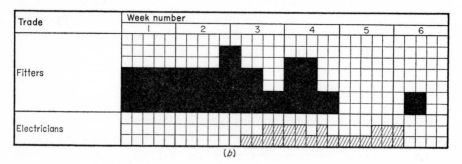

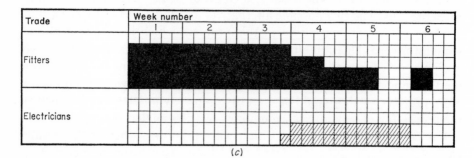

FIGURE 4:8   RESOURCE LEVELLING BY BAR CHART

The project depicted in (*a*) is the same as that in Figure 4:6. The positions of some of the activities have, however, been rearranged in order to produce a smoother usage of resources. The results can be seen by comparing the two histograms in (*b*) and (*c*). In (*b*), the resources which would be required to operate the plan of Figure 4:6 are shown, whilst (*c*) shows the effect obtained by rescheduling to remove unwanted peaks and troughs

the jobs have been entered, the chart becomes, in effect, a statement of total departmental commitments.

| Name | Week ending | | | | | |
	3 Apr 70	10 Apr 70	17 Apr 70	24 Apr 70	I May 70	8 May 70
BRIGGS	4359		HOLIDAY	4359	4390	
COHEN	4405			TRAINING COURSE	4381	4382
DENTON	4321	4494	4363	4368		
EVANS	4374	4375	4376	4377	4381	4396
MURPHY	4300			TRAINING COURSE	4300	
McTAVISH	4401				4401A	
SMITH	4445			TRAINING COURSE	4450	

| Job number | Week ending | | | | | |
	3 Apr 70	10 Apr 70	17 Apr 70	24 Apr 70	I May 70	8 May 70
4300	MURPHY				MURPHY	
4321	DENTON					
4359	BRIGGS		DENTON	BRIGGS		
4368				DENTON		
4374	EVANS					
4375		EVANS				
4376			EVANS			
4377				EVANS		
4381					EVANS AND COHEN	
4382						COHEN
4390					BRIGGS	
4396						EVANS
4401	McTAVISH					
4401A					McTAVISH	
4405	COHEN					
4445	SMITH					
4450					SMITH	
4495	DENTON					

FIGURE 4:9 SCHEDULING DEPARTMENTAL LOADS WITH CHARTS

These two charts demonstrate alternative methods for scheduling departmental manpower loading. Each diagram shows the same plan of campaign—only the presentation is different. Neither option is entirely satisfactory, because in both cases there has been an attempt to cram too much information into one display. A practical solution combines both methods. One chart is arranged on the basis of that shown at (b), but key project events are depicted by symbols instead of any attempt to include people's names. This chart then becomes a statement of departmental commitments. A manpower loading chart, identical to that shown at (a) can then be used to translate commitments into a workplan, combining personal factors such as holidays and training

Translation of departmental commitments into a working schedule is achieved by the preparation of a second chart, where the names of resources, or individual people, are written down the left-hand side. The timescale chosen for this second chart must not be too long, because it is not feasible to attempt the planning of individuals' time for more than about two weeks ahead.

All of the jobs from the overall commitment schedule are entered against individuals' names on the manpower chart, according to the ability and availability of each man. Holidays, and other personal commitments can be superimposed on the loading chart, which can also be used to show the location of men when they are expected to be away from the office. The overall chart is then used as a progress tool, for the day-to-day checking of achievement for every job. The manpower loading chart, in addition to providing a means for the allocation of work across all the resources available, gives supervision and management a useful record of the personal performance of each man. Updating must be carried out every week, so that individuals can plan their time for at least one week ahead.

PLANNING DEPARTMENTAL LOADS BY GRAPH

Another very common method for the planning of total departmental loads depends upon the use of squared paper. The popularity of this system probably stems from the ease with which graph paper can be obtained. Figure 4:10 shows a typical specimen, where a chief engineer has attempted to plan his departmental loads for a period of three months.

Charts of this types are used to schedule all types of work. A central planning authority would be able to express forward loads for all departments, using one sheet of paper for every department planned. A clear indication is provided whenever the planned activity must exceed capacity if project commitments are to be met.

In the engineering example of Figure 4:10, the planner has not allowed any overload condition to occur, but has instead smoothed out his planned use of resources within departmental capacity. Although this may have a detrimental effect on some completion dates, it was probably necessary to recognise that in design work it is often difficult to accommodate overloads by the use of sub-contract labour or the working of overtime.

Load pictures drawn on graph paper provide a very clear indication of apparent forward loads for every department, together with projected underload and overload conditions. For that reason, they are well liked by higher management, who need no special instruction in order to be able to interpret them.

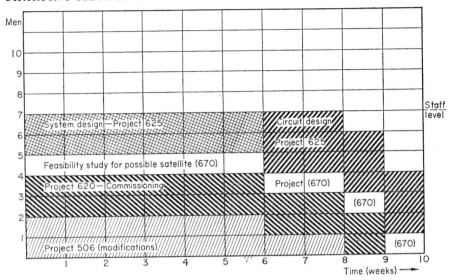

FIGURE 4:10 SCHEDULING DEPARTMENTAL LOADS
GRAPHICALLY

Here is another method by which departmental managers attempt to load
their departments. It is simple, and it has the advantage that ordinary graph
paper can be used. But, it is inflexible because whenever a change occurs
it is necessary to draw up an entirely new schedule. Schedules of this type
seldom remain valid for a significant portion of the timespan which they
attempt to depict

Unfortunately, all of these advantages are heavily outweighed by one
major drawback. It is well known that any plan, other than the very
simplest, is going to be liable to at least some change in the course of time.
It follows that if these plans are expressed on graphs, the graphs must be
redrawn completely every time a change occurs.

If a chief engineer were to draw up a plan like that shown in Figure 4:10,
he should not be surprised to find that it is completely out of date only one
week later, although he was attempting to show a three-months plan. What
is lacking is the ability to update the plan easily. There is no flexibility.

Planning by graph, therefore, cannot be recommended as an effective
method for scheduling project resources. In the short term, if no other
system has been devised, then a few graphs will be better than no planning
at all, and can provide a stopgap measure until something better can be
found. Otherwise they will take too much effort, and the results will not
repay the energy which has to be put into them.

It is stressed that these remarks only apply to the use of graphs for resource scheduling. Simple projects can be scheduled far better on adjustable bar charts, whilst for more ambitious planning a computer will be necessary. It is all a question of choosing the right technique for a given situation. For purposes of cost control, and to show trends, graphical methods will usually be preferred.

PROPRIETARY CHARTING SYSTEMS

A wide variety of proprietary charts is available to planners, and the choice must depend on a combination of individual preference and the requirements of specific applications. In general, the simplest method will stand the best chance of achieving long-term success. Many charts are purchased at considerable expense, set up and used for a few weeks, only to be discarded because they have proved too complicated and time consuming to maintain.

The simplest form of "mechanical aid" is the use of a glazed sheet, where the plan outline is indelible, and the actual schedule details are written on with wax crayons, such as Chinagraph. Schedule changes are simple, because details can be quickly erased and replaced. A well known proprietary version is that sold by Sasco Visual Planning Limited. Useful accessories include hinged wall panels, allowing a lot of information to be displayed in a small space.

Although Sasco charts are relatively cheap, an even simpler and cheaper system is provided if a dyeline printing machine is available. By producing an image on sensitised Mylar film, such as Ozaloft, an indelible framework is produced on a surface which allows the use of ordinary pencils and coloured crayons. Erasure is simple, either by surgical spirit, or by the use of plastic erasers. In either case, the plan is removed, but the charting framework is not.

Most manufactured charts are purchased because they embody some form of adjustable system to facilitate the manipulation of schedules. Proprietary charts usually manage to provide an overall effect which is more pleasing to the eye than that produced by "home-made" efforts, although there have been some notable exceptions. If a chart is going to be used for the purposes of calculating and scheduling resources, then a change in any one task shown will be reflected in the timing of all following jobs. In these circumstances, the planning system must allow for easy adjustment, and simple drafting methods have to give way to mechanical methods.

Pegboard, with a pattern of small holes arranged on a 5 mm grid, can provide a useful basis for charts where considerable detail has to be accommodated in a small space. Symbols in various shapes, or strips that can be cut to length, can be plugged in to the chart in any desired position. Both the symbols and strips are usually obtainable in a wide range of colours. It is also possible to use pairs of pegs joined by coloured elastic threads, which can be used as a vertical "today's date" cursor, or for setting up graphs.

Proprietary charts using the pegboard principle are sometimes provided with "rotating" panels, which can be removed and interchanged with one another. When the left-hand panel becomes outdated, it can be removed, stripped, and replaced at the right-hand side. The remaining panels can be slid to the left, and need not be rescheduled. Thus, charts of this type save much labour when rescheduling is due. It is not necessary to remove and replace hundreds of fiddly pieces of plastic after each planning period.

Another useful proprietary idea, is the use of a visible-edge card holder, attached to the left-hand side of the chart. Each card edge is arranged to line up with a corresponding row on the chart panel. Cards can be used to show details of each activity which would be impracticable to include on the main display. They can also be used to record actual results, such as achieved dates or incurred costs in relation to estimates. After project completion, a set of project cards can be very useful as a library from which future plans can benefit. Adapta-Charts Limited is one supplier capable of providing pegboard equipment combining rotating panels and a visible edge card index.

Other suppliers employ different methods for attaching symbols and strips onto panels. One obvious and simple solution is to use thin, flexible plastic symbols and tape, with self-adhesive backing, Sasco charts adopt this method. If the panels are made of steel, magnetic components can be used. Early versions of magnetic charts were not popular because they were prone to accidental "rescheduling" if a passer-by happened to brush the display with his clothing. In recent years, this problem has been overcome by providing positive location with grooves or slots, into which all the symbols are placed. The grooves are usually very narrow, and placed only a few millimetres apart, so that considerable detail can be included in a small space. MBC (Office Systems) Limited and Roneo Vickers are capable of supplying modern magnetic systems.

A high degree of sophistication is reached in the equipment supplied by

Modulex. This is based on a comprehensive range of interlocking plastic parts, bearing an uncanny resemblance to the children's constructional toy Lego. Not only can strips, symbols, letters and numerals be fixed onto panels, but the strips can be fitted one on top of another. Strips can thus be extended in thickness, outwards from the panel, to give a third dimension to the plan.

Whenever a new charting system is designed, the overall size of the display will depend on the number of items to be shown, and the total number of days or weeks that must be planned in advance. Sometimes the results of such calculations will indicate the need for an enormous wall, on which to mount several panels. Two ways of countering this problem are to search for equipment that is designed on a very small grid pattern, or to cut down on the scope of the plan.

If it is not possible to reduce the area of chart, then it may be necessary to consider a space-saving method of mounting the panels. Some suppliers can provide wall mounting brackets, from which chart panels can be pivoted like the pages of a book. If the panels can be made of flexible material, a rotating arrangement similar to the "roller towel" principle can be used. This roller arrangement is particularly convenient for coarse, blackboard and chalk planning.

One of the neatest, but expensive, space-saving solutions allows several penels to be mounted in the fashion of sliding doors, within a wooden frame. Any two charts can be viewed at one time, whilst the remaining half dozen or so can be slid away beneath them. By this means the total wall area necessary can be cut by a factor of four.

The range of proprietary charts has grown sufficiently fast in recent years to bewilder any newcomer to planning. A very wide choice of methods and prices exists, with some rather questionable gimmickry included. To some extent, however, each manufacturer specialises in his own particular system, which usually embodies one or two basic proprietary ideas as selling points. No single charting system can solve all planning problems, and it follows that no supplier can meet every planner's needs.

The user must first decide upon an arrangement of data which will please both himself and his management. Then he is free to seek out the supplier who can meet his needs, when he will find that the careful preparation has narrowed down his choice to manageable proportions. One of the comprehensive catalogues such as *Buyer's Guide* will serve as a useful introduction for those without previous experience. By following the rule of specifying needs first, and then seeking a source of supply, there will be less danger of being sold a planning chart that will become a useless white elephant within weeks of its purchase. One may even save hundreds of pounds, and discover that a simple blackboard and box of chalks happens to be the correct solution to a specific problem.

SCOPE OF CHARTING METHODS

Whatever the problem, planning with charts must be recognised as being infinitely better than no planning at all. It is true that any chart can only be as valid as the information which it contains, but this argument applies equally to all other planning methods.

For planning departmental resources, or for the planning of simple projects, adjustable wall charts may prove to be extremely effective. Careful design, using a restricted range of positively coloured symbols, can result in a striking display of committed project or departmental dates. Provided that the chart is openly displayed, it can by itself represent a dynamic means of communicating key schedule data. Unfortunately, charts can be too effective, and may need to be covered up to disguise proprietary commercial information when visitors are about.

In simple cases, any proposed change of plans can immediately be tested if the basic plan is represented on an adjustable board. The effects of such changes on project resource needs, and on the completion date, can be demonstrated within a few minutes. For larger applications, however, where there is a high degree of interdependence between different jobs, or where hundred of tasks have to be planned, rescheduling becomes more difficult and tedious. Immediate answers to changes in project requirements are no longer forthcoming, and might take days to work out with no assurance that the schedule derived is the optimum result.

In fact, the more difficult a plan becomes to revise, the greater the chance that no attempt at updating will be made at all. When flexibility is lost, or when the notation is not capable of showing all the task relationships essential to a workable schedule, charting methods will fail. If any problem is recognised as too complex for simple manual methods, one of the more powerful techniques must be adopted. Some of these are described in following chapters. By harnessing the power of a computer, projects can be scheduled in great depth of detail, and with a degree of flexibility impossible to achieve with charts.

The choice between the use of a computer or planning with charts may not always be cut and dried. In borderline cases both methods can be used with success. In other cases, skilled judgement may be necessary to determine the right answer. In general, it can be assumed that charting becomes difficult and inflexible when more than one hundred different activities have to be considered. There can be no hard and fast rule, because the results must depend on the interdependence of different tasks, the complexity of resources, and the skill of an individual planner.

It is interesting to consider the case of one computer bureau, which offers a service to customers who want to schedule large projects by computer. Although very powerful computer programs will be used to disentangle all the complexities of the customers' projects, the bureau uses a wall chart to allocate computer time between different customers. Each scheduling problem has its own solution and, even in the computer age, charting methods can be extremely relevant to the successful control of projects and resources.

5
CRITICAL PATH ANALYSIS

The increasing complexity of industrial projects has led to a corresponding search for improved methods of project planning and control. One of the major drawbacks to progress in this field has been the lack of a suitable form of notation, capable of expressing all the facets of an intricate plan. During the 1950s a new family of techniques was introduced in the United States. As a result, great advances were made in the planning, co-ordination and progressing of major defence projects, notable among which was the Polaris program.

These new developments fall into a class of project control known by the generic description "Network analysis." Two similar systems were born at about the same time, and became available to United Kingdom project managers around the year 1960. One was PERT, an acronym for Program Evaluation and Review Technique. The other was Critical Path Analysis (or Critical Path Method), known by the initials CPA or CPM. The two methods have much in common, and both are sometimes wrongly referred to as PERT. In this chapter, the critical path method will be described, because it has virtually dominated the network scene for the last ten years. The differences between PERT and CPA are described later in this chapter, but they are now largely academic. Both methods rely on the same basic notation, which is an "arrow diagram" or "network."

ARROW DIAGRAMS

When network analysis was first introduced, the reputation for dynamic project control that it earned was counterbalanced by a general dislike of the network diagrams themselves, which were not so immediately acceptable as the older bar charts. In fact, for some time it was necessary to convert the results of network analysis into bar chart form before senior executives would look at them. Even today, most computer programs contain routines for presenting the output data in bar chart form.

Fortunately, the provision of training seminars, internal company training courses, and widespread publicity have all combined with the reputation earned by networking to overcome most of the resistance. Initial difficulties in the interpretation of the new notation are understandable. Any new language has to be learned before it can be used as a form of communication. However, there is nothing particularly difficult about the appreciation of network diagrams, provided that the newcomer is taken through the set of rules by simple degrees, and in the correct sequence.

FIGURE 5:1 THE SIMPLEST OF ALL NETWORKS
Each circle represents an event in the life of a project, whilst the arrow joining the two events denotes the activity which is necessary in order to achieve the second event. The numbers written within the event circles enable the activity to be identified without ambiguity, so that in this case the activity is named activity 1,2

The simplest network of all is shown in Figure 5:1. Each of the circles represents a project event. An event does not occupy any time itself, but is some happening that can be identified for the purposes of progressing a project through to completion. Thus the start of a project is one significant event. The start and finish of every separately identified task necessary to complete the project can also be described as events. Events are positively identified on the diagram by writing numbers within the circles.

In order to progress from one event to the next in any project, some activity has to take place. In network diagrams these activities are represented by arrows, so that in this simple example the work necessary to achieve event 2, starting from event 1, is denoted by the arrow. Activity arrows are not drawn to timescale, and their lengths have no significance whatsoever. They are, however, always drawn from left to right, by convention.

Activities are identified positively by naming their start and finish events, sometimes called the preceding and succeeding events. In this example, the activity flows from event 1 to event 2 and is therefore described as activity 1, 2. In practice, the verbal description of the activity which the arrow denotes would be written below the arrow shaft.

Figure 5:2 shows a network containing four activities. Since the work must proceed in the direction of the arrows, that is from left to right, activity 4, 5 must finish last. In fact, the diagram indicates that it is dependent upon the completion of all preceding activities, so that activities 1, 4; 2, 4; and 3, 4 must all be finished before activity 4, 5 can start. Another way of saying this is that event 4 cannot be achieved until all preceding activities have been completed.

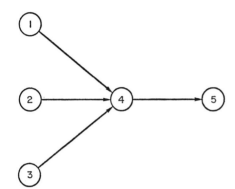

FIGURE 5:2 NETWORK
RESTRICTIONS
In this very simple network, activity 4,5 cannot be started until all three preceding activities have been completed. Another way of expressing this situation is to say that activity 4,5 cannot start until event 4 has been achieved

Now consider a very simple "project." A workshop is charged with the task of designing and manufacturing a small metal tray, and this will have welded corners and be drilled with fixing holes. A list of the steps necessary to produce the box is shown in the bar chart of Figure 5:3. Of course, such a simple example would not normally result in planning of any sort, but the bar chart does show the time relationship between the different operations to good effect.

If the tray project were to be depicted in network form, the result would be that shown in Figure 5:4. Here, a series of activities corresponding to the operations of the bar chart is shown taking place one after the other. Unlike the bar chart, the diagram has no scale. Instead, the estimated duration of each operation has been written above its arrow. No account is taken of manpower requirements at this stage. If two or more men have to work on the box simultaneously, this cannot be shown. The estimates refer to duration, or elapsed time, and not the work content.

It is important that the difference between estimates of duration and work content is clearly understood. Network analysis is basically a tool for analysing the time relationship between project activities, and does not take into account resource restrictions. This time analysis, as will be shown later

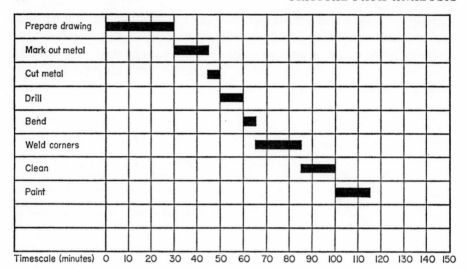

FIGURE 5:3   METAL TRAY PROJECT—BAR CHART VERSION
This bar chart shows the steps necessary to construct a metal tray. It is
drawn to scale, and gives a good, effective display. Restrictions between
different activities are, however, not shown

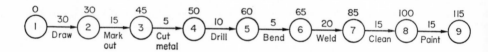

FIGURE 5:4   METAL TRAY PROJECT—NETWORK VERSION
This network carries the same data as the bar chart shown in Figure 5:3.
The display is not immediately so effective because it is not drawn to
scale. Notice, however, that the sequence of activities is much more
clearly shown. The numbers above each activity are the estimated
duration, in minutes. The number above each event is the earliest possible
time at which the event can be achieved, expressed in minutes measured
from the start of the network

does provide a basis for the allocation of resources, but these are calculated
as a follow-on step from the network calculations.

It follows that when estimates are being made for any particular activity,
it is not necessary to ask the question "Will resources be available, or will

they be tied up on another activity?" On the other hand, if there is an activity which could be done in (say) four days with two men or two days with four men, the planner would use the four day option for his duration estimate if he was aware that only two men were totally available.

In the bar chart version of the plan for making a tray, the total time required can be read off the scale. It is seen to be 115 minutes. The same answer is obtained from the network, where the estimates are added arithmetically, in sequence from left to right. The intermediate answer for each event is written above the appropriate circle. Whereas the bar chart timing is regarded as a fixed schedule, the network timing is considered from a slightly different aspect. The time written above each event is *the earliest possible time* at which that event can be achieved. This, therefore, means that 115 minutes is the earliest possible completion time for the whole project.

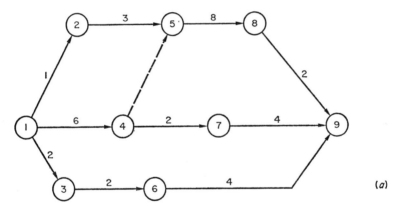

(a)

FIGURE 5:5 CALCULATION OF THE CRITICAL PATH
This diagram shows the basic steps necessary to arrive at time analysis, and location of the critical path. In (a), estimates have been made for the duration of each activity, and the results written immediately through above each arrow. In (b) the process has been carried to the next stage by adding up all these estimates along the various routes through the network. For each event it is possible to calculate the earliest possible completion time, and the results can be seen written above the event circles. In (c), the latest permissible completion time for each event has been found by subtracting the duration of each activity from the latest permissible time of its completion event. These latest times are written beneath the event circles. Events which have their earliest and latest completion times equal, must be finished at their earliest possible completion times if the project itself is to be finished in the shortest possible time. The activities joining these events lie on the critical path, which is shown here in heavy lines

In Figure 5:5 a more substantial network is illustrated. Consider first Figure 5:5(*a*). Notice that there is more than one possible path through the network to eventual completion of the project at event 9. One of these paths lies through the dotted arrow 4, 5. This activity does not represent any work, but implies a restriction on the start of activity 5, 8. Not only is activity 5, 8 dependent on completion of activity 2, 5 for "permission to start," but the dotted arrow has extended the restriction to include activity 1, 4 also. Another way of stating this is to say that event 5 cannot be considered achieved until both activities 2, 5 and 1, 4 have been finished. Dotted arrows, which usually have zero time value, are called *dummy activities*.

Now turn to Figure 5:5(*b*). The earliest possible completion times for all events have been calculated, and the results written above the circles, in just the same way as the first example of Figure 5:4. This time, however, care has to be taken in selecting the correct path to each event, since different answers can be obtained according to the path chosen. The estimates must be added up along each alternative route, and the *highest* value taken, since this must determine the earliest possible completion time for the particular event. Notice that for event 5 in this case, the longest path actually passes through the dummy.

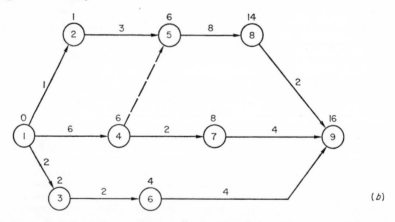

Assume that the units of time used in Figure 5:5 are working days. It follows that completion of the project, at event 9, will be sixteen days. This is the earliest possible time at which the project can be finished, provided that no unexpected delays are encountered and all estimates prove correct. Athough sixteen days represents the shortest feasible project duration, the real life situation may allow some relaxation in the program. Usually, some target completion date must be set for the finish, tied to a customer requirement or some other commitment. Any period by which the target date lags behind the earliest possible date is called the slack period or, more commonly, the project *float*.

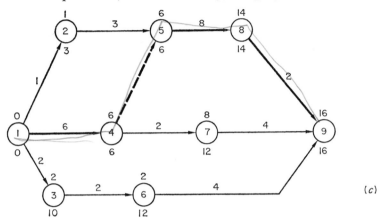

Unfortunately there is usually insufficient time available in everyday industrial life, and it is fairly safe to assume that if this project *can* be achieved in sixteen days, then that is when it *must* be finished. If this is indeed the case, the result is indicated on the network diagram by writing the latest permissible completion time underneath the final event. This has been done, and the figure 16 is seen written underneath event 9 in Figure 5:5(*c*). The effect of this action is to freeze the time at which event 9 can occur. No freedom of choice is left to the planner. The completion date for event 9 is a *critical* date, without any float.

It is now possible to consider the network in detail, in order that the significance of every activity can be assessed in relation to the overall goal of sixteen days. The analysis is carried through from right to left, in the reverse direction from the initial calculation of project duration. Starting at event 9, the duration for each activity is subtracted from the latest permissible completion time of its finish event. For activity 8, 9 therefore, the calculation is $16 - 2 = 14$. The result, 14, is the latest permissible date at which the start event for activity 8, 9 can be achieved if the project is to finish in sixteen days. This answer is written below event 8 which is, in this case, seen to be critical because the latest permissible time equals the earliest possible completion time, and there is zero float.

At event 7, a similar calculation shows that the latest permissible completion date is day 12 (16 — 4 = 12). But the earliest possible finish date for event 7 precedes this result by four days, at day 8. Event 7 is therefore said to have a float of four days. This amount of float can also be allowed for activity 4, 7 or activity 7, 9. If activity 4, 7 happens to be delayed from its earliest possible start, however, it will eat into the float available for the following event. The period of four days is therefore referred to as the *total float* for either of these activities. There are several other kinds of float, and the subject is dealt with more exhaustively in Chapter 6.

In any network where the completion event is critical, there will always be found one chain of activities which links a series of critical events. None of these activities will possess any float. The route through the network formed by these activities is called the *critical path*. These are the project tasks which most deserve close management supervision, since a delay in any one of them must delay the completion of the project by a corresponding amount. In Figure 5:5(*c*) the critical path is shown by heavy lines. It passes through events 1, 4, 5, 8 and 9. Note that networks can sometimes contain more than one critical path.

The procedure leading to evaluation of float for all activities, and therefore to the location of the critical path, is known as time analysis. The calculations are not usually difficult, and are feasible for networks containing several hundred activities. If, however, the analysis has to be repeated at frequent intervals because of schedule changes, then networks which exceed about one hundred activities will become too difficult to manage by normal mental arithmetic. A further complication is added when the day numbers have to be translated into calendar dates. It is all very well to do the translation once, but it becomes very tedious when frequent changes occur.

Translation of day numbers into calendar dates can be made easier by the provision of a key. This has been done in the case study which follows (see Figure 5:7). This method is far better than any attempt to write dates above and below the event circles. Dates look very fine initially, but the mess that results from the revision of a large network has to be seen to be believed. If networks are too big to be calculated by hand, effective computer programs exist which can take over. The use of computers is dealt with fully in following chapters.

The language of networking is simple, yet powerful. Because they are not drawn to scale, networks can be drawn without the aid of drawing boards or instruments. The vocabulary is limited to three items—events, activities and dummies. Even the most complicated plan can be expressed by deploying the methods so far described, provided that resource restrictions do not have to be taken into account. A simple, but practical example will now be introduced to illustrate the use of network analysis in planning the timescale of an actual project.

Case study—hearing aid project

Lenden-Ear Limited was a small company which employed some 200 people for the purpose of designing, making and marketing hearing aids. During the approximate period 1955 to 1965 this industry was able to achieve considerable progress towards the prime technical goal of hearing aids, namely that they should be so small as to be virtually invisible in use. The introduction of transistors, development of mercury cells in sub-miniature form and, more recently, the availability of integrated circuits have all helped towards this progress.

Encouraged by technological progress, and goaded by fierce competition, this particular company introduced new models to its range at the rate of about one each year. Engineering design was entrusted to "project engin-eers," each of whom had complete responsibility for the mechanical and electrical development of one hearing aid, right through to the time when successful batch production had been achieved. The total time elapsing between the birth of a new project and full scale production sometimes approached two years. The project engineer himself was expected to keep the program on schedule.

Now consider the situation at the start of a new project. In order to launch the design, a meeting was called between the chief engineer, market-ing manager, production manager and the project engineer appointed to carry out the work. It was decided to follow the company's usual practice of drawing up a critical path network to define the way in which the job should be followed through to completion. All of those present had received some network experience, but only the project engineer had any formal training, received at a two-day seminar run by an industrial training organisation. He was sufficiently competent to undertake the construction of the network, which is reproduced in Figure 5:6.

The first, and seemingly obvious, question asked by the project engineer was "What do you want me to design?" It is surprising how many projects are undertaken without definition of the problem. Contracts for the

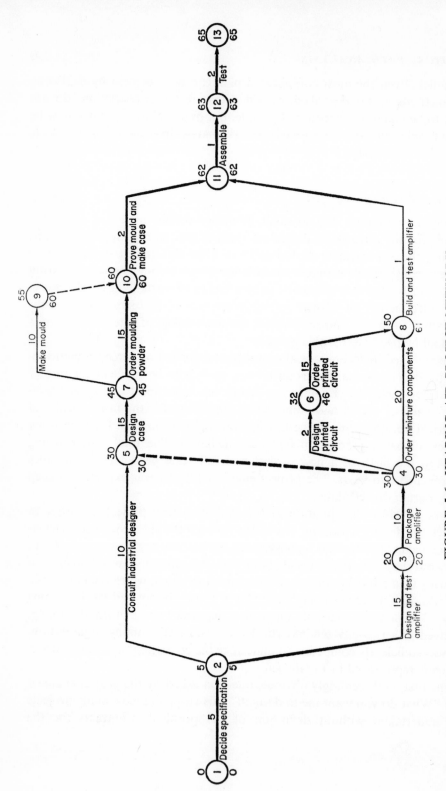

FIGURE 5:6 HEARING AID PROJECT NETWORK

This network was produced in order to plan and control the progress of a project to design and construct a prototype model of a hearing aid

fulfilment of customer orders may bear no relation to the actual intention of the proposal. If work proceeds without adequate preliminary definition, costs and timescale can be dangerously exceeded, and the results could be so different from those originally wanted as to be useless. Fortunately, these problems were well appreciated in the offices of Lenden-Ear Limited, and it was agreed that the first task was to write down a specification for the size, shape and performance of the new instrument. The start of the network reflects this decision. It is seen that activity 1, 2 has been allowed a duration of five working days, equivalent to one calendar week.

In order to continue development of the network diagram, and therefore the plan of campaign, those present at the initial project meeting had to project their thoughts forward to the time when the specification would be ready, and consider which steps to take next. It was decided that the firm's consultant industrial designer would be called in to advise on the styling of the case. This would be able to start as soon as the specification was known. At the same time, there was no reason why the project engineer should not start on the design of the electrical circuit. These decisions are shown as activities 2, 5 and 2, 3 on the network.

By following this process of thinking ahead, using their imagination, and progressing systematically through all the logical steps to making a working prototype, the project team was able to complete the network. Notice, for example, that the case design (activity 5, 7) cannot start until the industrial designer has been consulted (activity 2, 5). Also restricting the start of case design is the packaging of the electrical circuits at activity 3, 4. The engineer must know how big the amplifier will be before he can design the case round it. The dummy arrow 4, 5 was used to show this particular restriction.

The dummy activity 9, 10 was not strictly necessary in this example. Activity 7,9 "make mould" could have been terminated at event 10, as activity 7, 10. The dummy does not alter the logical significance of the network at all, and whether it is there or not both activities "make mould" and "order moulding powder" can take place in parallel. However, should it be wished to process the network by computer, the numerical identification of activities and not their verbal descriptions are the means of identification that the computer is programmed to recognise. Without the dummy, both activities would bear the identification "7, 10", and the computer would be confused and unable to distinguish between them.

Once the sequence of events had been agreed, it was necessary to make estimates for the duration of all activities and carry out time analysis. This was done, and the results are apparent in Figure 5:6. It is seen that the expected project duration is sixty-five working days, or thirteen calendar weeks. This is considerably less than the firm's customary performance in introducing a new model, but it must be remembered that most of the production snags will be encountered after the prototype stage, during the first production runs. Nevertheless, the use of this network can herald a speeding up of operations over former planning methods because of the more detailed control afforded. Introduction of full-scale production could

DAY NO.	DATE	DAY NO.	DATE	DAY NO.	DATE
1	30 Sep 68	26	4 Nov 68	51	9 Dec 68
2	1 Oct 68	27	5 Nov 68	52	10 Dec 68
3	2 Oct 68	28	6 Nov 68	53	11 Dec 68
4	3 Oct 68	29	7 Nov 68	54	12 Dec 68
5	4 Oct 68	30	8 Nov 68	55	13 Dec 68
6	7 Oct 68	31	11 Nov 68	56	16 Dec 68
7	8 Oct 68	32	12 Nov 68	57	17 Dec 68
8	9 Oct 68	33	13 Nov 68	58	18 Dec 68
9	10 Oct 68	34	14 Nov 68	59	19 Dec 68
10	11 Oct 68	35	15 Nov 68	60	20 Dec 68
11	14 Oct 68	36	18 Nov 68	61	23 Dec 68
12	15 Oct 68	37	19 Nov 68	62	24 Dec 68
13	16 Oct 68	38	20 Nov 68	63	30 Dec 68
14	17 Oct 68	39	21 Nov 68	64	31 Dec 68
15	18 Oct 68	40	22 Nov 68	65	1 Jan 69
16	21 Oct 68	41	25 Nov 68	66	2 Jan 69
17	22 Oct 68	42	26 Nov 68	67	3 Jan 69
18	23 Oct 68	43	27 Nov 68	68	6 Jan 69
19	24 Oct 68	44	28 Nov 68	69	7 Jan 69
20	25 Oct 68	45	29 Nov 68	70	8 Jan 69
21	28 Oct 68	46	2 Dec 68	71	9 Jan 69
22	29 Oct 68	47	3 Dec 68	72	10 Jan 69
23	30 Oct 68	48	4 Dec 68	73	13 Jan 69
24	31 Oct 68	49	5 Dec 68	74	14 Jan 69
25	1 Nov 68	50	6 Dec 68	75	15 Jan 69

FIGURE 5:7 NETWORK CALENDAR FOR LENDEN-EAR
PROJECT
It is convenient to calculate network times by day numbers on the network diagram, and convert them afterwards into calendar dates by the use of a table similar to that above. Notice that weekends and holidays have been omitted, since they are not valid working days

be planned in a series of further steps, resulting in another network diagram to take over control where that of Figure 5:6 finishes.

On leaving the project meeting, the engineer's first task was to copy out the network from the original, in order to tidy it up and remove the smudges and erasures left behind by changes of mind as the plan was thrashed out at the meeting. For this simple example, the original did not look too bad. For more complex projects it is sometimes advisable to redraw the network diagram before carrying out time analysis. There is no need for drafting perfection in networks, and the only tools necessary are a ruler for the arrows and a stencil for the circles. Twenty minutes would be an ample allowance for copying the Lenden-Ear network.

A useful accessory for any network that is to be controlled without a computer is a conversion chart for translating network day numbers into calendar dates. Although it would be possible to write actual dates above and below events on the actual diagram, any change of schedule will result in considerable difficulty when time analysis is repeated. It is easier to work with simple numbers on the network, and then convert them afterwards. The conversion chart produced for the Lenden-Ear project is shown at Figure 5:7.

Design of the new hearing aid started according to plan on day 1, or, as the network calendar indicates, 30 September. The specification was written in the allotted five days, and the first problem was encountered the following Monday, 7 October. A meeting with the industrial designer showed that he was too busy to undertake the work immediately, and could not meet his estimated time of ten days. In fairness to him, this estimate had been made without his consent, at a project meeting that he did not attend. Estimates frequently have to be made in this way, and project leaders should not be surprised to find that they have been mistaken in estimating functions over which they have no control or experience.

Reference to the network showed that although event 2 must be achieved by day 5, event 5 could be delayed until day 30 with no ill effect. An interval of twenty-five days existed for activity 2,5, defined by the latest permissible completion dates of its start and finish events. Since only ten days were required for the actual work, the engineer and the industrial designer were therefore able to come to a quick agreement to the effect that the styling sketches would not be required until day 30, or 8 November.

Later in the Lenden-Ear development program, the project engineer found that he was faced with a choice between two jobs. When the amplifier had been designed, tested and fitted into the smallest volume possible, he could either start designing the case or the printed circuit. A glance at the network showed him that the case was a critical item, and he therefore started that right away. Design of the case was achieved according to schedule, but as it was nearing completion the project engineer noticed from the network that activity 4,6 "design printed circuit" had not started, and was running out of float. If it could not be started by day 44, then it would be at least one day late. The problem was solved by taking the work home over one weekend, and working some overtime. Normally overtime and weekends are not built into plans, since they are useful reserves to set against unforeseen contingencies. It is only worth spending time in catching up late activities, however, if they are critical or in danger of becoming so.

Two points are worthy of comment here. Any plan which does not take resource restrictions into account is not a complete solution. The engineer should have been able to get extra help to design his circuit board. If that help could not be given, then the plan should have been arranged accordingly. Resource scheduling is a specialised planning function which takes the process of project control one step beyond network analysis. The subject will be dealt with in later chapters. Another feature of this hearing aid example is that the engineer was concerned that he was going to be only one day late. Many people in this situation would have shrugged this off as insignificant. Odd days have a nasty habit of being cumulative throughout a project, however, and it is always right to pay attention to even the smallest delay on a critical activity.

By adhering to the planned sequence of events, and by making certain that all events were achieved before their latest permissible dates, the prototype hearing aid was ready on time. Of course this project was very simple, and the network contained only sixteen activities. Nevertheless, the example is useful because, with the exception of resource scheduling, all the features essential for the planning of larger projects are illustrated. Note that the end objectives were defined by a specification at the outset. Use of a network aided the evolution of a sensible working plan and allowed the decisions to be expressed on paper.

As work proceeded, careful control of the timescale was possible because the significance of each event towards meeting the end date was known. Whenever a choice of action had to be made, the network was consulted and used to determine priorities. Those activities which were critical or had the least amount of float were given priority over those with greater float, and started first. If any activity threatened to exceed its estimated duration the project engineer was able to determine immediately the delay that would result in the overall project if no corrective action were to be taken. Even if the project had been of several years' duration, and not just a few weeks, it would have been possible to assess the effect of one late activity right at the start. The sounding of early warnings when things go wrong allow the management time in which to take effective counteraction.

A project of such small size could obviously have been achieved without network analysis. In fact, the bar chart shown in Figure 4:4 is an alternative method for expressing the same schedule as that shown in Figure 5:6, and the time scale is identical. At first sight, the bar chart version appears to offer a more acceptable display, mainly because it is drawn to scale so that the various activities are placed on the chart according to their time relationship. Restrictions on the start of any activity are shown in relation to other activities by vertical linking bars. Indeed, many project managers do convert the results of network analysis into bar charts of this type so that resources can be scheduled, and to improve the visual display.

However, linked bar charts are very difficult to draw for larger projects. Inclusion of all the restrictions between activities would prove to be impossible, or at least extremely tedious and inflexible to change. Even in this simple case there is an error contained in the logic, as expressed in Figure 4:4. Note that the bar chart has prevented the start of work on the design of the printed circuit board, on the ordering of miniature components and on the design of the case, until the industrial designer consultation has been finished. The network notation of Figure 5:6 is more powerful, and has allowed the correct restrictions to be shown. It is seen that the circuit design and component ordering are not, in fact, restricted at all by the industrial designer's report.

PLANNING FOR SHORTENED PROJECT DURATION

It has been shown that the use of CPA can provide management with the means for controlling project timescales. If a network were to be produced, for example, which predicted a project duration of 100 weeks, then provided that the plan was sensibly constructed and diligently followed up, the project would stand a far better chance of completion on time than if no network had been drawn. Suppose, however, that this project with a planned duration of 100 weeks had been sold to a customer against a firm delivery promise of only 80 weeks. In effect, planning by network has merely served to show that the original delivery promise was too optimistic. Many planners will be familiar with this situation, where the preparation of detailed plans after receipt of a customer's order apparently indicates that there is no hope whatever of meeting the promised delivery dates.

There are several ways open to a project manager who is faced with the need to condense his program into a smaller timespan. One possible approach would be to question the proposed technical design, and with it the methods of execution that must be employed. Technical management of projects falls outside the scope of this book, and will not always be within the authority of project planners. Nevertheless, when the planned timescale is too long, the technical approach, and not only the plan itself must be questioned. Of course the technical specification must be satisfied. However, the application of value engineering, and the arrangement of discussions between design staff and those responsible for purchasing and production can lead to significant results. Savings can be achieved either by reducing the amount of effort needed to produce the desired end results, or by altering material requirements to those which can be more quickly obtained. As a general rule it might be claimed that shortening a planned timescale by management decisions will increase both risk and costs, whereas timescale improvements achieved through technical decisions will generally reduce the timescale and project costs.

Assuming that even after consideration of design changes no improvement can be made in the project duration, there remain several other possible avenues of approach. One of these is to go through the network and chop all the estimates by a factor. It is not really necessary to labour the reasons why arbitrary reductions of activity durations should never be made. If a plan is not based on reliable estimates it will be suspect from the outset. As such a plan proceeds, those who are being controlled by its detailed instructions will become disillusioned and unwilling to co-operate in this, or any future plan. In any case, the project would be late. This does not, of course, mean that estimates can never be reduced, but if they are management must be able to say how the shortened duration is going to be achieved.

One method for expediting a project which often bears fruit is to carry out a re-examination of the network sequence. Sometimes critical activities can be started earlier, at the expense of accepting a degree of risk. An example of this is provided by the preparation of a set of manufacturing drawings. In one particular company, the preferred sequence for producing drawings is that shown in Figure 5:8(*a*). It is considered both convenient and safer to hand over work from each activity to the next as a complete, finished parcel. If the project commitments do not allow such clear-cut divisions it is possible to overlap the activities, as shown in Figure 5:8(*b*).

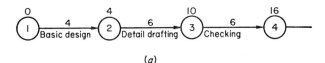

(*a*)

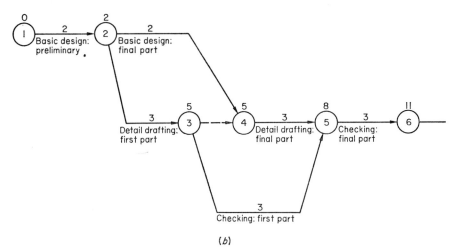

(*b*)

FIGURE 5:8 SAVING TIME BY OVERLAPPING ACTIVITIES
In the network at (*a*), the duration is seen to be sixteen days. If this prediction proves to be unacceptable, it is possible to consider shortening the duration by allowing activities to start before their preceding activities have been completely finished. In this example, for instance, the draughtsman could start to receive his detail drawing instructions before basic design has been entirely completed. The result, shown at (*b*), adds to the risk of later modifications, but saves an initial five days of project duration

Allowing activities to overlap reduces the time required to complete a set of drawings, but there is an associated risk of extra cost. If, for example, the design engineer gives bits and pieces of work to the detail draughtsman before the whole design has been completed, then some of the first detail drawings produced may have to be completely redrawn. Nevertheless, the expense of such risks, when weighed against the costs associated with the delay in project completion that must result if no overlapping were allowed, may be completely justified.

Some companies and computer bureaux use standard forms of network notation to indicate overlapping activities. These are referred to as ladder networks, and the example shown in Figure 5:9, because of its pictorial resemblance to a ladder, demonstrates the source of the conventional name. Planners who wish to make extensive use of overlapping activities would do well to consider the use of a more powerful network notation, introduced in recent years. This is the precedence method. An account of precedence networking is given in Chapter 11.

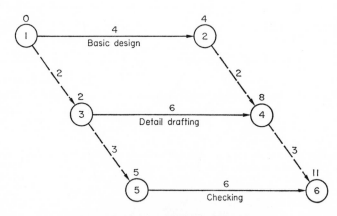

FIGURE 5:9   LADDER NETWORK
This is one way of expressing the network shown in Figure 5:8 (*b*), in a
slightly simpler form

If all else fails a project can usually be speeded up by spending more money in order to "crash" the times of one or more critical activities. CPM, in its complete form, takes account of this fact. A somewhat academic representation of the relationship between duration and cost is shown in Figure 5:10. In general, there is an economic duration for every activity. If this optimum time needs to be reduced by emergency crash action, then money must be spent. This extra cost might take the form of overtime premiums, hire of special plant, use of sub-contract labour, waiving of purchasing by competitive tender, the provision of special messengers and many other more extreme measures. On the other hand, if the optimum duration is exceeded by a significant amount, costs will be pushed up by the attraction of fixed expenses (overhead) and even the payment of higher prices for labour and materials because of inflation. The application of CPM to optimise the cost-time relationship is amplified in the case study which follows.

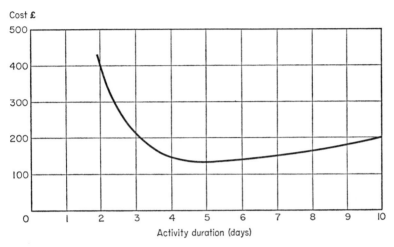

FIGURE 5:10   A TIME/COST CURVE
The lowest point on the curve corresponds to the most economic duration for completing an activity. The cost will increase if undue delays occur, owing to the attraction of overheads. Extra money could, on the other hand, be spent in order to shorten the timescale on a crash basis

Case study—kitchen project

A manufacturing company occupies premises which include a large works canteen, capable of seating some 600 employees. Each year, the company closes down completely for summer vacation. It is customary to carry out any major overhauls and maintenance of key plant and services during this period. This year, a complete refurbishing of the canteen kitchens is planned. All the work must be condensed into the two week shut-down period.

The job has been planned by network, and the initial result can be seen in Figure 5:11. All estimates on this network are expressed in half-day units. No weekend working is permitted at all, because of special site security restrictions. An estimate of ten units, therefore, is equivalent to five full working days or one calendar week. In terms of network time, the project start date at time "0" is six weeks in advance of the actual shut-down period.

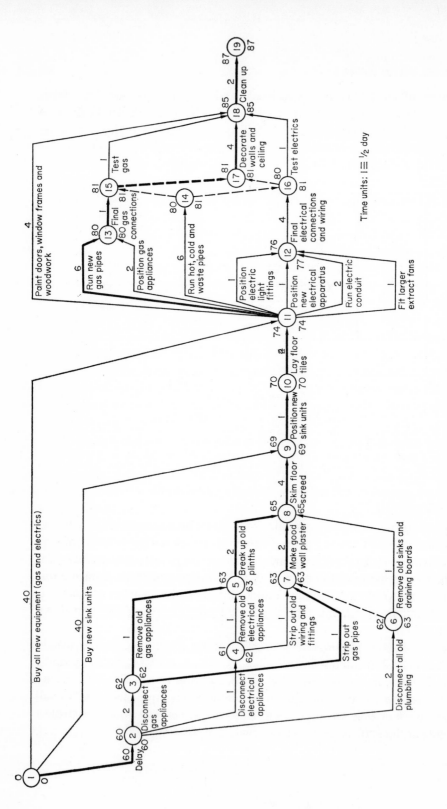

FIGURE 5:11 KITCHEN PROJECT—THE INITIAL NETWORK

This is a network showing the refurbishing of a factory canteen kitchen. The duration indicated is unacceptable, because if the project takes eighty-seven half days, the canteen cannot be back in operation when the workers return from the summer holiday shut-down

This gives sufficient time in which to procure all the new kitchen equipment. The network has been arranged to include this six weeks by introducing a "delay" activity of sixty units (activity 1,2).

In terms of half-day units, the two week shut-down is represented on the network by a duration of 20. Therefore, if the shut-down starts at time 60, completion of the work must be achieved on or before time 80. But the results of time analysis, as shown on the network of Figure 5:11, indicate a total duration of 87, which exceeds the time available by seven half-day units. Unless special steps can be taken, the workers will go short of canteen services on return from their annual holidays.

Now suppose that the project manager, aware of the need to take urgent planning action, considers all the activities which are capable of being speeded up by one means or another. He could list them, and make some assessment of the additional costs that might be incurred as a result of the crash action. This has been done, and the results are shown in the table of Figure 5:12. Activities not listed in this table have been omitted because they cannot be speeded up at all, no matter how much money is spent. Examples of the reasons for cost additions are the inability to shop around for lowest competitive prices for the kitchen equipment, and the payment of overtime premiums to some of the workmen. It is also well known that a job can be speeded up by putting more men in to help, but that the total man-hour content is likely to increase as a result, simply because they tend to get in each other's way at times, and therefore work inefficiently.

If, in desperation, the project manager allowed himself to take panic measures and order crash action for all activities, the total extra cost would amount to about £207. This amount is obtained by adding all the estimates in column 4 of the table in Figure 5:12. Such things do happen in practice. One can imagine the cry "We must get this job done on time at all costs." But, is it necessary to crash every activity in order to get this project completed by time 87?

Consider, for example, the purchase of all new kitchen equipment. The project manager does not need the network to tell him that he has ample time available in which to go out for competitive quotations. He only needs four weeks, and the start of the annual holiday is six weeks away. If £100 had been spent in reducing delivery of equipment from twenty to fifteen days, the money would have been wasted. In fact, the equipment might have proved embarrassing to store. The other activities, however, need more careful consideration.

1 ACTIVITY	2 ECONOMIC DURATION half days	3 CRASH DURATION half days	4 EXTRA COST OF CRASH ACTION £	5 COST FOR EACH TIME UNIT SAVED £
1–11 Buy all new equipment	40	30	100	10
2–3 Disconnect gas appliances	2	1	2	2
2–6 Disconnect all old plumbing	2	1	2	2
5–8 Break up old plinths	2	1	4	4
7–8 Make good plaster	2	1	5	5
8–9 Floor screed renewal	4	2	8	4
10–11 Lay floor tiles	4	2	7	3.5
11–12 Run new electric conduit	2	1	6	6
12–16 Final electrical connections and wiring	4	1	21	7
17–18 Decorate walls and ceiling	4	2	10	5
18–19 Clean up	2	1	nil	nil
11–18 Paint doors and window frames	4	3	2	2
11–14 Run hot, cold and waste pipes	6	2	24	8
11–13 Position gas appliances	2	1	nil	nil
11–13 Run gas pipes	6	2	16	4

FIGURE 5:12 KITCHEN PROJECT—TABLE OF COSTS FOR CRASHING ACTIVITY TIMES

The above table represents decisions made by the project manager for the kitchen project, the network for which appears in Figure 5:11. Activities included in the table can be shortened to durations less than those estimated for the original network. In most cases, however, this "crash" action will increase the costs. Some activities can be shortened for less expenditure than others, and the relative return on extra money spent for crashing has been calculated in the right-hand column. These comparative costs assist the project manager in choosing which activities to crash, in order to shorten the program to the required time

The first job of the planner is to eliminate all other activities which can produce no benefit to the overall timescale if they are subjected to crash action. The purchase of kitchen equipment was an obvious example, but the network must be examined to find all the others. Bearing in mind that a time reduction in total project timescale of seven half-days is required, there will be no point in shortening the times of activities which have float in excess of 7. Each activity in the table must be checked against the network, and crossed off the list if its float is equal to or greater than 7. The result is the deletion of activity 11,18, which has a float equal to 7. All other activities are either critical, or have insufficient float.

Each of the remaining activities can be assessed in two ways to determine the most effective way of spending extra money to reduce the project duration. First, it is possible to make an estimate of the relative cost of shortening the individual activities, and this has been done in Figure 5:12. Taking activity 12,16 as an example, note that three time units can be saved for the expenditure of an additional £21. Thus the cost of a time unit, or half-day, saved is £7. On the other hand, some of the activities can be shortened for as little as an additional £2 per half day, or even at no cost at all. Obviously, this factor should be taken into account when deciding on the final plan of action.

Now suppose that it was decided to crash the time of activity 5,8. A glance at the network, Figure 5:11, will show that this activity is critical. However, even if it is shortened, the parallel critical path through activities 3,7 and 7,8 will remain, so that the overall project will not be speeded up. The activity 7,8 would also have to be crashed, increasing the total cost of saving one half day to the sum of both crash actions, or £9. It is better, in this case, to choose at first those activities which lie along the single critical path, with no critical or near critical activities running in parallel.

A trial and error process is necessary from this point onwards, in order to determine the most economic course of action. The possible effect on cost and time of crashing each activity has to be looked at in turn, although experience and practice will soon teach the planner which activities are the most likely candidates for attention. The factors of least float and minimum cost are the two main criteria. In this particular example, there are several possible solutions. It has been found, for instance, that activities 10,11; 11,13; 11,14; 18,19 and 12,16 can be crashed to save the seven half days, at an additional cost of £48.

Compared with the cost of £207, which would have resulted from panic

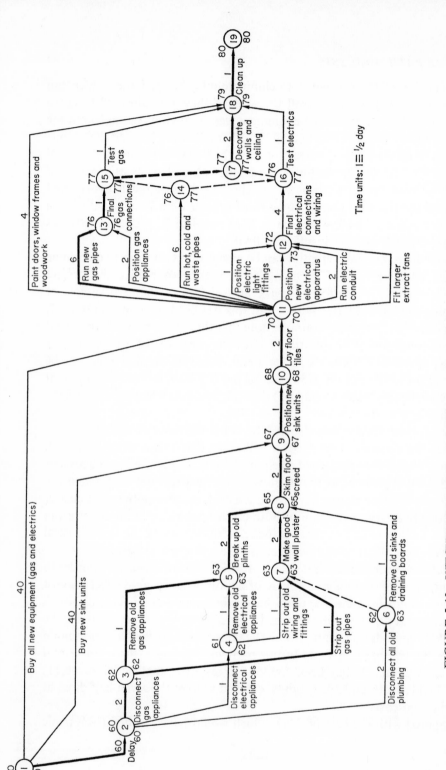

FIGURE 5:13   KITCHEN PROJECT NETWORK AFTER SELECTIVE CRASH ACTION

This is the same network as that shown in Figure 5:11, except that the overall duration of the project has been shortened to eighty half days. This was necessary in order to allow the canteen to re-open in time for workers returning from the company's annual shutdown. The important point here is that the network was used to decide which activities had to be subjected to crash action. By being selective, and choosing only critical activities, the project was speeded up at minimum cost

action in crashing all activities, this represents a considerable saving. But, continued attention to the network reveals that another, more effective solution remains. This is shown by the revised network in Figure 5:13. It is seen that by crashing activities 8,9; 10,11; 17,18 and 18,19 the seven half days can be saved for a cost of only £25. Network analysis has therefore provided the project manager with the means to cut his total cost risk from £207 to £25, for the effort of only a couple of hours planning with simple pencil and paper.

In the kitchen project it was only necessary to reduce the project duration by seven half days, but sometimes a planner is faced with the problem of planning his project for the shortest possible duration. If critical path analysis is used, and crash actions are considered, the process is just the same as that just described, but it has to be continued to the bitter end, until the critical path has been reduced to its shortest possible crash duration. Often, when a critical activity is shortened, an alternative path through the network is left with a longer duration, and therefore it takes over the critical role. In fact, it is not unusual for the critical path to undergo several changes of route when a large network is being systematically crashed. Ultimately, one critical path must emerge that is incapable of further shortening. It is then possible to consider relaxing the crash actions planned for all activities outside this path until they themselves are allowed to become just critical. In this way, a whole network can be crashed for minimum extra cost. The final result could be a network which has all its activities critical!

PERT

PERT, or Programme Evaluation and Review Technique, is another system of project planning, very similar in many respects to CPA. Both methods rely on networks for their notation, and this similarity has led to some confusion between the two systems. Most project planning by network is based on CPA, and when a project manager refers to his PERT network, the chances are that it will, on investigation, prove to be CPA.

The basic differences between PERT and CPA are to be found in the treatment given to duration estimates and time analysis. Whereas the CPA method concentrates attention onto the critical path, and to time/cost relationships, the PERT system is founded on a statistical approach. Three time estimates are made for each activity. These are:

t_o = *the most* optimistic *estimate*
t_m = *the most* likely *estimate*
t_p = *the most* pessimistic *estimate*

These three quantities are subjected to a simple mathematical treatment, in order to derive the *expected* time, t_e, for the activity. The standard formula assumes that estimates will not be biased either optimistically or pessimistically, but that the spread of actual results will be distributed equally about the arithmetic mean. The formula is:

$$t_e = \frac{t_o + 4t_m + t_p}{6}$$

By repeating this calculation throughout the network, for all activities, it is possible to calculate the probability of meeting the duration indicated by the critical path. In fact, it is well known that estimates tend to be optimistic, so that the actual duration is therefore more likely to be inclined towards the pessimistic end of the timescale. An allowance for this trend was made by one company using PERT by a slight modification to the basic formula. They skewed the result as follows:

$$t_e = \frac{t_o + 3t_m + 2t_p}{6}$$

Figure 5:14 illustrates the method of writing the three time estimates on a PERT network. However, the PERT system has now largely given way to CPA, and this account has been included primarily as a reference.

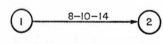

FIGURE 5:14   PERT ESTIMATES
In PERT notation, three time estimates are made for each activity. These are the optimistic, pessimistic and most likely time. This diagram shows how they are indicated on the network

IMPORTANCE OF USING CORRECT NETWORK LOGIC

The essential elements of network analysis can be taught in a few hours, and there is nothing difficult in their comprehension. Complete mastery of the art of network construction must take a little longer and a lot of practice. There are several pitfalls which can rob a potential network expert of his initial enthusiasm. Although the basic notation contains only a small number of symbols, it is not always easy to arrive at the sequence of activities which expresses the best way of carrying out a proposed project.

Two possible reasons can be cited for the construction of a network diagram whose logic is incorrect. Either the planner has been given the wrong technical information on which to build up his sequence of activities and events, or his own skill is insufficient to allow true appreciation of the logical significance of the network.

When a network is being drawn for the first time in a company, it is usual to convene a meeting of all the project key participants, in order that they can contribute to the plan of action. The role of the network analyst is to express their decisions as a written plan. A highly skilled planner can often help to ensure that the information given is both complete and correct by asking a series of check questions. For this reason, it is desirable that the planner himself has practical technical experience of the type of work being discussed.

Check questions can often take the form "Should not this activity be followed by inspection?" "Doesn't this panel need to be treated before it can be used in assembly?" or "Can this wall really be built immediately after the footings have been filled with concrete?" The task of the planner in this respect will be made easier if all the participants have received some basic training in network analysis, in order that they may be able to interpret the significance of the diagram as it grows in front of them. If a diagram emerges from an initial network meeting showing the scars of several erasures, this is a sign that active thought has been put into the logic. For this reason, the planner must never allow himself to become lazy, and reluctant to change the network when failure to do so would leave the logic incorrect.

An example of one process which can introduce an error into network logic is given in Figure 5:15. Imagine that a construction firm is drawing up an arrow diagram for the planning and control of a new building project. Figure 5:15(a) shows a small portion of the network during its development. Notice that, rather obviously, the roof frame cannot be started until the brick walls have been put up, and the timber purchased. So far, so good. Now suppose that the next activity to be added, as the network is built up, is "Point brickwork of walls." The network is consulted to find a suitable starting point, and in Figure 5:15(b) the most sensible one has been chosen. Pointing can commence as soon as the brick walls have been erected, at event 22.

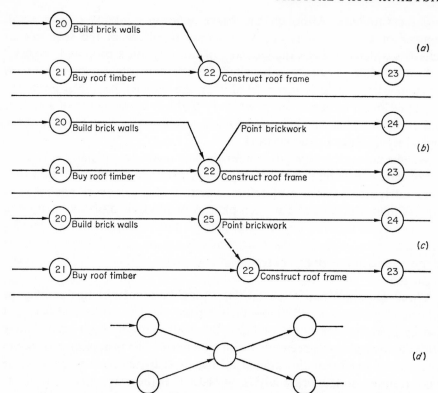

FIGURE 5:15   EXAMPLE OF AN ERROR IN NETWORK LOGIC
The network shown here, in (a), (b) and (c) is an extract from a larger
network. At (a), the diagram is under construction, whilst at (b) another
activity has been added. But this addition has introduced an error into
the logic. Although the pointing of the brickwork does depend on the
brick walls being built, it is not dependent at all on the purchase of timber
for the roof. The corrected version is shown at (c). In fact, whenever a
pattern is encountered like that shown at (d), where multiple activities enter
and leave an event, the planner must ask himself "Do all emerging
activities depend on all preceding activities?" If they do not, then the
logic must be corrected by the addition of dummies and isolating events

It is true that pointing cannot begin until the bricks have been laid. In
this respect the network logic is correct. However, notice that activity 20,21
is not the only restriction. Activity 21,22 also restricted the start of pointing,
so that according to the network it is necessary to purchase the roof timbers
before pointing can begin. This is not what the planner intended, and is
obviously wrong. The corrected logic is shown in Figure 5:15(c), where the
addition of another event and a dummy have succeeded in isolating the

unrelated activities. As a generalisation, it is always wise to question the network logic when an event has two or more activities leading into it, together with two or more activities emerging from it—see Figure 5:15(d).

USE OF DUMMIES TO IMPROVE VISUAL DISPLAY

Figure 5:15 illustrated one possible use of dummy activities in order to improve the logical meaning of a network. Other applications of dummies can aid the visual presentation of an arrow diagram, but they depend on whether or not a computer is going to be used to process the calculations of time analysis. The three networks in Figure 5:16 all carry exactly the same logical information, but their presentation has been affected by the different application of dummies. The networks all show part of a plan for an electronics project, where several subassemblies have to be made and tested, before being brought together to make one final assembly.

In Figure 5:16(a), the network is shown as it might have emerged from the planning meeting. Time analysis has been carried out and the results indicated above and below the relevant event circles. It is not possible, however, to show the earliest possible completion times for all the activities, because they share one completion event at event 40. In Figure 5:16(b), the addition of several dummies has allowed each activity to be given its own unique completion event, and it is now possible to record the earliest possible completion times on the network. Not only is the float of individual activities more obvious from a quick glance at the network, but it is also easier to use the network as a wall chart for the day-to-day control of the project. Each event can be checked off as it is achieved by colouring in the corresponding circle on the network. Such displays can be very effective.

If a computer is going to be used, however, these additional dummies can only add to the data processing costs. They become unnecessary, in any case, because the report produced by the computer will list each activity separately, together with as many time analysis details as the planner requires. Not all dummies can be deleted. If the network were to revert to that in Figure 5:16(a), the computer would be faced with two activities bearing the same identification 39,40. The network is shown adapted for computer use in Figure 5:16(c), where the dummy 45,40 has been used to give separate identities to the two parallel activities 39,45 and 39,40. The construction of a project network, therefore, must depend to some extent on whether or not it is going to be processed by a computer.

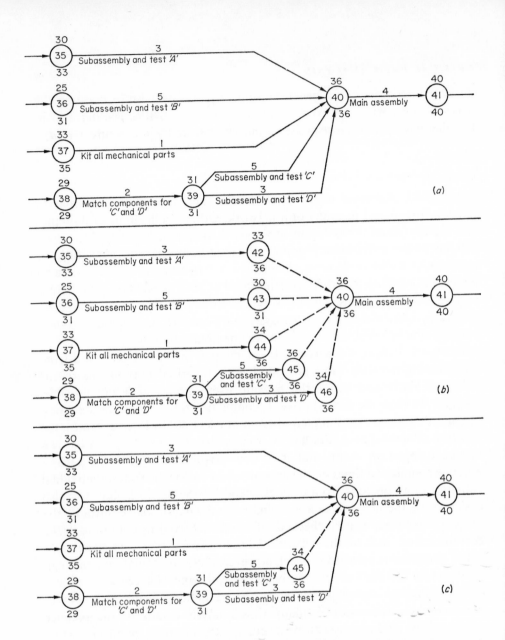

FIGURE 5:16 USE OF DUMMIES TO IMPROVE NETWORK PRESENTATION

The three networks in (a), (b) and (c) are all adapted from the same portion of a much larger network. All three versions are identical in their logical meaning. However, the addition of dummies at (b) has enabled the planner to write in the earliest possible completion times for all activities, where he was unable to do so before owing to the absence of suitable finish events for some of the activities. If this network is going to be calculated by a computer, however, these dummies will add to data processing costs. The computer version is shown at (c), where dummy 45,40 is essential in order to give activity 39,45 unique identification. If this dummy were absent, there would be two activities called 39,40, and the computer would be confused

FORWARDS OR BACKWARDS?

Most accounts of network analysis describe the construction of arrow diagrams starting at the front end, left-hand side, and proceeding to completion from left to right. Provided that a project can be planned right from the start, and picked up before any actual work has started, then this is probably the best sequence. However, when a network is drawn for a project already in progress, the start situation may be complex. This state of affairs is typical of "rescue attempts" when networking is introduced in order to pull a program back onto schedule. Under these circumstances, the finish event can often be imagined as a simple situation from which it is easy to work backwards.

One example of a backward-drawn network concerns a project which was aimed at the provision of a stand at a national exhibition of hospital equipment. The main exhibit on the stand was a complete, pre-fabricated operating theatre. Also exhibited was a wide range of associated medical equipment. This equipment included such items as heart–lung machines, steam sterilisers and racks full of electronic instrumentation for patient monitoring. As the program proceeded it became apparent to all concerned that there was a distinct danger of the exhibition opening with one stand empty. Since this was a prestige event at Olympia, this could not be allowed to happen. The state of progress was reviewed in detail, but an extremely complex situation was revealed, with bits and pieces all over the place, and in all stages of production. Some of the items had not even been designed.

Starting to draw a network under such circumstances is always difficult, but it was decided that a network had to be drawn if the project was to be achieved on time. The problem was solved by calling a meeting of all the key project members, and asking them to use their imagination to derive a plan of campaign, drawn in network form, but starting from the mental picture of the exhibition stand on the day of opening. Quite literally, these people were asked to project their thoughts forward in time, and think of visitors actually arriving on the stand. Then, they were asked, "What was the last activity immediately before opening?" The answer was, "clean up the stand." By starting from the simple situation, it was then possible for the network to be constructed, backwards.

The network grew, in a series of logical steps, working through each item on the stand in turn, until it terminated at the left-hand side in a number of start events. Each start event represented, in fact, a particular aspect of the current state of progress, or related to some activity that had not been thought of previously. Indeed, if the network had not been drawn backwards, the thought processes of the planning team would not have been directed to these forgotten activities, and they would have been remembered too late. By adapting the planning tactics to suit the requirements of the particular project situation, an apparently impossible state of affairs was retrieved. The exhibition opened on time.

6

RESOURCE ALLOCATION

One of the most important aspects of project management, and probably the most difficult, is the scheduling of resources. Project resources are usually thought of in terms of manpower, split into various degrees of skill or different trade categories. This chapter will be concerned with the relationship between network analysis and manpower scheduling. The purpose of this account is to prepare the reader for the following chapters, where the use of computers for resource scheduling will be discussed in some detail. It would be quite wrong, however, to ignore all the other resources which must be made available in sufficient quantities, and at the right time, if any project is to be completed successfully. Purchased materials, space, money and plant are perhaps the most obvious. Subcontract facilities are another example.

MATERIALS

The ordering of materials can be arranged as activities on the project network, and their deliveries can be requested from suppliers according to the dates indicated from time analysis. Provided that the lead times allowed on the network are sufficient, scheduling becomes the problem of the supplier, and not the project manager, although he may wish to reserve the right to follow up the progress of some of the firms supplying key materials.

SPACE

Space is not always a straightforward resource to plan in advance. If a fixed area of factory floorspace is set aside for assembly purposes, and all projects have to share the same area, then the parameters that have to be taken into account might be very complex. In the heavy machine tool industry, for example, not only the area has to be considered, but also many other factors such as the shape of the area, positions of factory hoists and cranes, and the saving of space that can be achieved by allowing one high machine to overhang part of a smaller unit. The best way of solving these problems is often found by presenting them to the company's production engineers. They will probably have the advantage of a physical model of the factory layout, and this can be used as a decision-making tool. Fortunately, these space problems usually work out fairly well in practice, owing to the fact that the scheduling of other resources has resulted in a smooth flow of work throughout the plant. In particular, the scheduling of assembly labour must contribute to an acceptable solution.

MONEY

A schedule of project costs, showing a predicted rate of expenditure against time, can be calculated directly from the network, provided that estimates can be made for the materials and labour necessary to complete each separate activity. The time when each activity cost must be incurred can be derived from the results of network time analysis, although there will be some choice if large amounts of float are present. Many computer programs are capable of carrying out summation of project activity costs, and scheduling them against a timescale. PERT/COST is one well established method. The use of computers in this context will be given fuller treatment in later chapters. If other resources are to be scheduled, resulting in modification of activity times, then it is obviously important that these cost calculations are performed after all scheduling has been done, and not before. Notice that cost scheduling is limited to a prediction of when money will be required. The actual provision of funds must be left to management at higher level, and the accountants, and is well outside the scope of this book. However, the cash flow situation must depend to a large extent on the performance of a company in meeting project deliveries, since if deliveries are late, then the resulting delays in receipts of customer payments must hold up the availability of funds for following projects. The project manager, therefore, has an indirect, but important, role to play in maintaining a healthy cash position for his employer.

MANUFACTURED PARTS

Parts which have to be specially manufactured for a project in a firm's own factory have to be scheduled not only to be available for the project when they are needed, but also with due regard for the economic use of the company's machining facilities. It is neither usual nor desirable for a project network to show the provision of each piece part as a separate activity. Indeed, this would normally be impossible, because most networks are drawn at a very early stage in project life, when the individual piece part requirements are not known. The logical solution is to use the network to schedule groups of manufactured parts, arranged according to project needs. Two examples can be given which illustrate this point.

Imagine a network that is designed to control the progress of a new computer development. It will be known that a power unit must be provided, and some idea of the physical size of the power unit and its manufacturing complexity can be estimated from experience gained in previous projects. The network activities relating to the provision of parts for this particular unit will be aimed at ensuring that all parts are ready when power unit assembly begins. In other words, all the mechanical parts on the power unit bill of material would be grouped together. This, of course, anticipates the actual bill of material, which may not be drawn up for several years to come. If more than one bill of material is envisaged, as will be the case if subassemblies are to be made, then it would be prudent to draw the network to this level of detail.

Another case that demonstrates a sensible choice of component grouping for network scheduling can be taken from a company which specialises in the design and manufacture of heavy, special purpose machine tool systems. Manufactured items are grouped according to the subassemblies that are known to be project requirements, although the actual physical content of these subassemblies will probably not be known until much later. These groupings correspond exactly to the forthcoming bills of material. Estimates for work content, in terms of man-hours, together with predictions of activity calendar durations, are taken from comparisons with actual results from previous project components of similar size and complexity. Groups might be defined as a complete machining head, a complete machine base together with slideways or a machining fixture. Purchased components are similarly grouped on the network.

Networks, therefore, are ideally suitable for scheduling groups of manufactured parts, linked to the needs of a single project. The earliest and latest start and finish times for every group of parts can be found by carrying out time analysis. The problem that remains is the preparation of detailed schedules which specify all the operations necessary to make individual parts, together with the timing of these operations to ensure efficient machine loading on a day to day basis. These are production control activities, and not project management functions. They should be within the capability of any well organised manufacturing organisation. However, if committed dates are being provided from flexible and dynamic project scheduling systems, then the production control systems must be able to match that flexibility, and respond to rapid changes whenever necessary.

SUBCONTRACT RESOURCES

Two basic categories of subcontract resources can be listed. Either the subcontractor is being asked to provide some specialist service, not within the scope of the project contractor, or he is being asked to provide additional capacity because similar facilities within the contractor's own plant are overloaded. For scheduling purposes, each of these categories is treated differently.

The purchase of specialised services can be regarded as an extension to the normal process of ordering materials. The services can be requested on a purchase order, prepared by the purchasing department. Delivery of the services will be asked for according to the program derived from the network. There is no need to attempt any scheduling of capacity, because this should lie within the control of the subcontractor's own organisation. There may, however, be sufficient justification for the project manager to carry out some supervision of the subcontractor's performance against his planned program.

If it ever becomes necessary to employ an outside organisation to provide facilities that are really an extension to existing project manufacturing capability, then this requirement must be planned in advance. Otherwise, the extra capacity might not be available when it is most needed. Subcontractors must be given adequate warning of the amount of work involved, and the period over which it is to be conducted. These facts are not usually determined by a conscious effort to schedule the subcontract load. Rather, they are found by attempting to schedule available internal capacity, and then observing by how much, and when, this capacity must be exceeded if the project is to be finished on the due date.

MANPOWER

When a project network is drawn, no account can be taken of the interaction between different activities from the point of view of resource clashes. Only logical restrictions can be considered at that stage, based on the method of working best suited to particular project circumstances. If the availability of manpower had to be considered as a further possible restriction on the start of activities in the network, there would be too many variables to cope with all at once. Project planning has to be approached in a series of progressive steps. Drawing the network is only one stage in the process.

The network is used to provide accurate data which specifies when each activity must take place, and how long it can be delayed without affecting the overall project duration. Resource scheduling must be carried out with due regard to these restrictions, but it is a separate, subsequent planning stage. Project schedules which are based on networks that have not been taken through to this final stage are not complete schedules, and may not be effective planning tools. The only exception to this rule applies to the unlikely possibility of unlimited resources being available. The most important resource of all, and that which usually forms the backbone of resource scheduling calculations, is manpower.

RESOURCE ALLOCATION CASE STUDY—WORKSHOP PROJECT

The following case study is introduced specifically to illustrate the principles of resource allocation in very simple terms. The project to be described would be within the scope of any project planner armed with an adjustable bar chart (Chapter 4). A computer becomes necessary to schedule resources for all but the very simplest projects, but before any attempt is made to harness the power of a computer the simple concepts outlined in this chapter must be fully appreciated. It should also be realised that although the following example is restricted to manpower scheduling, some of the other types of resource listed in the introduction to this chapter can be subjected to the same treatment if necessary.

Figure 6:1 shows a network for the construction of a brick-built workshop. The contractor carrying out this contract has a normal manpower availability of one strong labourer and one good all-round craftsman. When the network was drawn, each activity was coded to show the resource types and levels that it would need for its duration. Although the planner has observed the rule of drawing his network without regard for the deployment of

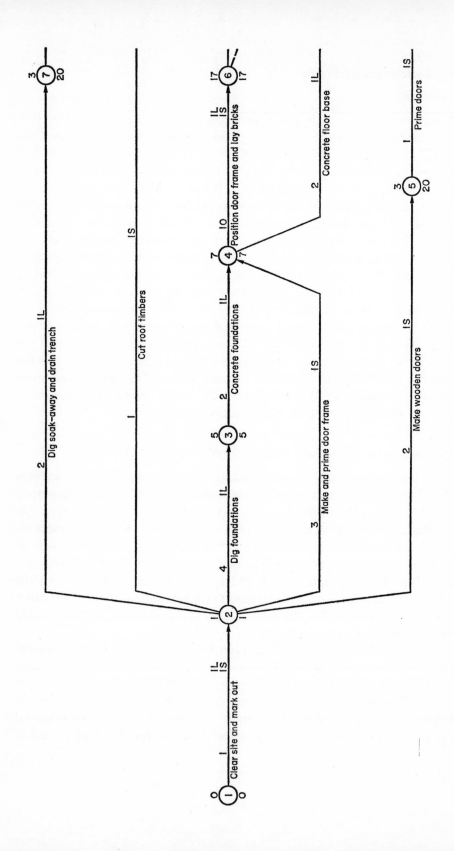

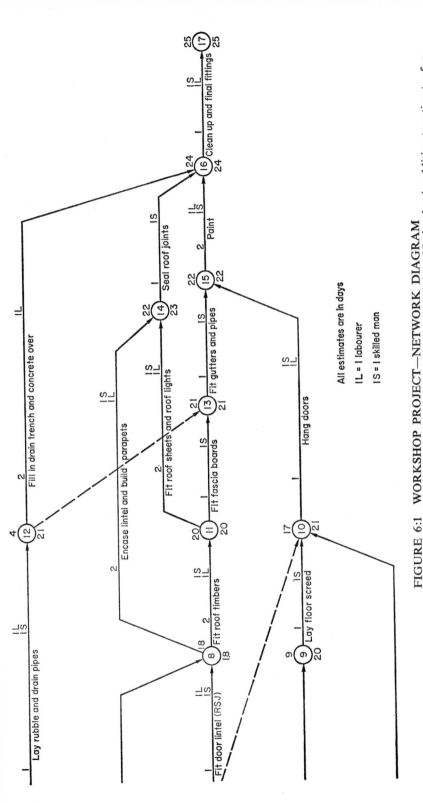

FIGURE 6:1 WORKSHOP PROJECT—NETWORK DIAGRAM

This network has been drawn in order to control the building program for a small workshop. Notice that in addition to estimates for the duration of each activity, a statement of resource requirements has also been given. When the final work schedule is produced, it must take resources into account, and compare the overall needs with those men who are available. Simple methods for performing this task are outlined in this chapter. The same network is used as a basis for more advanced methods, using a computer, demonstrated in Chapter 8

resources throughout all the different activities, he has used his common sense in not specifying resource levels for any single activity which exceed the total, known available levels. It would have been pointless, for example, to specify a resource usage of six labourers to dig the foundations, when it was well known that only one labourer was on the payroll.

The actual codes used are seen in Figure 6:1. In this case, L represents a labourer and S a skilled man. The figure placed in front of the alphabetic code denotes the rate of usage envisaged for the resource. An activity marked 4 $1L$, for example, means that a duration of four days has been estimated, and that one labourer will be needed for the whole of the activity.

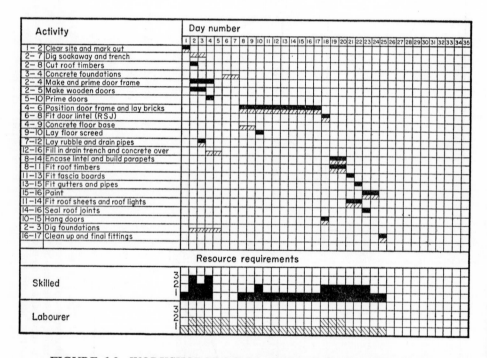

FIGURE 6:2 WORKSHOP PROJECT—RESOURCE AGGREGATION
In the upper diagram, a bar chart has been prepared with all activities shown starting at the earliest possible times calculated from the network of Figure 6:1. Summation of each column yields the resource requirements depicted in the histogram. It is easy to see that undesirable work peaks have been created, whilst at other times idle periods exist. There is obviously a need to refine this plan beyond simple aggregation of resources, in order to arrange a rate of working which is as smooth as possible

Resource aggregation

Networks are a poor method for displaying resource requirements. It is necessary to convert any plan into bar chart form if resources are going to be subjected to any calculations to determine day to day load requirements, unless a computer is going to be used. Figure 6:2 shows the result of a conversion from the network of Figure 6:1. Any float available has been ignored, and all activities have been placed on the chart at their earliest possible start times. The bar chart observes all the logical restrictions imposed by the network. No activity has been positioned at a time before its earliest possible start day.

Each activity on the bar chart has been coded to indicate the type or types of resource that it needs. The planner is then able to add up the day by day load for each different resource category. This has been done in Figure 6:2, and the results have been shown as histograms in order to provide a clear display. When all jobs have been started at their earliest possible start times, derived from network time analysis, it is apparent that no account has been taken of possible resource shortages. But if no people are available to carry out a particular activity, then the restrictions on its start become just as real as those imposed by the network logic. In fact, the schedule of Figure 6:2 would be a very undesirable plan in any case, even if unlimited resources were available, because the number of men needed fluctuates badly from day to day. However, the project duration is seen to be twenty-five days, the shortest possible time. Schedules produced by placing all activities at their earliest possible start times are called resource aggregations. They have a possible use as a means for summing total resource needs in order that project costs can be estimated. Otherwise, they are not sensible plans because of the uneven loading which results.

Resource smoothing—resource limited

In Figure 6:3 an attempt has been made to convert the workshop project network into a schedule which can be carried out within the limited resources available (one labourer, one skilled man). Apart from a one-day hiccup, when the skilled man is shown to be idle, the planner has achieved his objective of completing the project without exceeding his resource levels. He has still observed all the network restrictions between different activities, but resource limitations have compelled him to delay some activities beyond the amount of float available. The project, therefore, is going to take more than twenty-five days to complete. In fact, resource restrictions have added ten days to the planned program.

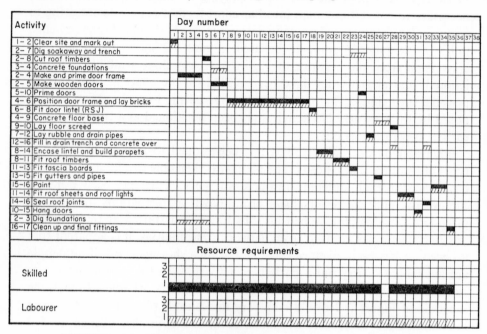

FIGURE 6:3 WORKSHOP PROJECT—RESOURCE LIMITED SCHEDULE

Realising that the resource aggregation plan shown in Figure 6:2 exceeds available resource levels, the planner has now rearranged his bar chart by delaying each activity in turn until the program can be completed within resource restrictions. The firm only has one skilled man and one labourer. The plan is now successful, in the sense that it can be completed by this work force, but this has been planned at the expense of duration. Whereas the earliest possible completion time calculated from the network is twenty-five days, resource restrictions have extended planned duration to thirty-five days

Although the program has been extended in duration by limiting the usage of resources to practical levels, the solution could be workable, provided that the customer agrees with the delivery promise. The arrangement of all activities in correct sequence is somewhat tedious, and an adjustable chart greatly speeds up the calculations. Once the size of a network exceeds about 100 activities, manual scheduling ceases to be a practical proposition, and the planner must seek the aid of a computer. The process of adjusting a schedule in order to flatten out the resource

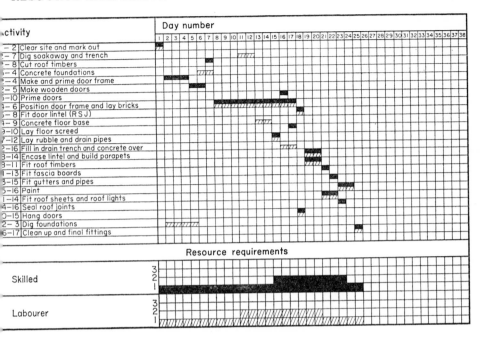

Activity		Day number 1–38
— 2	Clear site and mark out	
— 7	Dig soakaway and trench	
— 8	Cut roof timbers	
— 4	Concrete foundations	
— 4	Make and prime door frame	
— 5	Make wooden doors	
—10	Prime doors	
— 6	Position door frame and lay bricks	
— 8	Fit door lintel (R S J)	
— 9	Concrete floor base	
—10	Lay floor screed	
7—12	Lay rubble and drain pipes	
2—16	Fill in drain trench and concrete over	
3—14	Encase lintel and build parapets	
3—11	Fit roof timbers	
—13	Fit fascia boards	
3—15	Fit gutters and pipes	
5—16	Paint	
—14	Fit roof sheets and roof lights	
4—16	Seal roof joints	
0—15	Hang doors	
2— 3	Dig foundations	
6—17	Clean up and final fittings	

Resource requirements

Skilled

Labourer

FIGURE 6:4 WORKSHOP PROJECT—TIME LIMITED SCHEDULE
The workshop project cannot be completed within the shortest duration
indicated by the network unless the one man plus one labourer resource
levels are exceeded. In this schedule, the planner has managed to produce
a plan which is within the critical duration, whilst resource usage is as
smooth as possible. Excess loads do occur, but they are so arranged that
extra men can economically be brought in for well defined periods.
When this plan was devised, network restrictions were observed, so that
no activity is shown starting before completion of its preceding event. All
activities have been shuffled on the bar chart according to the amount of
float that they possess

histograms is called resource smoothing or resource allocation. If priority
is given to observing resource levels at the expense of timescale, the resource
smoothing is said to be resource limited.

Resource smoothing—time limited

If the customer had not been prepared to wait an extra ten days before he
could occupy his new workshop, the builder might have considered the use
of a few extra hands, hired on a temporary basis. The planner would then
have to adjust all the activity strips on his chart according to a different set
of rules. The schedule must be time limited, but in order to achieve this it

can be allowed to exceed the resource levels that are available normally. However, when resources are planned to exceed the set limits, the overloads must be kept to a minimum magnitude, and the usage pattern must be as smooth as possible.

One solution is shown in the schedule of Figure 6:4. It is emphasised that other arrangements of activities are possible which can also provide an acceptable plan, within the time limit of twenty-five days. Reference to the resource histograms at the foot of Figure 6:4 will show that although the usage levels have had to exceed the one labourer and one skilled man normally available, the overloads have been kept to minimum numbers, and spread over continuous, manageable periods. Once again, only small projects can be handled by bar charts in this way, and computers have to be employed to schedule really large projects. However, because a large number of different resource schedules are often possible which satisfy the time limited requirement, it is not always easy to arrange for the computer to select the smoothest. The rules are not easy to define. More will be said on this subject when the use of computers is discussed in detail.

It is sometimes useful to think of the work content of an industrial project in terms of a two-dimensional body filled with an incompressible fluid. The area of the body is constant, but the boundaries can be affected by external pressures. This concept is much simpler than it sounds, as reference to Figure 6:5 will show. If pressure is applied to condense the timescale, then resources overflow beyond their permitted level. Conversely, when resources are kept within their boundaries, the time scale must be expanded to take up the excess pressure in the system. The two cases illustrate time limited and resource limited schedules, respectively.

FLOAT

During the process of resource smoothing, two types of restraint limit the amount by which any activity can be advanced or delayed to remove unwanted peak loads. Network linkages must dictate the sequence in which jobs are scheduled, and no activity can be planned to take place before the completion of all its preceding activities. Network logic, therefore, determines the earliest time at which any activity can be started. At the other end of the scale, if it should prove necessary to delay the start of an activity owing to lack of available resources, this delay must not be allowed to exceed the float possessed by the activity if the project is to be completed

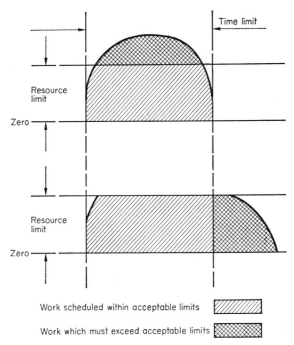

FIGURE 6:5 CONCEPT OF RESOURCE AND TIME LIMITED
SCHEDULES

The work involved in any project might be regarded as an incompressible
lump of material, bounded on the one hand by time limits and on the
other by the resources available. Timescale may be dependant only upon
the critical path duration of the network, or it could be imposed from
some other source such as contract requirements. Obviously, the timescale
can never be planned within a duration less than the critical path. When
a project demands a rate of working which exceeds available resources,
either more resources must be provided or the project must be allowed
more duration

on time. Float, therefore, determines the extent of permissible delay introduced during the resource smoothing calculations.

Float, however, is not always a simple quantity. It is usually shared
among several activities throughout a network, so that if an activity is
delayed there will probably be a reduction in the float available to remaining
activities. The exact relationship depends upon the network configuration
and its time analysis, but several types of float have been classified. These are
described in the following paragraphs, using the workshop project as a
source of illustration.

I.S.T.—D

Total float

Total float is the most common form of float. Whenever any event or activity is said to possess "float," without any further amplification of the type of float, then it is safe to assume that total float was intended. This is the maximum amount of float possible for an activity. It is provided by the condition when all preceding activities take place as early as possible, and all following activities can be delayed to their fullest extent. In other words, all the float in a particular network chain is ascribed to one of the activities in the chain.

Now refer to Figure 6:6. One activity has been extracted from the workshop project, and this is reproduced together with a fragment of bar chart showing the same activity drawn to scale. The job is shown starting at its earliest time, thus fulfilling the first condition for total float, namely that all preceding activities have been finished at their earliest possible times. If this activity is now allowed to slide out to its fullest extent along the bar chart strip, it can finish as late as day 20 before any following activities are affected. It is seen from the diagram that the total float is eleven days. This is the same result as that obtained when the difference is taken between the

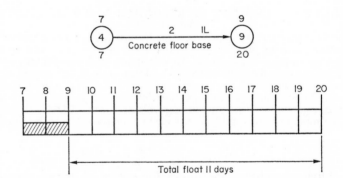

FIGURE 6:6   WORKSHOP PROJECT—FLOAT ANALYSIS OF
ACTIVITY 4,9

In this diagram, one activity has been extracted from the workshop project network of Figure 6:1 in order to examine the concept of float. By drawing the activity to scale, in bar chart form, it is possible to see that the activity can be allowed to float backwards or forwards between the outer limits of day 7 and day 20. The total amount of movement allowable is eleven days in this case. If the activity were to be delayed beyond completion on day 20, the overall project must also be finished late. Knowledge of available float is of prime importance when work is being scheduled to take account of resource restrictions

times written above and below the terminal events of the activity, although reference to the following examples will show that this difference does not always give the right answer.

For any activity therefore, total float is calculated using the expression:

Total float = latest permissible end event time—earliest possible start event time—duration of the activity itself.

When this is applied to activity 4,9 in Figure 6:6, the total float for this activity is found to be $(20 - 7 - 2) = 11$.

Free float

This is formally defined as the amount of float available when all preceding activities take place at their earliest possible times and all following activities can also be started as early as possible. The expression is:

Free float = earliest possible end event time—earliest possible start event time—duration of the activity itself.

When this expression is applied to activity 9,10, shown in Figure 6:7, free float is found to be $(17 - 9 - 1)$, or seven days.

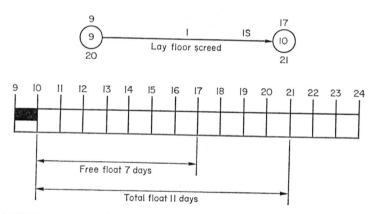

FIGURE 6:7 WORKSHOP PROJECT—FLOAT ANALYSIS OF ACTIVITY 9,10

This activity has a slightly more complex float characteristic than that shown in Figure 6:6. In common with activity 4,9 this activity also possesses a total float of eleven days. However, it could be delayed by seven days without causing similar delay to any following activity, because the earliest possible completion of event 10 is governed by other network restrictions (see Figure 6:1). This amount of seven days is free float

Independent float

This is a relatively rare kind of float, and occurs when all preceding activities take place at their latest possible times, whilst following activities start at their earliest times. In other words:

Independent float = earliest possible end event time—latest possible start
                              event time—duration of the activity itself.

Analysis of most networks will reveal very few, if any activities which possess independent float. One such activity is shown in Figure 6:8. When the appropriate figures from this example are substituted in the formula, independent float for activity 2,8 is found to be (18 — 1 — 1), or sixteen days.

Remaining float

From the practical point of view, most of these definitions of float are somewhat academic. They are included here for completeness, but most people talk simply of "float," without further qualification. In this respect they refer to total float. However, when the process of resource smoothing takes place, some total float will be lost whenever an activity is delayed to await a more favourable resource situation. Remaining float, therefore, is a useful concept, and it refers to the total amount of float remaining to any activity after resource scheduling has been carried out.

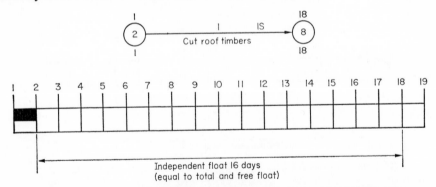

FIGURE 6:8 WORKSHOP PROJECT—FLOAT ANALYSIS OF
ACTIVITY 2,8

If event 2 finishes at its latest permissible time, and event 8 starts at its earliest possible time, this activity still has a float of sixteen days. Independent float, of which this is an example, is relatively uncommon. It occurs in conditions where the activity has other paths linking its terminal events (see Figure 6:1)

7

SCHEDULING BY COMPUTER

A project schedule cannot be considered complete until timescale requirements have been related to resources. In order to achieve resource allocation, it has already been shown that several discrete steps are necessary, ranging through the provision of estimates, preparation of a network, time analysis, conversion to bar chart form and resource allocation. By far the most tedious and time consuming part of this procedure is the conversion of the network to a bar chart. Once the bar chart has been produced, many of the original advantages of the network will have been lost, and in particular the resulting plan will be inflexible to change.

If the network contained more than about one hundred activities, the bar chart conversion would be difficult and time consuming, whilst it would become altogether impossible when larger networks were involved. In practice, it is not unusual to work with networks containing several thousand activities, and any attempt to convert these to bar chart form for the purpose of resource allocation would hardly be practical. Some other means has to be found. The answer lies in the use of a computer.

Advantages of computer scheduling

The most obvious advantage to be derived from the use of a computer lies in the ability of the machine to process large volumes of data with low risk of error, and in a short space of time. These characteristics enable a planner to produce his schedule with a speed and accuracy which would otherwise be impossible. If a change in project circumstances is foreseen, then it is only necessary to make a corresponding change to the data supplied to the computer, and a new, revised schedule can be calculated within a few hours. Normal mental and manual processes could not hope to compete with the speed of the machine.

Another benefit is discovered in the presentation of the reports printed out by the computer. It is possible to edit the output, so that only certain items are included in the reports. For example, dummies can be omitted.

By this means, reports can be produced which relate to individual managers, or to departments. In addition to the process of editing, the computer is also able to sort the printed out data into a specified sequence, making it easier to find any particular item among the lists of jobs to be done. Two examples would be sorting by order of scheduled start date, or by sequence of job number.

From the point of view of line management and other members of the project team, the introduction of a computer for project control is likely to give rise to some apprehension, if not actual hostility. Several reasons can be cited. Whenever any new procedure is implemented there is a risk of resistance to the change from old and familiar practice. Computers are often surrounded with an aura of mystery, and there are several hair-raising stories of disasters associated with the implementation of computer systems. Under these circumstances, the first project schedule produced by computer is apt to be seen as an embodiment of all fears. Paradoxically, it is the ability of the computer to provide a printed report which is edited, sorted and tabulated that can remove much of the clerical burden from line managers, and provide them with work schedules which are extremely convenient to use.

Requirements

No attempt to use a computer should start without the provision of certain basic facilities. These are:

1   A computer installation of sufficient capacity
2   A suitable program or "software package"
3   Computer operators trained for network appreciation
4   Good communications between the computer and the planning
     team

Computers with sufficient capacity to carry out resource allocation on a useful scale are expensive items of capital equipment. In addition to the cost of the hardware, supporting staff and provision of air-conditioned accommodation add to the capital and running costs. Quite obviously therefore, companies exist which cannot justify the installation of a computer for project control, even where the projects themselves are substantial in complexity and value.

On the other hand, many large companies and other organisations own computers which are not fully utilised. In order to help the recovery of overhead and depreciation expenses it is prudent for these computer owners to allow other companies access to the machines. This arrangement, which usually includes the operating staff along with the computer itself, provides many small firms with the opportunity to use the power of a large installation without any capital outlay. Another, perhaps more obvious source of computer capacity is available from the computer companies which operate bureaux.

Many small companies may be deterred from using a computer because of the danger of high operating costs, even on a rental basis. However, provided that a satisfactory agreement is reached between the user and the owner, time need only be paid for as and when it is actually used. Any firm wishing to introduce computer project scheduling, therefore, is able to make a start with no long-term financial commitment. Of course, project planning staff must be assigned or appointed, but any effective project management system demands the assignment of qualified staff, whether computer assisted or not. Should it be decided to discontinue computer based scheduling at any time, the expenditure on hiring machine time can be cut off at once. In other words, the use of a bureau or other form of hiring allows a small company the opportunity of experimentation, without the risk of badly burned fingers.

Suppose now that a firm, equipped with a competent planning engineer, decides to seek the aid of a computer for scheduling resources. A search for computer capacity within the neighbourhood might well reveal the existence of several installations, containing hardware of different capacities, ages and manufacture. One of the principal factors determining the installation eventually chosen must be the range of programs available for the machine in question. Most readers are probably well aware that a computer is unable to think in human terms. Instead, it must be programmed so that each calculation step is meticulously defined. The basis for any "decision" governing alternative calculation steps must be written into the program, and will consist of a simple yes/no comparison between two quantities.

An analogy which illustrates the role of a computer program is provided by the old-time fairground organs. These machines were able to play music according to instructions punched in the form of slots in folded cardboard "books." Each book had to be cut to fulfil a primary purpose, namely to cause a particular piece of music to be played. The range of different pipe tones and percussion effects that could be punched onto the card depended upon the capacity of the particular organ, and the final result would be proportional to the skill of the man punching the card. Thus one is able to compare the man who arranges and cuts music books to the modern computer programmer, and the range of orchestration allowed by a particular organ to the volume of data that a computer can store and manipulate. Payroll, stock control, production schedules and network analysis programs correspond to different tunes.

Most network analysis programs which are commercially available do not have the ability to smooth resource loads for large networks. Although several companies, including some of the large organisations, offer programs claimed to be capable of producing resource schedules, closer examination often reveals them to be designed only for resource aggregation. Basic requirements of an effective program demand that it can control time analysis of a large network, detect any obvious clerical errors contained in the input data, and then produce a schedule of activities against calendar dates. This schedule must fall within the constraints imposed by network logic, time analysis and resource availabilities. All of these calculations should be achieved within the shortest possible computing time in order that data processing costs are kept to a minimum.

Development of a suitable program requires considerable skill and effort from computer programmers who have a good knowledge of the requirements of project management. Although some computers are faster in operation than others, the speed of schedule calculation will also be dependent upon the mathematical rules and sequences adopted so that different programs could arrive at the same solution, using the same computer, but for different data processing time and cost. Once the program has been written it must be subjected to prolonged testing, in order to prove that it contains no inbuilt flaws and can meet its objectives. All of this work, together with the use of computer time for testing, represents a considerable investment. Not all computer companies have regarded programs for resource allocation as being potentially worthwhile commercial ventures.

Although network analysis was initially more fully exploited within the US, the tendency of American computer companies has been to provide programs for duration and cost control without consideration of resources. In contrast, the British project manager is provided with a choice of several programs, a few of which become very powerful scheduling tools indeed, when sensibly applied. Two of these systems have been used to process example projects for later chapters in this book. A useful survey, comparing many aspects of available programs, was published by Loughborough University of Technology. (See: Campbell, JY; *Computer User Report Number 5*, Loughborough University of Technology, 1968.) Although this report was produced primarily for the construction industry, it has direct relevance to many other users. Any final choice between rival programs must, however, be subject to an up-to-date assessment of their capabilities and operating costs, since programs are constantly being extended, modified and improved.

Now suppose that a planning engineer has drawn his network, and made his choice of program and computer. When the network information is delivered to the computer console, someone has to be asked to feed in the data and push all the buttons at the right time. Any computer operator is, of course, trained to carry out these very functions. Provided that operating staff are included in the agreement for the use of computer facilities, all should apparently be well. But if the amount of data is considerable, there will almost certainly be some clerical errors, resulting in the inclusion of some bad data among the good. These mistakes must be rooted out if a good schedule is to be produced.

Error detection is a feature of all practical project scheduling programs, and the nature of some of the checking facilities will be described later. Whenever the computer does detect an obvious input error, the printer is made to print out an "error message," whilst the calculations may automatically stop until the error is corrected. The operator may then have to communicate with the project planner, or make a decision himself on whether or not to restart the computer and allow the run to continue without error correction. Ideally, the computer operator should have sufficient familiarity with critical path techniques to be capable of discussing errors sensibly and appreciating their implication.

The degree of responsibility vested in the operator will vary according to the specific arrangements made governing the use of the computer. If the whole of the data processing is carried out within the premises shared by the project planner, then provided that the schedules are run during daytime he can be called to settle any problems promptly, and the operator need only be able to recognise that an error exists. At the other extreme, a project manager who relies on a computer bureau located many miles away will not feel disposed to travel to the machine, along with the data, for every schedule run. Instead, he will expect the operator to be able to recognise errors, and indeed correct the more obvious ones by reference to a copy of the network diagram.

It is unlikely that the computer will be located within a few yards of the project management team. Quite often it is necessary for network data to be sent several miles to the computer, and for the completed reports to be returned by the same route. If, for example, normal mail services were to be used, the delays resulting from the two-way journey might add up to nearly a week. There would also be some risk of loss or damage to the data parcel, which would be at the least very inconvenient. Clearance of data errors could easily add to transit delays, and to cap all this, the computer may be so heavily loaded that the work must join a queue, and wait its turn according to some priority decision. One advantage of the use of a bureau, compared with internal computing facilities, is that the user is a cash paying customer who can demand fair priority, whereas a myriad of reasons can force work to the back of a queue when the computer is dealing with departmental managers from one organisation, each screaming for his own report. Schedules must obviously be issued promptly, before they become outdated by events. Communications, in all respects, must therefore be swift between the project planner and his computer service.

Direct link between the computer and the user by means of telephone or teleprinter affords one way of overcoming communication problems. These methods become expensive and tedious, however, when large networks are being processed although they are invaluable when errors have to be discussed and corrected in a hurry. Some organisations offer a specialised service for the fast and secure carriage of data by road. Data Express and Securicor are two well known examples. The project manager himself must decide how much delay is tolerable, and this in turn must depend upon the nature of the project, depth of planning detail, and the intervals which elapse between regular schedule revisions.

Sometimes it is possible to accept delays in data transmission by means of sensible arrangements designed to minimise their effect. For example, it would be possible to post the data off to the computer on a Friday evening, using ordinary first-class mail. The computer run would be reserved in advance, in order to avoid queueing time, so that the first run could be carried out on the following Monday morning. Should any errors be present, these can be cleared in time for a re-run on Monday afternoon. Printed reports can be despatched from the computer to the project manager by one of the special data collection services, who will be able to deliver the results before start of work on Tuesday morning. Although about three days have elapsed, only one working day has been involved and the completed schedule should be fresh and accurate. Whatever arrangements are made to secure a quick turn-round of computer processing, these problems must be considered and overcome before any agreement is signed for the rental of computing services.

NETWORK NOTATION

Networks drawn for computer processing need not differ materially from those intended only for time analysis by normal mental processes. There are, however, three specific aspects of notation which must be observed. These are:

1　Event numbering
2　Avoidance of activities sharing identical start and finish events (activities in parallel)
3　Special treatment of start and finish events

Every event in the network must be given a unique identity number, in order that the computer can recognise it be a file reference. Each activity is recognised within the computer by the reference numbers of its terminal events. The number of digits that may be used for these event codes, and the ability to mix figures (numeric) with letters (alpha) will be a characteristic of the program in use. In most programs events can be numbered in random order throughout the network. Programs which demand that events should be numbered in ascending numerical sequence from left ro right must be avoided because of the problems caused whenever network logic is re-arranged.

Use of identification numbers for events and activities is illustrated in Figure 7:1(*a*). This diagram is intended to depict a very small portion of a large network, containing perhaps thousands of activities. The first event has been numbered 1122, and will be identified within the computer under that reference. Any associated descriptions or data for this event will always be fed to the computer with the identification 1122 included. Similarly, the first activity shown in the diagram will always be associated with the numbers 1122, 1123. Whenever any data is added or changed for this activity, the input to the computer will include the activity identification 1122,1123.

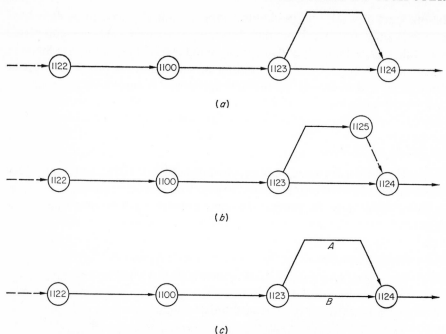

(a)

(b)

(c)

FIGURE 7:1   IDENTIFICATION OF ACTIVITIES AND EVENTS
The computer is programmed to recognise events by their serial numbers,
which must be allocated by the planner on his network. Each activity is
identified within the computer by its terminal events. In this diagram,
four activities from a larger network are shown. In (a), the first activity is
designated 1122, 1100. But a deliberate mistake has been made in this
diagram. Notice that two activities occur in parallel, each of which is
defined by the events 1123, 1124. The computer would not be able to
distinguish between these two activities, because it can only recognise
them by their numbers. The solution to this problem is found by adding
a special dummy, as shown in (b). Now each parallel activity has its
own identity, so that the computer sees 1123, 1125 and 1123, 1124 as two
separate activities. Parallel activities are permitted, however, when the
ICL 1900 program is being used. This is achieved by the addition of identifying letters, as shown in (c). In this case, the two activities are designated
1123,1124A and 1123,1124B

In the right-hand side of Figure 7:1(a) a pair of activities are shown
which bear identical terminal event numbers, 1123 and 1124. Thus each
activity could be described as 1123,1124. The computer would not be able
to distinguish between the two in this case, and this condition is therefore
not allowed. In many cases, the computer would be programmed to accept
the first activity read, and treat the second as a duplicate entry, to be rejected. One activity would be omitted from the subsequent scheduling

calculations and reports altogether. Figure 7:1(*b*) shows a dummy, whose sole purpose is to provide the same two activities which coincided in 7:1(*a*) with separate identities. Now there is no confusion, and two distinct reference numbers emerge, 1123,1125 and 1123,1124. The addition of this dummy in no way upsets the network logic.

It should be mentioned here that the very comprehensive program offered by International Computers Limited (ICL) does make provision for parallel activities. This is the ICL PERT 1900 system, and the method employed to identify parallel activities is shown in Figure 7:1(*c*). Each activity is given its own code letter, to single it out from its neighbour, so that the two references become, in this case, 1123, 1124(*A*) and 1123,1124(*B*).

It is mandatory with some programs, and usually desirable in any case to arrange networks with only one start and one finish event. All start and finish events are identified during error checking by the computer and they must all be accounted for. Time spent on the computer is greatly reduced if only one start and one finish event number have to be checked against the network diagram. Any unexpected numbers reported by the computer may signify that an activity has been omitted from the input, leaving events unconnected in the middle of the network so that they appear to be starts or finishes. Dummies can be used to link multiple starts and finishes together (Figure 7:2). Error detection will be fully discussed later.

INPUT

The collection of data comprising all characteristics of any project must be translated into some form that the computer is able to "read." Present-day technology does not allow the network diagram itself to be used, although the idea of feeding it into a machine through a set of rollers would be very attractive. Perhaps, one day, optical reading systems will enable this to be done. Several practical possibilities exist for input, including direct injection from an electric typewriter at the console, a remote teleprinter, magnetic tape, punched paper tape or punched cards. Punched cards are used very widely, and they offer the facility of rapid error correction or network alteration, because it is only necessary to punch cards for the affected data and substitute them in the card deck for the unwanted cards. The resource allocation examples used in this book were input to the computer on punched cards.

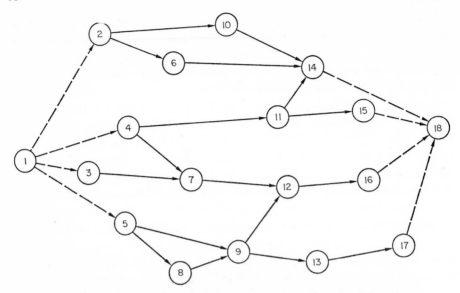

FIGURE 7:2   MULTIPLE START AND FINISH EVENTS
Although many programs can accept networks with more than one start
or finish event, it is often convenient to work with only one start and one
finish. If the original network has been drawn with multiple starts and
finishes, dummy activities can be added to tie in all the loose ends, without
altering the logic. This procedure may be preferable to extending the
start and finish activities themselves into the first and last events because
the use of dummies allows each start and finish event to retain its own
identity. This is often important when the network is being time analysed
by hand as a preliminary check. It is also useful when target start and
finish dates are to be applied to different parts of the network

Figure 7:3 is an illustration of a standard eighty-column punched card.
This particular example was taken from the deck of cards used to input the
workshop project described in Chapter 9. It contains all data specific to
one activity, and is punched in an arrangement suitable for the ICL PERT
1900 system. This arrangement will be described fully in Chapter 9.
Planners wishing to make the changeover from manual to computer
methods reach their first major hurdle when data has to be prepared in
punched card form. Somehow all the facts and estimates pertaining to the
project have to be represented by thousands of small slots punched onto the
faces of cards. Instruction manuals are usually provided by the computer
companies, but they are often badly organised, inadequately indexed, and
assume some previous knowledge of data preparation. The problem is best

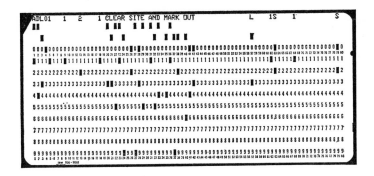

FIGURE 7:3 TYPICAL PUNCHED CARD FOR NETWORK
INPUT
Computer input can take many forms but the most common is the
standard eighty-column punched card. This example carries data
sufficient to input all information specific to one activity. It is arranged in
a format which is suitable for the ICL 1900 series of programs (see
Chapter 9)

overcome by seeking practical demonstration and coaching, at first hand,
from the firm who wrote the program. Proficiency will take a week or two
to acquire, but the basic elements can be learned very rapidly, possibly in
one day.

If a planner has access to a data processing department within his own
company, card punching facilities should present no problem. Otherwise
he can arrange for an external bureau to carry out the work. This bureau
need not be associated with that entrusted to process the project schedule.
Costs will vary considerably, depending on the method adopted. In general,
the most expensive procedure would be to choose the company who are
going to process the data. They will possibly add an amount to the actual
punching costs in order to indemnify themselves against the possibility of
a non-valid computer run resulting from punching errors. The costs of
additional computer time incurred from these errors has to be met, and if
the punching error was made by the bureau itself, then they could not
expect to pass the costs on to the customer. Card punching costs are likely
to vary between £25 and £15 per thousand, depending on the arrangement
chosen.

Class	Project	Sub project	Preceding event	Succeeding event	Activity duration	Activity description		Resource 1 Code / Quantity	Resource 2 Code / Quantity		Card Type
A D	L	1	1	2	1	CLEAR SITE AND MARK OUT		L 1	S 1		S

FIGURE 7:4   ACTIVITY CODING SHEET
Whenever cards are to be punched for the purpose of feeding new data to the computer, it is necessary to provide the punch operators with clear, precise instructions. This can be achieved by the use of coding sheets, such as that shown here. Each column is numbered to correspond to one of the eighty columns on the punched card. Every row of the coding sheet carries instructions for one card. This example has twenty-nine rows, and can therefore carry sufficient data for twenty-nine standard eighty-column cards.

In this example a blank coding sheet has been modified by the addition of column headings. It has been transformed, in effect, into a document which carries coding instructions that serve to assist the planner. This form is arranged for the input of network activities according to the requirements of the ICL 1900 program, as used by one particular company. The shaded headings indicate card fields that are not used, because this company does not wish to make use of all facilities offered by the program. Each row carries one activity. It will be seen that the first row has been filled in, and the punched card which would result from these instructions is that shown in Figure 7:3. See Chapter 9 for a more detailed description of the preparation of input data

CODING SHEETS

Instructions for card punch operators must be written in clear, non ambiguous style. They must also be arranged in accordance with specific requirements of the program being used. These objectives are aided by the use of standard punching instruction forms, often called "coding sheets." An example of a typical coding sheet is given in Figure 7:4. Each row on the sheet corresponds to one punched card, whilst the squares along the row refer to particular columns on the card. Columns are numbered from 1 to 80, in sequence from left to right, corresponding exactly to the column numbering convention for eighty-column cards.

Actual completion of coding sheets is best described by example and demonstration (see Chapter 9). In any case, training must be geared to the program chosen. However, certain basic disciplines are common to the writing of coding sheets for any purpose. When the computer reads a card, it must first be told the primary function of that card. Examples of these functions would be cards used to define fixed holiday periods, input network activities, specify a project title, fix the schedule start date, start and stop calculations, control the print-out, and so on. Each card, and therefore its corresponding row on the coding sheet, must bear a code character which signals its main function to the computer. These codes are defined in the program, and there is no choice for the planner; he follows the instructions provided in the specific manual.

Now it is obvious that a card intended (say) to give instructions to the printer to start printing will carry information of a substantially different character from a card intended to input a network activity. In each case the same column will be reserved for the letter or number code identifying the basic card type. The use of the remaining seventy-nine columns must be dictated by the program, because the computer is instructed to recognise specific columns as being reserved for the inclusion of particular types of data. For example, columns 6, 7 and 8 on an activity card might always be used to carry the estimated project duration. Groups of columns which are combined in this way are referred to as "fields." Because card types carry basically different information, it follows that the arrangement of fields must be specific to any card type, and that the writing of data onto coding sheets must conform both to program requirements and to the actual card type being generated.

A project planner must learn the functions of different card types in the system being used, and the associated arrangements of fields. Of course he can always refer to his instruction manual, but this can become time consuming and tedious. A useful aid to data preparation is provided by the use of coding sheets printed for each of the more common types of card, as shown in Figure 7:4. It will be seen that this particular sheet contains one entry which would cause the card of Figure 7:3 to be punched. Coding sheets with field headings printed in this way speed up the clerical process and help to prevent errors. Their use should be regarded as essential.

CONTROL CARDS

Although a complete project card deck may contain over a dozen different basic types of card, the most common card of all will undoubtedly be that used to input separate activities. Usually one activity card will be used for each activity on the network, although in some circumstances two will be needed. In a network containing 1000 activities, therefore, one can expect to find at least 1000 activity cards in the input deck, all of the same basic type. Among the 100 or so remaining cards will be found a diversity of card types. Some of these will be used to provide project support information, such as the level of available resources, resource codes used, project start date, cost rates, and many other details governing the preparation of a workable schedule. However, there must also be several cards whose function is connected not with the project, but with the operation of the computer.

Cards intended for the purpose of starting, stopping or in any other way controlling functions of the computing apparatus are called control cards. They form no part of the project schedule, except that they will be arranged in a manner designed to generate reports in the format required by the project manager. For example, the cards used to differentiate between a resource limited or a time limited run do affect the output, but they are strictly speaking control cards. In general, the appreciation of control card techniques offers a far greater problem to the newcomer to computer scheduling than the preparation of data input. In many cases the symbols required by the program include commas, asterisks and other non-obvious characters which must appear very strange to the novice.

At this point it is necessary to question the role of a planning engineer with respect to data preparation. He is not expected to be a data processing expert. Rather, he must be regarded as a customer of the computer facility, being provided with a data processing service. If computer scheduling is going to be introduced into an organisation, scheduling problems must be the responsibility of the project manager, and data processing routines left to the data centre employed. Control cards fall more logically into the realm of data processing than project management. Certainly for the first schedule, and if possible for all following computer runs, the data processing team should be persuaded to prepare control cards. The degree of success achieved in shedding this responsibility will depend on the attitude of the computer organisation employed. It should be mentioned here that the bureau service offered by *K* and *H* Business Consultants Limited is particularly helpful in this respect, and contributes to a painless introduction of computer scheduling.

SCHEDULING STEPS

A computer produces a complete project schedule after proceeding through a number of logical steps. Some of these processes are concerned with reading the input data and placing it into various "files," whence it can be searched or extracted at will. These are not, of course, files in the familiar office sense, but devices which contain magnetic or other physical states which can be sensed by electronic circuits to determine their content. Magnetic tapes and discs are the most common types of file, and the actual location of any piece of data among the various storage devices available at the computer will be decided by programmed instructions. The choice, made by the programmer, will in turn depend upon the speed with which it is necessary for the computer to be able to retrieve the data, because there is a considerable difference in the access time between alternative devices. These times are usually measured in thousandths or millionths of a second, and have to be compatible with the extremely rapid calculating speeds of modern computers.

From the planning engineer's point of view the computer follows a series of major steps which correspond to those that he would carry out himself during manual scheduling. The first of these steps is time analysis. Results are derived in unit numbers, corresponding to the estimating units used on the network. If days were used, for example, all time analysis results would be produced in day numbers from the starting day of the project. For each activity, its earliest and latest starts, earliest and latest finishes, and float are worked out and placed on file. Critical activities are therefore identified.

However, during this time analysis process, the computer must search its files systematically, and by means of the event serial numbers, trace out all possible paths through the network. If any unexpected loose ends turn up in the middle of the network, this may indicate that one or more activities have been accidentally omitted from the input card deck. The computer is therefore able to identify certain obvious input errors. Error detection is dealt with more fully later in this chapter, but it forms an essential part of the time analysis phase at the computer. Indeed, *K* and *H* Business Consultants refer to time analysis as a check list. This emphasises the point that a project schedule only deserves that description after resources have been considered, and that a time analysis schedule is therefore a document of limited use.

Error messages from the computer are checked against the coding sheets and the network diagrams, in order to determine the reason for each mistake. The card input deck is amended by the extraction of any surplus cards, and the substitution of wrongly punched cards with correct replacements. When all known errors have been accounted for the computer is restarted. Time analysis is repeated, in order that correct data can be established within the computer files. During this repeat run, the standard error-checking routines are once again performed by the computer. It is possible that some input errors still exist, being undetected during the first error check owing to the swamping effects of one large error. Alternatively, the corrected data may itself be wrong.

Quite often there will be no errors at all, but when a large network is being processed for the first time thousands of different items have to be written, and then punched onto cards. Some clerical ambiguities or errors are very difficult to prevent. One incorrect time analysis run is, therefore, not uncommon but the second should normally be free of trouble. It is always useful, at this stage, to obtain a print-out in order to determine whether the project duration is acceptable. Should the time estimates along the critical path add up to a total which exceeds that allowed by imposed target dates, negative float must result. A decision is therefore necessary, before proceeding with resource analysis, regarding the acceptability of these implications; namely that the project is going to be scheduled late from the start. Obviously, if the project must be completed by the target dates set, the network and its estimates must be re-examined before going on with the computer schedule.

Once a valid time analysis has been achieved, the computer is able to proceed to the major step of resource allocation. The computer attempts to schedule each activity at the earliest possible time indicated from time analysis. However, the resource requirements of every activity have to be tested against competition from other activities. If resources are not available at sufficient level to meet all demands, some activities must be delayed. The computer will therefore allow some activities to start, and delay those which would cause a resource overload. This mechanism entails a decision. Which activity should receive priority in its claim for limited resources? Because the computer is not able to think for itself, the program makes provision for competing activities to be allocated priorities on the basis of numerical rules. Several different rules are possible, and the project manager is often given the facility for making his own choice. He is able to specify his preference on one of the input control cards. An example of one very effective priority rule is that which assigns first priority to activities which have least remaining float.

If the network estimates for durations were given in working days, or parts of days, then it is useful to have the results specified in calendar dates. Both of the resource allocation programs demonstrated in this book have this capability. During this translation, the computer can be programmed to omit non-working days such as weekends and statutory holidays. When all calculations have been finished, the results are held in various files within the computer, whence they can be extracted for inclusion in output reports as required.

OUTPUT

After a large network has been processed, a very large volume of data will be stored within the computer. Usually this quantity of information greatly exceeds that necessary for project management. If it were all to be printed out, the result would be a great pile of unmanageable paper. It follows that the content of any printed reports must be carefully selected from all the data held on file. This is the process of editing. For example, a report might be produced which showed only critical activities. Another example, of great practical use, is a series of reports, each of which is edited to contain only activities pertinent to particular departments. Each department has a code which the computer can recognise. The code is added, as necessary, to each activity card at the time of input preparation. By this means, reports are directed at the areas where they will do most good, and at the same time their recipients are shielded from irrelevant data. It is surprising how this editing procedure, when sensibly applied, can reduce the size of departmental reports to only a few sheets where the networks contain thousands of activities.

Editing, therefore, can be used to determine the content of each report. This leaves the problem of arranging the information on the printed page in a form convenient to the reader. Suppose that a report is needed which shows the following information about each activity.

1   Preceding event number (sometimes called the *I* node number)
2   Succeeding event number (sometimes called the *J* node number)
3   Estimated duration
4   Departmental report code
5   Description of the work involved in the activity
6   Scheduled start date
7   Scheduled finish date
8   Remaining float
9   Resources needed
10   Earliest possible start date
11   Latest permissible start date

It is obvious that printing out all data in a completely random sequence must result in a report that is entirely unacceptable. Quick reference to any item depends upon the imposition of a logical and systematic order on the printed page. In project schedules, the reports are always tabulated in columns, with one column reserved for each type of information item. Thus there would be, in this case, a column for preceding event numbers, another for succeeding event numbers, and so on. Activities will be printed in rows, each spanning all the columns. Some programs allow no choice in these arrangements, and always generate printed reports that follow the same format. Others, including those used to produce the examples of resource scheduling used in this book, are called "free format." Free format reports allow the project manager to discuss the layout of his reports with the computer company, and his schedules can be laid out to his own individual requirements. These details are specified on control cards included with the original input deck, which combine with instructions contained in the program. The degree of freedom is usually considerable. Column headings, their sequence from left to right across the page, and their widths can be specially controlled. A planner might wish, for instance, to reduce the widths of some columns in order to allow more space within the column carrying activity descriptions.

Another option governing the presentation of data is the sequence in which activities are to be listed. For example, it would be possible to list all activities in order of preceding event number. Alternatively, they could be sorted into ascending values of float. An arrangement often found most useful is to prepare a schedule which lists according to scheduled starting dates. Many variations are possible, including sorts within sorts. This means, for example, that activities could be listed in order of scheduled start date, but that any groups of activities scheduled to start on the same day are themselves sorted into order of least remaining float. A report edited to include only information for an expediting department is best sorted in order of scheduled completion dates, because these are the dates that are most important to that specific function.

Computers, therefore, together with a suitable program, allow project managers to design their own reports. The wealth of detail produced after calculations on a major project resource smoothing run can be edited to extract only information which is going to be of real use; that information can then be printed onto a page whose layout can be chosen, and all the items can be sorted into almost any desired sequence. Careful use of these facilities can result in output reports that are extremely convenient in the hands of departmental managers. Conversely, if the reports are not sensibly chosen and designed, initial acceptance of computer scheduling within a company must be more painful, and the ultimate results less effective.

DIAGRAMMATIC OUTPUTS

Apart from the tabular types of output, computers can also be programmed to produce printed reports in the form of graphs or bar charts. Resource histograms can also be generated. For very large projects, and in fact for most projects which would justify the use of a computer by their size, these diagrams can become clumsy. A bar chart for a project of long duration, and containing many activities, would result in a print-out requiring several sheets extension in the left to right direction in order to accommodate the timescale. At the same time, this whole pattern must be extended downwards, because of the large number of activities which must be shown. Of course it would be possible to limit the extent of the output by only showing a selection of activities, and cutting the schedule off before the whole timescale had been plotted. There is still a great risk, however, of finishing up with a document which resembles an enlarged version of an *A* to *Z* street guide of London.

Nevertheless, there are many situations where personal preferences will demand outputs in diagrammatic form. For small projects these can provide useful control documents. In larger projects they can be made more convenient to use by designating certain activities as key activities. Reports are then prepared which contain only these important activities, so that the

```
I.C.T. 1900 SERIES PERT                              11/04/67                    OUTPUT SHEET NUMBER   58

                PROJECT   DB   SAMPLE PRINTOUT                                   TIME NOW 5DEC66   PAGE   1
BAR CHART OF TIME LIMITED RESOURCE ANALYSIS

                                                     5        19       2        16       30       13       27
    PREC  SUCC  REPORT  DESCRIPTION         DUR   DEC66     DEC66    JAN67    JAN67    JAN67    FEB67    FEB67
    EVENT EVENT CODE                               X...I....I....I....I....I....I....I....I....I....I....I....I...
      1     2   TEC     DESIGN              3.0   •CCCCCCCCCCCCC •    I    •    I    •    I    •    I    •    I
      1     2   TEC     DESIGN              5.0   CCCCCCCCCCCCCCCCCCCCCCCC•    I    •    I    •    I    •    I
      1    22   TEC     SPECIFY DRIVE MO    1.0   AAAAA•••••••••••••••••••••••••••••••I•••••••••I•••••••••I•••
                        TOR                        X •         I    •    I    •    I    •    I    •    I    •    I
     22    28   PUR     OBTAIN MOTORS       14.0  X   AAAAAAAAAAAAAAAAAAAAAAAAAAAAAAAAAAAAAAAAAAAAAAAAAAAAAAAAAA•
      1    18   QAD     DESGN & PLN RNNG    2.0   •••••AAAAAAAAAA•    I    •    I    •    I    •    I    •    I
                        •IN RIG                    X •        I    •    I    •    I    •    I    •    I    •    I
      2     4   TEC     PLAN CASTINGS       2.0   X •        I •CCCCCCCCCC•    I    •    I    •    I    •    I
      2     5   TEC     PLAN COMPONENTS     3.0   X •        I   AAAAAAAAAAAAAA•    I    •    I    •    I    •    I
     22    23   TEC     DESIGN CONTROLS     2.0   X ••••••••••••AAAAAAAAAA••••••••••••••••••••••••••••••••••I
     18    19   PUR     OBTAIN Q.O.PARTS    8.0   X •        I    •AAAAAAAAAAAAAAAAAAAAAAAAAAAAAAA•••••••••••I
      2    20   TEC     DESGN ASSEMBLY J    1.0   X •        I   AAAAA•••••••••••••••••••••••••••••••••••••••••
                        IGS                        X •        I    •    I    •    I    •    I    •    I    •    I
     20    16   PRO     MAKE JIGS           5.6   X •        I    •  AAAAA••••••••••••••••••••••••••••••••••••••
      4    14   PUR     OBTAIN CASTINGS     12.0  X •        I    •    I •CCCCCCCCCCCCCCCCCCCCCCCCCCCCCCCCCCCCC•
      2    13   TEC     DESIGN BASE FRAM    10.0  X •        I    •    I  CCCCCCCCCCCCCCCCCCCCCCCCCCCCCCCCCCCCCC•
                        E                           X •        I    •    I    •    I    •    I    •    I    •    I
      2     6           LEAD                1.0   X •        I    •    I    • AAAAA•••• I    •    I    •    I
      4    13   TEC     DESIGN TOOLS        4.0   X •        I    •    I    • AAAAAAAAAAAAAAAAAAAA•••••••• I    •    I
      2     6           LEAD                1.0   X •        I    •    I    • AAAAA•••••••••••••••••••• I    •••• I
      2    14   TEC     DESIGN CIRCUITS     3.0   X •        I    •    I    • AAAAA•••••••••••••••••• I    •••• I
      2     3   TEC     PLANNING            3.0   X •        I    •    I    • AAAAAAAAAAAAAAA••••••••••••••••••••
                        X •        I    •    I    •    I    •    I    •    I    •    I
     23    24   TEC     PLAN                2.0   X •        I    •••••••••AAAAAAAAAA• I    •    I    •    I
      6     8           LEAD                2.0   X •        I    •    I    • AAAAAAAAAA• •    I    •    I    •    I
      6     5   •PUR    OBTAIN RAW MAT'L    9.0   X •        I    •    I    •   AAAAAAAAAAAAAAAAAAAAAAAAAAAAAAAAA•
      6    10           LEAD                3.0   X •        I    •    I    • AAAAAAAAAAAAAA•••••••••••••••
      6     7   TEC     TOOL DESIGN         6.0   X •        I    •    I    • ••••AAAAAAAAAAAAAAAAAAAAAAAAAAAAAAA•
     24    25   PUR     OBTAIN B.O. PART    9.0   X •        I    •    I   ••••••••AAAAAAAAAAAAAAAAAAAAAAAAAAAAA•
                        S                           X •        I    •    I    •    I    •    I    •    I    •    I
      8    10           LEAD                3.0   X •        I    •    I    • •    I •    I AAAAAAAAAAAAAA• •    I
      5     7   PRD     MAKE COMPONENTS     6.0   X •        I    •    I    • •    I    •AAAAAAAAAAAAAAAAAAA•
     14    15   PUR     OBTAIN B.O.ITEMS    11.0  X •        I    •    I    • •••••••AAAAAAAAAAAAAAAAAAAAAAAA•
     18    19   PRD     MAKE PARTS          6.0   X ••••••••••••••••••••••••AAAAA••••AAAA••••••••••••••••
      3     7           LAG                 2.0   X •        I    •    I    • •    I    •AAAAAAAAAAA••••
      3     5           LAG                 4.0   X •        I    •    I    • •    I    • AAAAAAAAAAAAAAAA••••
     24    25   PRD     MAKE PARTS          5.0   X •        I    • I •    I    •    I AAAAAAAAAAAAAAAAAA••••
     14    15   PRD     MAKE SPECIAL ITE    5.0   X •        I    •    I    • •    I    •AAAAAAAAAAAAAAAAAAA
                        MS                          X •        I    •    I    • •    I    • I    •    I    •    I
      8     9   PRD     TOOL MANUFACTURE    10.0  X •        I    •    I    • •    I    • I ••••CCCCCCCCCCCCCCCCCCC•
      13    14  PRD     MAKE TOOLS          6.0   X •        I    •    I    •    I    •    I AAAAAAAAAAAAAAAAAA•
      10    11  PRD     P/P MANU            8.0   X •        I    •    I    •    I    • I    •••••A.AAA•
```

FIGURE 7:5   PRINTED BAR CHART

For those who prefer bar charts to network diagrams or tabulated
reports, the computer can be programmed to print out schedules in bar
chart form. In this diagram, bars formed from the letter *C* represent
critical activities. Those which are made up from the letter *A* are non-
critical, and the dots extending from the bars show the amount of float
available. When dots appear in front of an activity they indicate that the
start of that activity has been delayed beyond its earliest possible date in
order to achieve some resource smoothing. Time limited resource
schedules, of which this is an example, will not allow any resource to be
delayed beyond its available float
(*International Computers Limited*)

charts can be condensed in size. An example of a bar chart for a small
project is shown in Figure 7:5. This particular chart was prepared by
International Computers Limited, and is only one of a large variety of
outputs possible with their 1900 series PERT program. A resource histogram
is shown at Figure 7:6, and a curve which relates project cost estimates to
timescale is included at Figure 7:7. Tabular versions of all these outputs are
illustrated in full in following chapters, as they occur in the course of case
studies.

```
I.C.T. 1900 SERIES PERT                          13/04/67              OUTPUT SHEET NUMBER   22

                 PROJECT   DB    SAMPLE PRINTOUT                       TIME-NOW  5DEC66    PAGE   2

                          TIME LIMITED RESOURCES-SCALE 10 TO 1

               C   /TOOL ROOM H      0        100     200     300     400     500     600
        DATE       AV       REQ   REM  I.........I.........I.........I.........I.........I.........I        DATE

       8FEB67     200      190    10   I         I       #/I         I         I         I         I        9.2
       9FEB67     200      190    10   I         I       #/I         I         I         I         I        9.3
      10FEB67     200      190    10   I         I       #/I         I         I         I         I        9.4
      13FEB67     200      190    10   I         I       #/I         I         I         I         I       10.0
      14FEB67     200      190    10   I         I       #/I         I         I         I         I       10.1
      15FEB67     200      190    10   I         I       #/I         I         I         I         I       10.2
      16FEB67     200      190    10   I         I       #/I         I         I         I         I       10.3
      17FEB67     200      210   -10   I         I       ##I         I         I         I         I       10.4
      20FEB67     200      230   -30   I         I     / ##         I         I         I         I       11.0
      21FEB67     200      230   -30   I         I     / #          I         I         I         I       11.1
      22FEB67     200      230   -30   I         I     / #          I         I         I         I       11.2
      23FEB67     200      230   -30   I         I     / #          I         I         I         I       11.3
      24FEB67     200      270   -70   I         I     / ####       I         I         I         I       11.4
      27FEB67     200      230   -30   I         I     / ####       I         I         I         I       12.0
      28FEB67     200      270   -70   I         I     / ####       I         I         I         I       12.1
       1MAR67     200      270   -70   I         I     / #          I         I         I         I       12.2
       2MAR67     200      270   -70   I         I     / #          I         I         I         I       12.3
       3MAR67     200      270   -70   I         I     / #          I         I         I         I       12.4
       6MAR67     200      210   -10   I         I     /######      I         I         I         I       13.0
       7MAR67     200      210   -10   I         I     /#           I         I         I         I       13.1
       8MAR67     200      190    10   I         I    ##           I         I         I         I       13.2
       9MAR67     200      210   -10   I         I     ##          I         I         I         I       13.3
      10MAR67     200      210   -10   I         I     /#          I         I         I         I       13.4
      13MAR67     200      400  -200   I         I     /#############I#########I         I         I       14.0
      14MAR67     200      400  -200   I         I     /           I         #         I         I       14.1
      15MAR67     200      400  -200   I         I     /           I         #         I         I       14.2
      16MAR67     200      400  -200   I         I     /           I         #         I         I       14.3
      17MAR67     200      360  -160   I         I     /           I #####I   I         I         I       14.4
      18MAR67     200      400  -200   I         I     /           I    ####I         I         I       14.5
      19MAR67     200      400  -200   I         I     /           I         #         I         I       14.6
      20MAR67     200      400  -200   I         I     /           I         #         I         I       15.0
      21MAR67     200      400  -200   I         I     /           I         #         I         I       15.1
      22MAR67     200      400  -200   I         I     /           I         #         I         I       15.2
      23MAR67     200      200     0   I         I     ############I#########I         I         I       15.3
      28MAR67     200      200     0   I         I     #           I         I         I         I       16.1
      29MAR67     200      200     0   I         I     #           I         I         I         I       16.2
      30MAR67     200      200     0   I         I     #           I         I         I         I       16.3
      31MAR67     200      160    40   I         I ####/           I         I         I         I       16.4
       3APR67     200      180    20   I         I  ## /           I         I         I         I       17.0
       4APR67     200      180    20   I         I   # /           I         I         I         I       17.1
       5APR67     200      180    20   I         I   # /           I         I         I         I       17.2
       6APR67     200      140    60   I         I #### /           I         I         I         I       17.3
       7APR67     200      140    60   I         I #   /           I         I         I         I       17.4
      10APR67     200      160    40   I         I  ## /           I         I         I         I       18.0
      11APR67     200      160    40   I         I   # /           I         I         I         I       18.1
      12APR67     200      160    40   I         I   # /           I         I         I         I       18.2
      13APR67     200      160    40   I         I   # /           I         I         I         I       18.3
```

FIGURE 7:6   RESOURCE HISTOGRAM

This is an example of a computer-produced histogram. One such report
would be needed for every department which supplies project resources.
Although histograms are very suitable for displaying trends at a glance,
tabular presentations can condense more information onto a single page.
This histogram was produced using the ICL 1900 program, and is only one
of a large number of possible variations which that program can provide.
Tabular reports generated by the ICL program are demonstrated in
Chapter 9
(*International Computers Limited*)

COST SCHEDULES

Once a computer has calculated a resource allocation schedule, it has in
fact determined a rate of working for the project, and therefore, indirectly,
the rate of expenditure. If cost rates can be applied, either to whole activities,
or to units of resource usage, then programs can be extended to allow the
necessary calculations to be made. Very useful charts or tables can result,
which show the expected daily and cumulative total expenditure throughout
the life of a project. Both of the programs used in this book have inbuilt
cost scheduling facilities, although they differ in their methods and scope of
control. One immediate outcome of any schedule which includes a cost

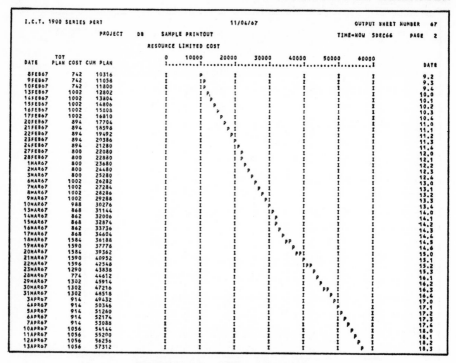

FIGURE 7:7   COST SCHEDULE

Once the computer has calculated a resource schedule, it can be programmed to carry out simple arithmetic calculations in order to compile cost
schedules which relate the work plan to spending. Either cost rates for
each resource, or an estimated cost for each activity must be input. Daily
and cumulative cost totals are calculated. When the ICL 1900 program
is used, graphical reports can be printed. One of these is shown here,
which displays planned expenditure against time. This example is labelled
"resource limited," which means that the schedule from which it has been
derived was resource smoothed with resource limits observed rigidly,
even if this meant exceeding the critical path duration of the original
network. Cost reports can also be printed as tables. Cost tables produced
by the *K* and *H* Business Consultants' program are demonstrated in
Chapter 10

(*International Computers Limited*)

calculation is that a revised overall project cost estimate is available for
comparison with the original pre-schedule budget. This can be a useful
early warning system, suggesting economies if there is a signal of possible
overspending.

This book is primarily concerned with resource schedules, but some further comments on the treatment of cost control and scheduling may be

found useful. In general, there are two ways in which estimated costs can be fed to the computer. For labour costs, it is possible to specify the rate for each type of resource to be scheduled. Care must be taken to give the rate for the network standard unit of time. It would be wrong, for example, to give the rate for machinists as 0.75, implying £0.75 an hour, when the time estimates are in days. Assuming an eight-hour day, one would have to give the cost rate in this case as $(8 \times 0.75) = 6$, implying £6 a day. Overheads can be included, if desired, by adding the relevant percentage to the direct cost rate. Cost rates for each resource being scheduled are added by means of special input cards.

Cost control of materials is best achieved by considering committed costs, rather than waiting for invoice payments to be recorded. This entails summing the values of all material orders at the time of purchase order issues (see Lock, *Project Management*, Gower Press). By carrying out two simple rules, it is possible for the project manager to have a schedule of expected expenditure prepared for him by the computer, and at the same time smooth the load in the clerical department of the purchasing office. The first rule is to split each procurement activity into two—place order and await delivery. By allocating a resource unit to the first part, and specifying a related level of resource, the situation is avoided where the computer prints out an impossible list of ordering activities on the same day. Instead, they will be scheduled in order of priority, on dates which allow the department to write its orders within its resource limitations. Estimated costs of these orders are also scheduled on the "place order" activity. They therefore become integrated into the total project cost schedule at the time of commitment.

The first special rule to be observed in scheduling costs for materials activities lies, therefore, in the treatment of the original network diagram. The second rule determines the method of cost estimate input to the computer. Whereas labour costs can be input as a rate per unit time, material costs are specified as total cost per activity. In this case, the input data is fed in by punching activity costs on their input cards. Labour costs can also be input as lumped quantities in this way, and another choice is to input both labour and material costs as one combined sum for each activity, using once again the activity cards for this purpose. This last case will prove necessary if purchasing activities are not shown separately on the network, which might arise when standard stock materials are being used.

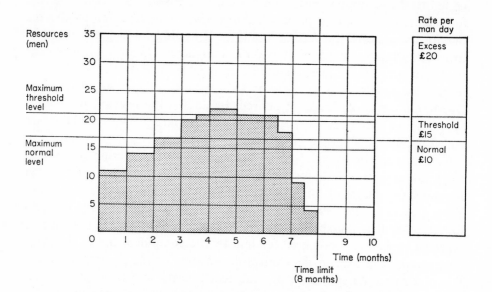

FIGURE 7:8   CONCEPT OF THRESHOLD RESOURCES

When a schedule has to be time limited, the ICL 1900 program allows the planner to specify a second level for each resource, to which it can be loaded when absolutely necessary in order to meet the time limit. The computer will attempt to smooth resource usage at the normal level of availability which the planner has stated. The schedule will be calculated at threshold levels when the time limit would otherwise not be met, and at the same time excess costs can be taken into account, on the assumption that it will cost money to work at resource levels higher than those economically available. Overtime, or the use of subcontract labour are two possible sources of extra cost. These concepts are illustrated in the histogram. In this case, the normal availability of the resource type shown is twelve men per day, at a rate of £10 per man day. If the level has to rise, a threshold number of sixteen men has been input as acceptable, but the cost rate of these extra men will be £15 per man-day. If the computer cannot meet the time limit restriction even with threshold levels, then it has no option other than to take infinity as its limit, and proceed to load resources at a level sufficient to meet the program of the project. Then the cost rate will go up to £20 for every man-day used above threshold. When the planner uses this facility he must input normal and threshold levels of availability for each category of resource. When costs are to be scheduled, he must also provide the appropriate cost rate for each level

THRESHOLD RESOURCES AND COSTS

The ICL 1900 series PERT program offers so many possible variations in the treatment of resources and costs that only a selection can be described. In any case, most proprietary programs for project management undergo improvements and extensions from time to time, so that a project manager is advised to consult the computer companies direct. Only by this means can he discover all possible facilities available to him. However, one feature of 1900 PERT worthy of mention is its treatment of threshold resources.

Suppose that a project cannot be completed within its allotted timespan unless resource levels exceed those available. It may be possible for the project manager to arrange extra resources by means of overtime and weekend working. Alternatively, he may be able to draw upon additional labour from a subcontractor. Normally available resources have a known, well defined availability level, obviously referred to as "the normal level." This is the level usually specified to the computer, and for which cost rates apply. However, the additional resources made available by emergency measures also have a practical limit. This can be considered a "threshold level." 1900 PERT allows this level to be specified together with its own cost rate. Threshold resources are then scheduled whenever they are needed to maintain the project on time. The computer automatically charges these additional resources at their own rate.

Occasions may arise when even resources set at threshold levels do not allow achievement of a plan that satisfies target dates. If the computer is operating with the instruction to produce a time limited schedule, it will have no option other than to plan for higher resource usage. Provision is made in the program to calculate these extreme excesses at an even higher cost rate than that used for threshold labour. These concepts are illustrated in Figure 7:8.

COMPLEX RESOURCES AND ACTIVITY SPLITTING

It is easiest to think of every activity as a continuous piece of work which employs the same number of men from start to finish. In fact, most activities do follow this course, but there are possible variations, and it helps if the program can deal with more complex cases. The project manager must decide his needs, and then match them against the program that he intends using. Once again, this is a question that must be resolved by discussion with the computer company. Three major departures from the simplest condition are possible, from a practicable scheduling viewpoint. These are as follows:

1 *Complex resources.* An activity may require more than one type of labour skill. An example is the wiring of a house, where skilled electricians and electrician's mates must be scheduled for the duration of the activity.

2 *Rate variable resources.* Most activities have rate constant resources. This means that the number of people specified for an activity is expected to be valid for every hour or day of that job. Even if small fluctuations are expected, provided the average rate of usage remains fairly level no special scheduling measures are necessary. But conditions sometimes exist where the number of people planned on one activity can be expected to change from day to day in some predetermined fashion. An example of this is given by the assembly of a structure in a confined space. As the assembly proceeds, fewer people can be used because working room becomes smaller. Some programs allow this situation to be preplanned.

3 *Splittable activities.* It is sometimes convenient to interrupt an activity, and then restart it in order to divert resources to a more critical area. At other times, and in fact in most cases, it is undesirable to interrupt work because of risks of error or high cost. The planner is usually able to specify his requirements in this direction on each activity card. Some programs assume activities to be splittable unless otherwise stated, whilst others operate in the reverse direction and will not split activities unless given special permission in the form of a code letter on the activity cards.

OVERLAPPING ACTIVITIES

During early network training one is taught the inviolate rule that no activity can start until its preceding activities have all been finished. This is, after all, one of the most important precepts of network notation and logic. However, there are sometimes occasions when the planner would like a little more freedom in this respect. He might often be aware of a situation where the logic is not strictly correct, so that activities can start some time before final completion of all preceding activities. In this sense, the activities can be said to overlap. An example is provided by a design engineering activity which is followed by detail drafting. Quite often, the drafting can start before completion of the entire design. Information is passed over to the draftsman on a continuous basis, and not in one final package.

Several methods can be adopted to schedule overlapping tasks. If they are ignored, a serious cumulative effect on timescale might be produced throughout a large project with many potentially overlapping jobs. ICL 1900 series PERT uses ladder networks. The *K* and *H* program allows special instructions to be provided on activity cards which provide for overlaps or even gaps between activities in a comprehensive set of combinations. A further development, discussed later in this book, lies in the use of a different type of network altogether, known as the "precedence system." Without the use of a computer none of these methods would be feasible at all.

ERROR DETECTION

Every precaution must be taken to avoid the introduction of clerical errors during the preparation of input data. Unfortunately, when networks contain many thousands of activities a few mistakes may slip through. Most computer programs are designed to recognise human fallibility and have inbuilt checking procedures that can identify some of the more obvious mistakes. But these checks cannot cover every possibility. If, for example, a duration of a hundred days has been input for an activity when only ten days were intended the computer will be unable to recognise that an error has occurred. A bad schedule must result. If, on the other hand, two activities are input with identical start and finish event numbers, the computer can be programmed to react. This time, one of the basic rules has been broken.

Not all errors, therefore, can be detected. This means that error prevention is better than error cure. One effective routine can be carried out whenever sufficient time is available. Two people are required, one to call out the essential data from each punched card whilst the other ticks off each correct item on a print of the network. Nevertheless, error checks made by the computer are very powerful and capable of detecting several categories of invalid input. These checks can only be described here in general terms because specific treatment will depend on the program chosen. In each case the computer prints out an error message for every mistake discovered. This is done during or just after initial time analysis. For the actual wording used in these messages, and their exact interpretation, the relevant program instruction manual must be consulted. The more common errors are as follows:

I node equal to J node

An activity has been input with its preceding event (*I* node) number identical to its succeeding event (*J* node) number. Obviously one or both of these serial numbers is wrong, and a correction should be made before allowing the run to continue.

Dangling arrows

"Dangling arrows" or "dangles" are the most common errors of all. They are caused when one or more activities are accidentally omitted from the input, or when incorrect event serial numbers have been punched. In each of these cases, the result is an effective interruption to network continuity, leaving activity arrows "dangling" unexpectedly. This is illustrated in Figure 7:9, which depicts a small portion of a complete network. If activity 12,13 in Figure 7:9(*a*) were to be input by mistake as activity 12,14 the computer would interpret the network logic as that shown in Figure 7:9(*b*). Although the incorrect activity would itself be accepted, since the numbers 12,14 do allow a sensible arrow link, event 13 has been left unconnected, to become a "start dangle." This state of affairs can be recognised by the computer, and a message would be printed out listing event 13 as a start dangle.

Now suppose that the punched card for activity 12,13 was missed from the input completely. The network logic, as seen by the computer, must be that shown in Figure 7:9(*c*). Events 12 and 13 have both become dangles. All genuine start and finish events in the network are identified by the computer as start and finish dangles, respectively. Special measures are necessary to prevent legitimate starts and finishes from being listed among the errors. Some of these methods are demonstrated in Chapters 9 and 10.

Loops

Figure 7:10 demonstrates the generation of another unwelcome error—a loop. The planner intended to input the data shown in Figure 7:10(*a*), but he inadvertently reversed the terminal event numbers of activity 10,13. Thus this activity was wrongly input as activity 13,10 and the computer "saw" the network of Figure 7:10(*b*). Now this incorrect version of the network breaks a rule of networking because it contains a chain of activities which link together to form a continuous loop. These activities, 10,11; 11,12; 12,13; and 13,10 resemble London's inner circle trains—the journey has no end and there can be no completion of work. All activities comprising a loop are printed out as an error message, leaving the planner to check his input in order to root out the delinquent activity.

Duplicate activities

If an activity is input twice by mistake, two punched cards will be present in the input card deck with the same event serial numbers. The computer will read in the first card, and effectively shout "snap!" when the second appears. If, on examination the two cards are found to be identical in every way, then one must be removed and destroyed. Sometimes, however, only the event numbers will match. Descriptions and other data will be different,

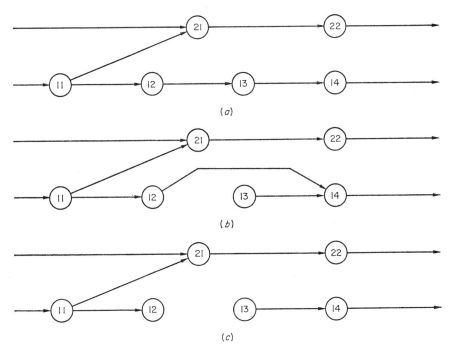

FIGURE 7:9   ERROR DETECTION—DANGLING ARROWS
In (*a*), a small portion of a larger network is depicted. If, by mistake, activity 12,13 were to be input as 12,14, the computer would interpret the input as representing the logic shown in (*b*). Event 13 now appears as an unexpected start event, and can be recognised as such by the computer. An error report would result, listing event 13 as a "start dangle." Should the punched card for activity 12,13 have been omitted altogether from the input card deck, the network of (*c*) would be read by the computer. In this case event 13 again becomes an unwanted start dangle, and event 12 is also left unconnected, to be reported as an end dangle

I.S.T.—E

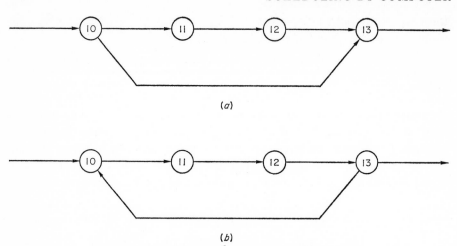

(a)

(b)

FIGURE 7:10   ERROR DETECTION—LOOPS
If activity 10,13 in (a) were to be input, by mistake, as activity 13,10
the computer must read this portion of network as the logic shown in (b)
Now it is seen that activities 10,11; 11,12; 12,13 and 13,10 form a continuous loop. This is a vicious circle without end. Continuous loops are
obviously not allowed, and the computer would print out an error
message listing all activities contained within the loop. The planner must
then use this information as a strong clue from which to identify and
correct his mistake

making it clear that two different activities are involved. In this case one of
the event serial numbers must be wrong. Both activities must be examined
against the network diagram in order that the incorrect event number can
be traced and rectified. Incidentally, if the duplication of activities did result
from a wrong event number, a dangle could have been caused at the same
time. In that case two different error messages would arise from the same
initial mistake. This is illustrated in Figure 7:11. Figure 7:11(a) shows a
small segment of a project network, Figure 7:11(b) shows the result, as seen
by the computer, of an input error causing the card for activity 219,220 to
be punched as 219,202. Two error messages must result. One will list
duplicate activities with event numbers 219,202. The other will declare
event 220 a start dangle.

UPDATING

Unfortunately, plans seldom work out exactly in practice. One can always
expect to encounter some unavoidable change in a project situation, or

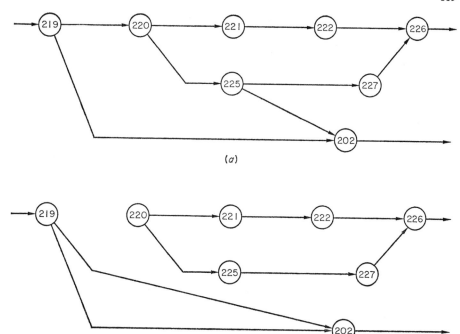

(a)

(b)

FIGURE 7:11   DUPLICATE ACTIVITIES

Suppose that activity 219,220 in (a) were to be incorrectly input as activity 219,202. Transposition of digits occurs very easily when large volumes of data are being handwritten onto coding sheets, so that this type of mistake is quite common. The network pattern, as seen by the computer must become that shown at (b). Event 220 is now left high and dry as a start dangle, and a suitable error report would be printed out. But there are two activities which now bear the identification 219,202. In practice the computer would call the equivalent of "snap!" and print out the event numbers of the duplicate activities. Examination of descriptions and other activity characteristics in the card deck would soon reveal to the planner whether or not two cards had been input in error for the same activity. In this case the descriptions would be different, indicating an error in the event numbering of one of the two activities. From this knowledge, and by reference to the network, the planner can find the source of his mistake

discover that estimates were inaccurate. Changes can arise from a variety of causes ranging from technical modifications to fire and earthquake. It follows that there always exists some risk of an initial plan becoming outdated by actual events or catastrophe. If effective control is to be maintained the project must be kept in step with the plan. When all efforts fail, the plan itself has to be changed to a new, feasible alternative solution.

Otherwise project progress must degenerate into hit and miss methods and the plan will be discredited.

So far all discussions have been directed at techniques and facilities which have the preparation of project schedules as their end objectives. Most of the remainder of this book is devoted to extensions of these methods. But project scheduling is only part of project management. It has to be supported by systems for monitoring progress and, whenever necessary, revising the schedules accordingly. With manual scheduling of small projects the plan can usually be revised at very short notice whenever a significant need arises. Computer-controlled projects can only be rescheduled at the expense of a complete computer re-run. Although each re-run might cost almost as much as the initial schedule calculation, and must take a day or two to arrange, complex projects would be impossible to schedule at all without computer aid. All project scheduling programs have special provisions for recalculating plans in line with actual progress. One system is demonstrated in detail in Chapter 10.

Updating procedures involve reporting activities that have been finished, and signalling those which have been started. A reference date is chosen for the revised schedule, from which the computer starts all new time analysis calculations. This date is called "time-now," and is usually chosen to coincide with the date when the revised schedules are printed out. Thus, during the preparation of input data for a re-run, some forecasting of progress has to be done, because the progress information actually collected will be a few days out of date when "time-now" is reached. Activities in progress, or which are expected to be in progress at time-now, must have their durations re-estimated, so that the remaining duration from time-now to activity completion is input. Updating also provides the project manager with an opportunity to make changes to his network logic, or to any other project conditions such as resource levels, target dates and cost rates.

The concept of time-now is sometimes difficult to grasp, and the choice of a date set slightly into the future contributes nothing to the familiarisation process. It would, of course, be simpler to record actual progress up to the end of a week, update information during the following week, and declare the date on which progress was actually measured as time-now. By this means a new schedule could be produced within seven days of receiving all progress reports. Indeed, this sort of time delay between gathering information and seeing a new schedule must result, whatever date is chosen for time-now. But this schedule must be seven days out of date from the minute the sheets leave the printer. When a future time-now is used, it is true that facts have to be supplemented with forecasts. However, the risk should be very small in a well controlled project. Against this small risk one must weigh the benefit of a schedule which is completely up to date.

Perhaps the most important aspect of updating a schedule for any complex project is the gathering of accurate and reliable progress information. But this is a problem common to all project management systems, and by no means peculiar to computer control. Assuming that effective communications and information systems exist, the question remains "How often must the project schedule be revised on the computer?" Most authorities teach that updating should be conducted at regular intervals, in order that the effects of actual progress can be gauged against target dates. Some companies might re-run a large project network schedule every two weeks as a matter of routine. However, one must always consider the return benefits resulting from money spent on computer time in this way. Taking an extreme example, suppose that a project of two years planned duration ran exactly according to the original schedule produced by a computer. Now suppose that the schedule cost £100 to prepare. If this company carried out an updating run every two weeks, something like £5000 must have been spent to no purpose.

Should progress depart very slightly from schedule, so that one activity slips to become a few days late, it is not necessary to return to the computer in order to learn the effect on project completion date. This result is known immediately from the amount of remaining float possessed by the late activity. Small deviations from plan can usually be absorbed without recourse to a complete schedule revision. Every endeavour is made to recoup the slippage by taking some emergency action on following activities, especially where the amount of remaining float is small or zero. It is often possible to restore a project to plan in this way. The method is, in fact, using the two essential ingredients of exception reporting, complemented by prompt management response. Nevertheless, there will be occasions when a whole new computer run must be ordered. These needs arise whenever project delivery requirements are changed, when a new order is received that competes for the same resources, or when progress slips cannot be contained. Very large projects obviously carry greater risk of deviations from plan, so that when complexity extends to several departments, carrying out many thousands of activities, regular updating does become a necessary and justifiable expense.

The frequency of updating, therefore, depends entirely on the nature of the project being controlled. It should be decided by the project manager, according to his needs and not by any established convention.

COST OF DATA PROCESSING

Computer programs for network analysis and resource allocation differ greatly in running costs from one to another. Companies also adopt different methods for assessing charges. If a large computer is being used, it will generally cost more for each minute or second of time used than a smaller machine, but the calculations will take less time. As a very general guide, one should budget for about £75 for every thousand activities in a resource allocation run. This sum should be sufficient to cover card punching costs, an error run, the actual scheduling run and printing out of a reasonable number of reports. But because of variations between programs one might expect a price range of between £50 and £150 to cover all methods.

Total project management costs include, of course, supporting staff and facilities. However, it must be assumed that staff would be needed whatever the form of control adopted. Annual budgeted computer costs are also dependent upon the frequency of updating. The total budget for planning staff and computer costs could reasonably be expected to be only a small fraction of 1 per cent of the annual cost of sales of all work scheduled. In one company, for example, annual sales totalled about £4 000 000. All the networks together contained some 10 000 activities. Updating was scheduled at monthly intervals. The total annual budget for the department amounted to £10 000.

Justification for scheduling costs is not always easy to prove. When top management are asked to vote the necessary funds one argument, unlikely to succeed, should be avoided at all costs. This is the overworn question "What will it cost us if we do not install computer scheduling?" Another equally undesirable phrase would be to call expenditure an "act of faith." If hard cash has to be provided for any industrial purpose, some estimate of the return must be made. One suggestion, quantifiable in terms most likely to impress top management is to consider the financial reward of speeding up project completion times. Suppose that the project planning department accepts an objective which directly relates their efforts to improvement in average project duration. For each day gained, a value can be calculated in proportion to total company turnover. If the company is operating management by objectives, so much the better. A gain of two weeks in every project lasting two years would represent a modest but entirely feasible target. Similar gains spread throughout all projects might be argued as an increase of 2 per cent in productivity.

Later chapters examine experience of computer scheduling in the light of case studies. Before that point the next chapter describes the principles of computer-assisted planning techniques in the area of time sharing and bureau service.

8 USE OF A
REMOTE COMPUTER TERMINAL

Any planning department which relies upon a data processing machine for producing schedules will know the frustration that can result from delays between initial data preparation and the receipt of error-free print-outs. If the data has to be transported to an outside bureau, processed, error-corrected, reprocessed, and then conveyed back to the client, delays may prove very inconvenient, to say the least. If, for example, the whole cycle takes three days, discovery of an error in the final print-out might mean that the total effective turn round is extended to six days. The significance of such delays must depend to a large extent on the degree of detail, and relative timescale of the schedule being calculated. At worst, the results could be hopelessly out of date by the time they have been corrected.

Most bureaux offer excellent service. Some guarantee a turn-round time not exceeding twenty-four hours. The use of fast messenger services, such as Data Express or Securicor, coupled with careful checking for errors in input data are the usual measures taken to defeat delays. Other methods will be described later, particularly in connection with the updating of multiproject schedules. Nevertheless, in situations where alternative scheduling solutions have to be tested in a planned sequence, or where errors are found in final results, total turn-round times which exceed a few hours may be inconvenient. There is also a possibility that a sequence of schedule tests must be run, each new step of which depends on the use of data from previous runs in the same series.

Even planning teams which have access to a computer owned by their company, and which are housed in the same building, can be subjected to delays. Regular payroll calculations and other heavy demands on computer time may result in clashes of priority. This in turn causes queueing at the computer console, so that several hours or days may pass by before the schedule can be processed. Perhaps the planner's dream would be a computer installed in his own department, complete with trained operating staff and an effective program, and assigned entirely for his own use. It is, of course, most unlikely that such an investment could ever be justified, especially since most scheduling programs need medium or large scale computers.

PRINCIPLE OF TIME SHARING

There is an answer which can yield a virtually immediate turn-around of information within economic cost limits, provided that the networks to be processed do not exceed about 250 activities in size and need no resource scheduling. The system is based on the use of a large, central computer in a bureau. Operating consoles, which resemble teleprinters, are connected into the computer from remote locations. Special electronic devices, called modems, convert the data signals into a form which can be transmitted over ordinary telephone lines. It is therefore possible to set up a terminal in any office, which for this example would include a planning department.

Access to the computer is obtained by dialling in from a normal telephone handset, and the use of Post Office lines is charged at the same rates as conversational telephone calls for the distance covered. Terminals and modems are rented on a monthly basis, and there is an additional charge for the use of computer time. The actual computer charges, however, are far less than the overall operating costs of the computer for the duration of the telephone call. This is achieved by an ingenious system of electronic switching between several clients connected to the computer simultaneously. This is made possible because of the speed at which the computer is able to carry out its calculations. The computer operating speed is far faster than that at which any individual user can type in his instructions, or receive his print-out. In fact, whilst the computer is transmitting print-out information to one customer, it could be storing input from several others, and calculating the data received from yet another terminal.

All of the remote users are sharing the time of the computer, and therefore the overall operating cost. The system is logically called "time sharing," and a large bureau service is available from Time Sharing Limited, who processed the example used in this chapter. The effectiveness of any computer system is directly related to the range of programs that are available. In the case of time sharing, the user is offered a choice of several standard programs, or he can write and test his own program from his remote terminal. One of these standard programs is designed for critical path analysis. It is called "Telpert 4."

Several companies offer time sharing facilities. Resource aggregation can be undertaken by some programs, and the largest networks that can be handled conveniently contain around two or three hundred activities. No doubt technical advances will allow the processing of larger networks before very long, and will even enable some simple resource levelling to be carried out. Charges for the use of a terminal are made up from a variety of elements. The actual rates experienced must obviously depend on the system chosen. It is usual to expect rental charges from the PO for the handset, but this cost can be ignored if a PO telephone is already installed since the new handset can be used instead for all ordinary calls. A further small PO charge will be made for the rental of the data conversion unit (the modem) which is necessary to render the electrical signals from the teletype machine suitable for transmission over normal telephone lines. But the largest monthly rental will be incurred for the teletype machine itself. As a rough guide, one might expect all of these monthly rental charges to total about £50. It is, of course, also possible to purchase the teletype machine outright.

Apart from the teletype rentals, the computer bureau will also levy charges according to the amount of computing time used. Methods vary, but costs should not be very different from about £10 per hour, measured according to the connection time between the teleprinter and the computer. In addition to this computer charge, the user will be charged for each telephone call to the computer, just as if he were making a normal conversational call. If more sophisticated terminal equipment is used, or if the bureau itself has to provide other equipment for special purposes, then additional costs must be expected. However, in order to carry out network analysis as demonstrated in this chapter, and to use many other programs, the simplest and cheapest equipment will prove adequate. If the user wishes to leave his data stored within the computer files after completing his calculations, then the normal bureau practice is followed and a rental charge will be made according to the amount of data stored and the period of time involved.

TIME SHARING DEMONSTRATION: NETWORK FOR A CONSTRUCTION PROJECT

Industrial Development and Construction Limited (IDC) use networks for planning and controlling all their major projects. One of their contracts concerned the erection of a computer centre in the South of England. The network was processed by BARIC at their Kidsgrove bureau, using the ICL KDF9 computer. Library subnetworks were employed, so that although the original network diagram contained about 100 activities, the effective network size was increased to over 500 by inclusion of the library sub-networks from the computer (see Chapter 12). Figure 8:1 shows a slightly simplified version of the original IDC network. Its size makes it an ideal example for demonstrating the application of a remote computer terminal for time analysis. The teleprinter output which resulted from this demonstration was printed onto a normal teleprinter roll of paper, so that the full amount of data printed was spread over a strip of paper several feet in length. For convenience of discussion, this output has been divided up into a series of tables for inclusion in this book. The first of these appears in Figure 8:2.

In order that the user can communicate directly with the computer, he has to work within a precise and limited vocabulary whenever he wishes to pass some instruction. The computer has been specially programmed to respond to particular words. This will become clearer as the example proceeds. Another aspect of the program is that the computer, via the teleprinter, can ask questions that tend to lead the user into giving the correct replies. Although the program is written to accept everyday words as commands, each fresh instruction sent from the terminal must use the appropriate word for each purpose, or in other words the particular codewords for which the program was written. Some effort is therefore necessary from the user, who must learn the specific vocabulary of the program and the customary sequence in which the command words are typed in. However, the program demonstrated here has a helpful feature, designed to guide the user. This is the so-called "how" facility. Whenever there is doubt of the correct reply to any question which is generated by the computer, the answer "how" can be typed in. The computer program then arranges a helpful reply from the computer that gives the user a description of the type of answer expected. The teletype roll records both outgoing messages to the computer and the automatic computer replies. These together form a conversation, using everyday words. The special language developed for this purpose and used in this chapter is TELCOMP.

Input

Strictly speaking it is not correct to consider the input of network data as a separate function from computer output when a time-sharing exercise is undertaken. The whole operation is far more akin to a conversation, with questions and answers being passed between the user and the computer.

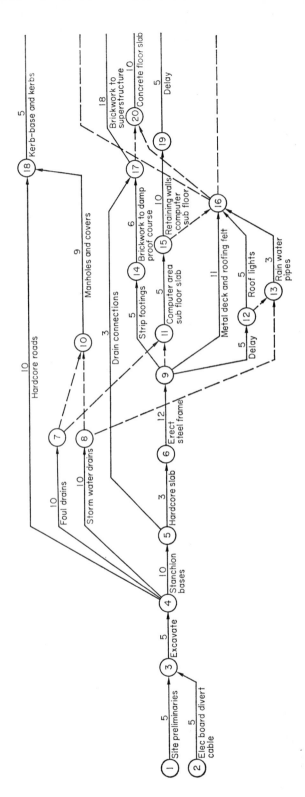

FIGURE 8:1 NETWORK DIAGRAM FOR THE CONSTRUCTION OF A COMPUTER CENTRE

This network has been adapted from one which was actually used to control a construction project for the erection of a computer centre in the South of England. It is reproduced here by courtesy of Industrial Development and Construction Limited (IDC)

continued on next page

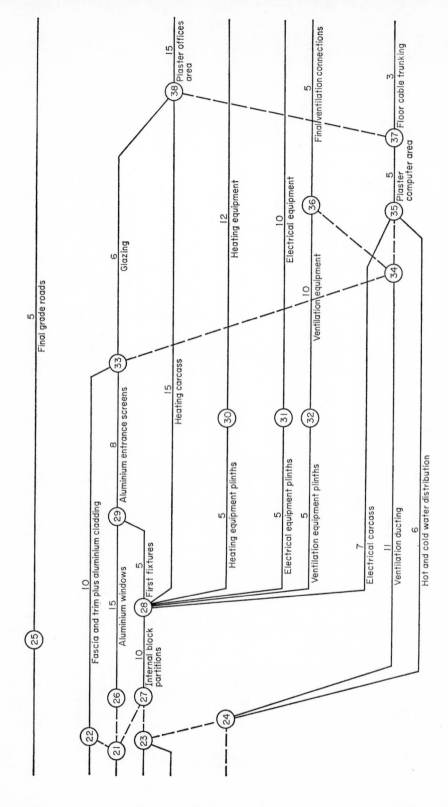

FIGURE 8:1 continued

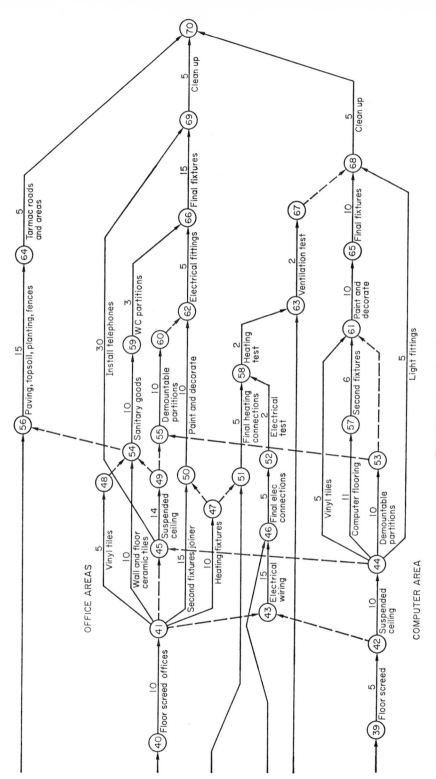

FIGURE 8:1 continued

TEXT KEY	
1	←DELETE ALL ←LOAD %PERT4
2	TELPERT CRITICAL PATH ANALYSIS PROGRAM IN MODULAR FORM HOW FACILITY INCLUDED
3	PERT OPTION DATA
4	TABLE OF ACTIVITIES,USE CONTROL I AS TERMINATOR

	ACTIVITY NUMBER I	START EVENT A[I]	FINISH EVENT B[I]	DURATION (DAYS) DW[I]	DEPT NUMBER W[I]
5	1	1	3	5	0
	2	3	4	5	0
	3	4	5	10	0
	4	4	7	10	0
	5	4	8	10	0
	6	4	18	10	0
	7.	5	17	3	0
	8	6	9	12	0
	9	7	10	0	.0
	10	7	11	0	0
	105	68	70	5	0
	106	69	70	5	0
	END				

6	PERT OPTION DATE DAY : 1 MONTH : MAR YEAR : 1971
7	PERT OPTION WEEK DAYS IN WEEK ? 5
8	PERT OPTION TITLE ENTER OR CHANGE YOUR PROJECT TITLE NOW ↑TIME SHARING EXAMPLE FOR DENNIS LOCK BOOK

FIGURE 8:2 TIME SHARING CASE STUDY—COMPUTER
INPUT

This is an abridged version of the teleprinter roll produced at the remote
terminal when the case study used in this chapter was input to the computer. Text key numbers have been added since, in order to allow easy
reference from the text to particular items as they are described

But Figure 8:2 is a section of the teleprinter roll that was used to pass over
the network data to the computer, and it corresponds approximately to the
input stage when a computer is being used from punched card or other
type of input. In each section of the teleprinter roll that has been included
in this chapter, key reference numbers have been added as a guide for
discussion. These follow sequentially throughout all the separate diagrams

as a reminder that the original messages were typed onto a continuous teleprinter roll, split into sections only for the convenience of inclusion in this book.

The actual messages concerned with establishing initial contact between the computer from the remote terminal are not shown. This example starts with an instruction from the user, at Key 1, to delete all previous data held on his file. This is immediately followed by another instruction from the user to tell the computer to "Load PERT 4." Ignore the odd arrows and percentage signs which crop up from time to time. These are necessary in order to operate the system, but need only be learned by the actual user. They are not relevant to the general intention of this chapter, which is intended to illustrate the principles of the system rather than to provide detailed instruction to an intending user. Any person who does want to install a terminal and use it for access to a time-sharing computer installation will be well advised to approach the computer company for a short course of instruction. The techniques are not difficult to learn, but they do demand some practice at an actual terminal installation under the guidance of the instructor.

Many programs are available to the user through the medium of his terminal. They are stored at the computer centre within the various electronic files, controlled by a range of magnetic tape and disk units connected to the computer. The command "Load PERT 4" is necessary in order to set an automatic process in operation at the computer centre. The "PERT 4" program is selected, and "loaded" ready for use. Once the program has been automatically connected to the computer, the user receives a message to this effect over the teletype machine. It appears at Key 2 in Figure 8:2. Three lines of type are printed out by the machine which give the program title and description in more helpful detail. The "How facility" which is mentioned in the third of these lines refers to a specific feature of the program that allows the user to type out the word "How" whenever he is uncertain of the correct response to any question from the computer. The program then generates an automatic instruction to describe the method of response appropriate to the type of data being transmitted. It has not been used in this example.

Because the user is sharing the total computer time available with other users he has to await his turn for each stage of the operation. But the electronic circuits are designed to work at extremely rapid speeds, with data being handled in intervals of time measured in millionths of one second.

Complex electronic control equipment arranges for each user's messages to be placed in a "queue," and then released to different parts of the computing system for processing as soon as capacity becomes available. The control system is so rapid and efficient that no individual user is aware of delays lasting more than a few seconds and there is no sense of any interference from any of the other users. The conversation between one user and the computer gives the illusion of being entirely private and immediate.

At Key 3 the first question has been posed by the computer. The words "PERT option" are typed out automatically. They demand some response from the user, who must of course be familiar with the system and know what is expected of him. In this case, the user wishes to give the computer all the input data from his network. "Data" is the specific response that is used. Remember that, at Key 3, the computer has transmitted the question "PERT option," whilst the terminal operator has typed in the reply "DATA" on the same line.

Once the response "DATA" has been sent out, the computer arranges for the headings shown at Key 4 to be typed out. These headings guide the user, who proceeds to type out his network data one line at a time, as shown from Key 5 onwards. Notice that each activity is given a sequential reference number, and each entry in this column is followed by the start and finish event numbers peculiar to the activity. Durations are given in days, and the final column gives the user the opportunity to enter a departmental code that can be used for sorting reports. The code in this example was chosen as zero (∅) throughout because it was not intended to carry out any departmental sorting of output data. No activity descriptions can be specified in the input, and therefore no descriptions can be expected to appear in the output. These are limitations of the program, and of the range of output possible to show on the narrow teletype roll. Activities are identified solely by their reference numbers, and by their start and finish event numbers. Each output report must, therefore, be read in conjunction with the network diagram. Dummy activities are input in the same way as real activities, but are given zero duration. It is seen, for instance, that activities 9 and 10 are dummies.

Typing of input data can be a tedious and time-consuming process. When the user is paying for connection time to the computer, and also for the cost of his telephone call, some method for speeding up the transmission process is always welcome. This can be achieved by more than one method, but the simplest is similar to that employed by any operator of a teletype machine for the transmission of cables and telex messages. A punched paper tape can be prepared in advance, checked, and then transmitted automatically in a fraction of the time needed to type out the data by hand. A network containing 107 activities, as this example does, provides a good case for the use of such economy. It was not considered necessary to reproduce the complete set of input data here. The method used to input the first activity does not vary from the method used to input all the rest, so the list in Figure 8:2 has been edited considerably to show only the first ten and last two activities from the total input. The word "End" is typed in by the user to signal to the computer that all data has been input.

At Key 6, the computer has reacted to receipt of a complete set of data by typing out the question "PERT option" again. Every time that one major stage of the total process has been completed, the user is asked for a decision on what should be done next. This time, he has chosen to specify the start date for all calculations, or in other words, the "Time-now." He has done this by replying "Date." The reaction from the computer, shown in the second line of the Key 6 section, is to ask in turn for the day, the month and the year. The teletype operator has supplied the answers that are seen interspersed between the computer questions, establishing the "Time-now" as 1 March 1971.

The computer has an insatiable appetite for information, and will go on demanding "PERT option" until the answer "End" is supplied. At Key 7, the user is asked again which option he wishes to use, and he has decided that he should tell the computer how many days are to be worked during each calendar week. He has therefore typed out the word "Week," and the computer has immediately come back with the question "Days in week?" The answer "5" has been supplied from the terminal, resulting in the digestion of this piece of data and the repetition yet again of the question from the computer "PERT option." On this occasion, it has been decided to give the project a title. Here again, the conversational nature of the system is demonstrated, with the computer giving the instruction "Enter or change your title now." Entry of the title by the teletype operator completes the input of data for this example, and the computer is ready to go ahead with any calculations that the user may need. Although it is necessary for the man at the teletype to know what responses are needed against each "PERT option" message for the computer, he can enter his data, time-now, title and so on in any order; not necessarily the sequence shown here.

Input error checking

Some automatic error checking routines are built into the program. In order to demonstrate one of these, a deliberate mistake was introduced in the input data by the omission of activity 5,6. Reference to the original network diagram in Figure 8:1 will show that this has the effect of leaving event 6 high and dry as a start dangle. The actual abortive attempt to make a time analysis calculation with the incomplete set of data appears at the head of Figure 8:3. At Key 9, the instruction "Run" has been given by the

```
TEXT
KEY

 9        PERT OPTION    RUN

10        EVENT    6 DOES NOT FINISH AN ACTIVITY

11        PERT OPTION     DATA

12        TABLE OF ACTIVITIES,USE CONTROL I AS TERMINATOR

          ACTIVITY    START    FINISH  DURATION  DEPT
          NUMBER      EVENT     EVENT   (DAYS)   NUMBER
            I        A[I]      B[I]     DW[I]    W[I]
          ------------------------------------------------
13            7          5        6        3        0
            END
          ------------------------------------------------

14        PERT OPTION    RUN

15        FINISH DATE IS    21 OCT

16        PERT OPTION    CRIT

17        TIME SHARING EXAMPLE FOR DENNIS LOCK BOOK
          ACT.  EVENTS    DUR.    START  FINISH   DEPT
          ------------------------------------------------
            1 (  1-»  3)    5     1 MAR   8 MAR    0
            2 (  3-»  4)    5     8 MAR  15 MAR    0
            3 (  4-»  5)   10    15 MAR  29 MAR    0
            7 (  5-»  6)    3    29 MAR   1 APR    0
            9 (  6-»  9)   12     1 APR  19 APR    0
           16 (  9-» 14)    5    19 APR  26 APR    0
           23 ( 14-» 17)    6    26 APR   4 MAY    0
           30 ( 17-» 21)   18     4 MAY  28 MAY    0
           35 ( 21-» 26)    0    28 MAY  28 MAY    0
           36 ( 21-» 27)    0    28 MAY  28 MAY    0
           43 ( 26-» 29)   15    28 MAY  18 JUN    0
           44 ( 27-» 28)   10    28 MAY  11 JUN    0
           45 ( 28-» 29)    5    11 JUN  18 JUN    0
           51 ( 29-» 33)    8    18 JUN  30 JUN    0
           55 ( 33-» 38)    6    30 JUN   8 JUL    0
           62 ( 38-» 40)   15     8 JUL  29 JUL    0
           64 ( 40-» 41)   10    29 JUL  12 AUG    0
           69 ( 41-» 50)   15    12 AUG   2 SEP    0
           87 ( 50-» 62)   10     2 SEP  16 SEP    0
          100 ( 62-» 66)    5    16 SEP  23 SEP    0
          104 ( 66-» 69)   15    23 SEP  14 OCT    0
          107 ( 69-» 70)    5    14 OCT  21 OCT    0
          ------------------------------------------------
```

FIGURE 8:3   TIME SHARING CASE STUDY—ERROR CHECK
AND FIRST REPORT

In this part of the print roll, error correction has taken place, enabling the computer to proceed with its calculations. The first report requested is seen to be a list of all critical activities

operator to the "PERT option" request from the computer. The user's intention here was that he should receive back a statement of the project finish date. But he was disappointed.

At Key 10, the computer has printed out the reason for failure to make a time analysis calculation. Although the terminology varies from one computer company to another, and from one program to another, there is no difficulty in recognising that the message "Event 6 does not finish an activity" places event 6 firmly in the category of a start dangle. The operator has corrected the mistake by responding to the next "PERT option" message with the reply "Data." This, once again, causes the computer to print out the tabulated column headings in readiness for the transmission of basic network data (Key 12). The operator can then go ahead and input the missing activity, as shown at Key 13.

Output reports

At the stage represented by Key 13 on Figure 8:3, all input has been made to the computer from the terminal and all errors have been corrected. A network data file now exists within the computer from which a useful range of calculations and reports can be demanded from the terminal. The first question that the teletype operator wants to solve is the finish date of his project, based on the logic of the network, the time-now date given to the computer, the activity durations estimated and the fact that a five-day week is to be worked. After the input of the missing activity at Key 13, the computer has automatically ruled the dotted line, moved the typewriter carriage, and once again typed out "PERT option" (Key 14). In order to generate a time analysis calculation, the answer "Run" has been given for the second time, but there are no longer any errors to impede the calculation. Almost immediately the answer is received at the terminal, "Finish date is 21 Oct."

The steps leading up to calculation of the finish date have taken some time to describe here, but in practice this result could be obtained quite quickly. So far, however, nothing has been achieved that could not have been done as well, and as quickly, without the aid of the computer. The remainder of this chapter is devoted to a few examples which illustrate the flexibility and speed of calculation that can be harnessed as aids to project management decisions. Once the computer file has been established reports can be generated, and then regenerated according to a variety of changed project parameters. The probable effect of any management decision can be tested on the computer, and the answer received at the expense of only one or two key depressions from the teletype machine and a few seconds' pause.

Now suppose that the project manager for the computer centre construction project has been informed of the computer result, and suppose also that the forecast completion date of 21 October is unacceptable to him. He can use the computer in several ways to assist him in obtaining a working schedule that will achieve faster project completion. He could, for example, demand a list of all critical activities. This is arranged very simply by responding "Crit" to the "PERT option" message from the computer. The result for this project is shown in Figure 8:3, where all critical activities have been printed out in the table which starts at Key 17.

Under these circumstances it may become possible for a project manager to load in more people, or to reassess his original estimates, in order that durations of some activities on the critical path can be reduced. Alternatively, the network logic can be re-examined. It has been assumed in this case that neither one nor the other of these two possibilities could be pursued fruitfully. With the teletype machine still connected to the computer, and with the inevitable "PERT option" message displayed, some action is demanded. In Figure 8:4, at Key 18, the project manager's next idea is tested. It has been decided to test the effect of changing over from a five- to a six-day week. By typing out "Week," the computer is triggered off to ask the question "Days in week?" once again. When the figure "6" is sent back by the operator, the scene has been set for a recalculation of all project calendar dates on the basis of Saturday overtime working.

Over one calendar month has been gained by the decision to work every Saturday. This is seen from the revised forceast completion date of 13 September, which has been printed out at Key 22. It is now assumed that this result is acceptable to the project manager. The computer has, therefore, come up with an acceptable solution, based on the input data from the network and management decisions on overtime policy. If the result had not been acceptable, other management decisions could have been tested very rapidly. These might have included a seven-day week, for example, or an earlier project start date. Whatever the change of working rules, a revised schedule can be received back from the computer within seconds.

Having achieved an acceptable solution, it remains to translate that answer into a working schedule that shows the start and finish date of every activity. At Key 22 the computer has been commanded to print out the

```
TEXT
KEY

 18        PERT OPTION     WEEK

 19        DAYS IN WEEK ?    6


 20        PERT OPTION     RUN

 21        FINISH DATE IS    13 SEP



 22        PERT OPTION     CRIT


           TIME SHARING EXAMPLE FOR DENNIS LOCK BOOK
 23        ACT.  EVENTS    DUR.    START  FINISH   DEPT
           ----------------------------------------------
             1 (   1->   3)    5    1 MAR   6 MAR     0
             2 (   3->   4)    5    6 MAR  12 MAR     0
             3 (   4->   5)   10   12 MAR  24 MAR     0
             7 (   5->   6)    3   24 MAR  27 MAR     0
             9 (   6->   9)   12   27 MAR  10 APR     0
            16 (   9->  14)    5   10 APR  16 APR     0
            23 (  14->  17)    6   16 APR  23 APR     0
            30 (  17->  21)   18   23 APR  14 MAY     0
            35 (  21->  26)    0   14 MAY  14 MAY     0
            36 (  21->  27)    0   14 MAY  14 MAY     0
            43 (  26->  29)   15   14 MAY   1 JUN     0
            44 (  27->  28)   10   14 MAY  26 MAY     0
            45 (  28->  29)    5   26 MAY   1 JUN     0
            51 (  29->  33)    8    1 JUN  10 JUN     0
            55 (  33->  38)    6   10 JUN  17 JUN     0
            62 (  38->  40)   15   17 JUN   5 JUL     0
            64 (  40->  41)   10    5 JUL  16 JUL     0
            69 (  41->  50)   15   16 JUL   3 AUG     0
            87 (  50->  62)   10    3 AUG  14 AUG     0
           100 (  62->  66)    5   14 AUG  20 AUG     0
           104 (  66->  69)   15   20 AUG   7 SEP     0
           107 (  69->  70)    5    7 SEP  13 SEP     0
           ----------------------------------------------
```

FIGURE   8:4 TIME   SHARING   CASE   STUDY—REVISED
SCHEDULE
The first report of critical activities showed a predicted project completion
date of 21 October. Here, management have tested the effect of working
a six-day week. The result is seen to be an earlier completion date of
13 September

final schedule of critical activities, and the result follows immediately in the
shape of the table that starts at Key 23. The critical activity list is of
limited use in controlling the project. A more practical schedule is shown in
Figure 8:5, which completes this computer centre construction example.
From the "PERT option" question of the computer, the operator has
replied "Order." The computer has been told by this command that data
has to be sorted into some order before printing. Naturally enough the
computer has to be told in which order the data must be sorted, and this
question has been cleared up in the "conversation" shown at Key 25. At
Key 26, the operator has answered "Lot" to the next "PERT option." This
means that every activity is wanted in the printed schedule. It would have
been possible, for example, to restrict the output to a particular department,

TEXT
KEY

24	PERT OPTION	ORDER
25	ORDER ON ?	START
26	PERT OPTION	LOT
27	TIME SHARING EXAMPLE FOR DENNIS LOCK BOOK	

ACT.	EVENTS	DUR.	ESTART	LSTART	EFINISH	LFINISH	FLOAT	DEPT
1 (	1-> 3)	5	1 MAR	1 MAR	6 MAR	6 MAR	0	0
2 (	3-> 4)	5	6 MAR	6 MAR	12 MAR	12 MAR	0	0
3 (	4-> 5)	10	12 MAR	12 MAR	24 MAR	24 MAR	0	0
4 (	4-> 7)	10	12 MAR	9 APR	24 MAR	21 APR	24	0
5 (	4-> 8)	10	12 MAR	17 APR	24 MAR	29 APR	31	0
6 (	4-> 18)	10	12 MAR	28 JUL	24 MAR	9 AUG	118	0
7 (	5-> 6)	3	24 MAR	24 MAR	27 MAR	27 MAR	0	0
8 (	5-> 17)	3	24 MAR	20 APR	27 MAR	23 APR	23	0
18 (	10-> 18)	9	24 MAR	29 JUL	3 APR	9 AUG	109	0
9 (	6-> 9)	12	27 MAR	27 MAR	10 APR	10 APR	0	0
31 (	18-> 25)	5	3 APR	9 AUG	9 APR	14 AUG	109	0
42 (	25-> 56)	5	9 APR	14 AUG	15 APR	20 AUG	109	0
17 (	9-> 16)	11	10 APR	20 APR	23 APR	3 MAY	8	0
19 (	11-> 15)	5	10 APR	21 APR	16 APR	27 APR	9	0
15 (	9-> 12)	5	10 APR	21 APR	16 APR	27 APR	9	0
16 (	9-> 14)	5	10 APR	10 APR	16 APR	16 APR	0	0
22 (	13-> 16)	3	16 APR	29 APR	20 APR	3 MAY	11	0
23 (	14-> 17)	6	16 APR	16 APR	23 APR	23 APR	0	0
25 (	15-> 19)	10	16 APR	27 APR	28 APR	8 MAY	9	0
21 (	12-> 16)	5	16 APR	27 APR	22 APR	3 MAY	9	0
30 (	17-> 21)	18	23 APR	23 APR	14 MAY	14 MAY	0	0
33 (	20-> 23)	10	23 APR	3 MAY	5 MAY	14 MAY	8	0
32 (	19-> 23)	5	28 APR	8 MAY	4 MAY	14 MAY	9	0
40 (	24-> 34)	11	5 MAY	29 MAY	18 MAY	11 JUN	21	0
41 (	24-> 35)	6	5 MAY	4 JUN	12 MAY	11 JUN	26	0
37 (	22-> 33)	10	14 MAY	29 MAY	26 MAY	10 JUN	13	0
43 (	26-> 29)	15	14 MAY	14 MAY	1 JUN	1 JUN	0	0
44 (	27-> 28)	10	14 MAY	14 MAY	26 MAY	26 MAY	0	0
47 (	28-> 31)	5	26 MAY	7 AUG	1 JUN	13 AUG	63	0
48 (	28-> 32)	5	26 MAY	12 AUG	1 JUN	18 AUG	67	0
49 (	28-> 35)	7	26 MAY	3 JUN	3 JUN	11 JUN	7	0
50 (	28-> 38)	15	26 MAY	31 MAY	12 JUN	17 JUN	4	0
45 (	28-> 29)	5	26 MAY	26 MAY	1 JUN	1 JUN	0	0
46 (	28-> 30)	5	26 MAY	7 AUG	1 JUN	13 AUG	63	0
53 (	31-> 46)	10	1 JUN	13 AUG	12 JUN	25 AUG	63	0
54 (	32-> 36)	10	1 JUN	18 AUG	12 JUN	30 AUG	67	0
51 (	29-> 33)	8	1 JUN	1 JUN	10 JUN	10 JUN	0	0
52 (	30-> 51)	12	1 JUN	13 AUG	15 JUN	27 AUG	63	0
58 (	35-> 37)	5	3 JUN	11 JUN	9 JUN	17 JUN	7	0
61 (	37-> 39)	3	9 JUN	26 JUN	12 JUN	30 JUN	15	0
55 (	33-> 38)	6	10 JUN	10 JUN	17 JUN	17 JUN	0	0
59 (	36-> 63)	5	12 JUN	30 AUG	18 JUN	4 SEP	67	0
63 (	39-> 42)	3	12 JUN	30 JUN	18 JUN	6 JUL	15	0
62 (	38-> 40)	15	17 JUN	17 JUN	5 JUL	5 JUL	0	0
72 (	42-> 44)	10	18 JUN	6 JUL	30 JUN	17 JUL	15	0
75 (	44-> 53)	10	30 JUN	3 AUG	12 JUL	14 AUG	29	0
76 (	44-> 57)	11	30 JUN	26 JUL	13 JUL	7 AUG	22	0
77 (	44-> 61)	5	30 JUN	9 AUG	6 JUL	14 AUG	34	0
78 (	44-> 68)	5	30 JUN	1 SEP	6 JUL	7 SEP	54	0
64 (	40-> 41)	10	5 JUL	5 JUL	16 JUL	16 JUL	0	0
95 (	57-> 61)	6	13 JUL	7 AUG	20 JUL	14 AUG	22	0
67 (	41-> 47)	10	16 JUL	22 JUL	28 JUL	3 AUG	5	0
68 (	41-> 48)	5	16 JUL	30 JUL	22 JUL	5 AUG	12	0
69 (	41-> 50)	15	16 JUL	16 JUL	3 AUG	3 AUG	0	0
70 (	41-> 54)	10	16 JUL	24 JUL	28 JUL	5 AUG	7	0
79 (	45-> 49)	14	16 JUL	17 JUL	2 AUG	3 AUG	1	0
80 (	45-> 69)	30	16 JUL	3 AUG	20 AUG	7 SEP	15	0
73 (	43-> 46)	15	16 JUL	7 AUG	3 AUG	25 AUG	19	0
99 (	61-> 65)	10	20 JUL	14 AUG	31 JUL	26 AUG	22	0
88 (	51-> 58)	5	28 JUL	27 AUG	3 AUG	2 SEP	26	0
103 (	65-> 68)	10	31 JUL	26 AUG	12 AUG	7 SEP	22	0
92 (	54-> 59)	10	2 AUG	5 AUG	13 AUG	17 AUG	3	0
93 (	55-> 60)	10	2 AUG	3 AUG	13 AUG	14 AUG	1	0
94 (	56-> 64)	15	2 AUG	20 AUG	19 AUG	7 SEP	16	0
87 (	50-> 62)	10	3 AUG	3 AUG	14 AUG	14 AUG	0	0
81 (	46-> 52)	5	3 AUG	25 AUG	9 AUG	31 AUG	19	0
89 (	52-> 58)	2	9 AUG	31 AUG	11 AUG	2 SEP	19	0
96 (	58-> 63)	2	11 AUG	2 SEP	13 AUG	4 SEP	19	0
97 (	59-> 66)	3	13 AUG	17 AUG	17 AUG	20 AUG	3	0
101 (	63-> 67)	2	13 AUG	4 SEP	16 AUG	7 SEP	19	0
100 (	62-> 66)	5	14 AUG	14 AUG	20 AUG	20 AUG	0	0
106 (	68-> 70)	5	16 AUG	7 SEP	21 AUG	13 SEP	19	0
102 (	64-> 70)	5	19 AUG	7 SEP	25 AUG	13 SEP	16	0
104 (	66-> 69)	15	20 AUG	20 AUG	7 SEP	7 SEP	0	0
107 (	69-> 70)	5	7 SEP	7 SEP	13 SEP	13 SEP	0	0

PERT OPTION   END

FIGURE 8:5   TIME SHARING CASE STUDY—FINAL ACTIVITY LISTING

Here is the list of activities, complete with their time analysis data, calculated according to a decision that a six-day week will be worked. The limited width of the teleprinter roll does not allow activity descriptions to be handled. It is therefore necessary to refer to the original network diagram (Figure 8:1) in order to be able to use the schedule fully

had input codes been provided for all activities in the original input data. The final schedule is shown starting at Key 27. All time analysis data is shown, there are no arithmetic errors, and the data is conveniently tabulated and sorted. Anyone who has ever been faced with the task of updating or changing a network manually, with the results shown in calendar dates for each event, will appreciate the amount of work saved by the application of this computer technique, quite apart from the advantages of speed and accuracy.

The final schedule for this construction project was, however, derived without consideration of project resources. It therefore remains an incomplete solution. Progress in the development of computer programs for time-sharing operation will, no doubt, remove this obstacle in due course. Already there are programs that can produce resource aggregation tables. However, the results cannot be dismissed as having no practical use. The system can be seen as a very effective tool for decision-making in the early stages of a new project. The project team can set up a detailed network for input to a computer from the more conventional punched cards. Resource scheduling can take place at this later stage. The results obtained from the use of time sharing can prove useful in the establishment of feasible target completion dates. Many first attempts at resource scheduling for new projects are expensive failures, in terms of computer time, because the basic time analysis results prevent the achievement of target dates even before consideration of resource constraints.

9 SINGLE PROJECT SCHEDULING: A CASE STUDY

In Chapter 6 a small construction project was introduced for the purpose of demonstrating conversion of a network into a practical resource schedule. Then, clerical methods were used. In this chapter the same project will be subjected to time analysis and resource allocation once more, but this time a computer will be used. The sole objective of this case study is the derivation of a practicable resource allocation for the project. Progress reporting, and subsequent updating of the schedule will not be discussed, since these topics are illustrated by slightly more complex examples in Chapter 10.

Choice of the simple workshop project allows comparison between the results obtained by manual and computer methods. It will be seen that the computer does not necessarily produce the optimum solution in terms of smooth resource usage. But larger projects do not allow such comparison, because their complexity is too great to allow any attempt at manual scheduling at all. In those cases, schedules calculated by computer may have to be recognised as compromise solutions, falling somewhat short of perfection. In any case, a perfect schedule in which all activities dovetail exactly to provide continuous and smooth resource loading is hardly ever possible at all. When complex network patterns are combined with the need to plan several categories of labour, one could not reasonably expect every resource to come out of the calculation with a constant usage rate. Even if that did happen, it is almost certain that some real-life condition must upset the balance, and prevent the exact detail of such a plan from being achieved.

A computer stands its best chance of producing an optimum schedule when resource requirements are almost equal to the resource levels declared available. If resource requirements are much lower than available levels, the computer will simply go ahead and produce a resource aggregation schedule, with all activities able to start at their earliest times without exceeding resource limits. If, during a time limited schedule calculation, the computer finds it necessary to load resources beyond their stated limits, critical path priority rules will assume highest significance, and once again there will be no shuffling around of activities in order to achieve smoothing, In the project which follows, attempts will be made to overcome these problems by testing the calculations with different resource limits, in order that the program is given its best chance to produce a reasonable result. In practice, any remaining hiccups in the schedules would be overcome by on-the-spot man-made decisions.

Computer facilities

This project was processed at the Manchester bureau of Baric Computing Services Limited. ICL 1900 range equipment was used, and the program was the ICL 1900 series PERT. Only a small portion of the comprehensive potential of the program can be demonstrated in this book. Details of basic hardware requirements, together with full details of the many scheduling calculations and reports possible will be found in the *User's Guide*, published by International Computers Limited. The program allows input to be made in simple form, using four-character event names, or in more comprehensive form with event names containing up to six characters. Notice that event names, rather than numbers are used for this program. This arises from the capability of the program to accept alpha characters (letters) in addition to the more customary numbers. For this example, the simple form of input card coding has been used, which allows event names to contain up to four characters. Even in this form, extremely large networks can be processed, containing many thousands of activities.

PROJECT SPECIFICATION

A very small company, whose staff comprises one skilled man and one labourer, has contracted to build a small workshop. Construction is of brick walls, without windows. Natural lighting is to be admitted through transparent roofing sheets. The workshop has been designed, and the sequence of working has been determined with the aid of a network diagram. This is the same project as that described in Chapter 6, and Figure 6:1 is the relevant network diagram. In addition to estimates for the duration of each activity, the resources needed for each task have also been determined. In no case do these resources change during the course of any one activity, but they remain rate constant. In other words, if one man is needed to lay bricks, it is understood for this project that he will be continuously employed for that task until all bricks have been laid, and he will not require an additional bricklayer to assist him at any stage.

Work can start on 7 December 1970, and the customer desires completion of the workshop not later than 11 January 1971. It is recognised by the builder that his very limited resources might not be able to achieve this timescale, so a decision has been made to produce several alternative schedules to test resource implications. Three reports are to be prepared, according to the following rules.

Report 1. A resource schedule which will attempt to meet the target date of 11 January 1971, but which will not permit resource loading to exceed one skilled man plus one labourer at any time. This, therefore, is to be a resource limited schedule, based on available resource levels. Network float will be calculated from the target date of 11 January. Because this schedule is to be resource limited, it is recognised that the scheduled completion date may have to be later than this critical target date. *Report 2.* A time limited schedule with the target date of 11 January 1971 mandatory. This means that the computer must produce a schedule which satisfies this completion date, even if available resource levels must be exceeded. The only possibility of failure to calculate a plan which meets the scheduled date would be a critical path duration in the network which is greater than the time allowed by the target date set. In this project, time analysis has already been carried out by hand, and it is known that the target date will indeed fall a few days short of the critical network duration. *Report 3.* Another time limited schedule, with the same target date as all other reports. However, this time the resource levels will be set higher, at two skilled men and two labourers being normally available. This report, therefore, will produce a plan that embodies the decision of the builder to accept the employment of additional labour as a necessary policy decision. Although resource levels will be exceeded in Report 2, in order to meet the completion date, setting the available levels higher from the outset will produce a different resource smoothing solution.

When the computer is asked to schedule a project within time limits, it attempts to load resources up to their specified availability levels by scheduling each activity in turn. However, if any activity is delayed until all its float has been accounted for, the computer, in the time limited option, has no choice other than to load the activity and exceed planned resources. Once the computer has passed the resource "ceiling," it ceases to have a reference against which to carry out load calculations. Time limit priorities have completely taken over, and the computer proceeds to assume infinite resource capacities. This is a limitation of the program, and it can lead to some very unacceptable solutions. The level of each resource specified as normal availability is therefore a factor in producing a smooth usage pattern. In practice, however, most companies will be aware of their capacity to fulfil orders, in general terms. Their annual budgets and long-range planning will have been used to provide facilities which match, on a broad basis, their annual market plan. Any project manager should, therefore, be working under conditions where his own experience, coupled with general company planning, assists him in determining resource levels which are likely to be within striking distance of actual requirements. In a completely new industrial environment, where previous experience does not exist to allow reasonable resource levels to be set before a computer run, it may be necessary to carry out test runs. This, in effect, has been done in this example, with Reports 2 and 3 testing different levels of resource availabilities within the same time project time limits.

Other project conditions which must be reported to the computer include the number of days normally worked in any week. This company works five days in any week, from Monday to Friday inclusive. Statutory holidays are also specified, in order that they can be removed from the calendar of days available for work. It is important to distinguish between statutory holidays and individual holidays by members of the work force. In the former case, whole days are extracted from the calendar as being unavailable for any work. Individual holidays, however, represent a depletion of resource capacity, and must be allowed for either on a percentage basis or a seasonal calculation when resource availabilities are set. In this project, should one of the men have gone on holiday, the schedule could have been corrected in several ways. The holiday might have been input as an activity, between events fixed by target dates. Alternatively, the resource levels input as normal capacity could have been changed for the relevant period, because the program does allow for planned changes in resource levels. It is possible, for example, to take into account the effects of planned recruitment and expansion or contraction. However, no individual staff holidays are expected during the workshop project.

DATA PREPARATION

Figure 9:1 is the coding sheet from which all input cards for the workshop project were punched. This does not include the control cards, used to activate particular parts of the program or to arrange the format of printed reports. Control cards were prepared for this project by the computer bureau, a practice which can usually be adopted in order to save the time of the project manager. The arrangement of data in columns is in accordance with instructions contained in the *User's Guide* for the ICL 1900 PERT program.

Notice that every letter *O* has been struck across by a diagonal line. This is to instruct the punch operator to punch a letter, and not the quantity zero. Although both of these possibilities share the same written character, different codes must be used on the punched cards in order that the computer can distinguish between them. It is customary to cross the zero, and not the letter, but the data for this project is written in line with the normal practice of the particular punch operators who keypunched the input cards.

Activity cards

The first twenty-five rows on the coding sheet have been used to specify the punched cards that will give the computer input data on every network activity. Each row, and therefore each card, carries all data for one activity. Data is written as follows (the numbers refer to the columns):

1   Letter *A*, placed in this column, means add the information contained in this card to the computer file. Other letters could have been written in this column to give different instructions. For example, *N* signifies that this card carries new information for an activity already on file. *D* means that the activity is to be deleted from the file altogether, whilst *C* indicates that any data contained on this card is a change to data already on file for this activity. In all cases the activity must be identified by its start and finish event names. Remember also that all of these instructions are only relevant to this ICL program, and that the input significance for other manufacturers' programs will be entirely different. Because this is data for a new project, all data is being added to the file, so that letter *A* is used throughout.

2 to 3   Project code. These letters are allocated to a particular bureau user in order to distinguish his projects from all other projects in the computer files. This code is chosen by agreement between the user and the bureau.

Line	ID	i	j	Act.	Description	Dur	Code
1	ADLO1	1	2	1	CLEAR SITE AND MARK OUT	1	S
2		2	7	2	DIG SOAKAWAY AND TRENCH	1	L
3		7	12	2	LAY RUBBLE AND DRAIN	1	L S
4		12	6	2	FILL TRENCH AND CONCRETE	1	L
5		6	3		DUMMY		
6		6	2		DUMMY		
7		2	8	1	CUT ROOF TIMBERS	1	
8		8	14	2	CASE LINTEL & BUILD PPET	1	S
9		14	1	2	FIT ROOF SHEETS & LIGHTS	1	L S
10		4	6		SEAL ROOF JOINTS	1	S
11		3	4	4	DIG FOUNDATIONS	1	S
12		4	4	2	CONCRETE FOUNDATIONS	1	L S
13		4	6	10	FIT DOOR FRM & LAY BRIX	1	L S
14		6	8	1	FIT DOOR LINTEL (CRST)	1	L
15		8		2	FIT ROOF TIMBERS	1	
16		1	13	1	FIT FASCIA BOARDS	1	S
17		13	15	1	FIT GUTTERS AND PIPES	1	S S
18		16	17	2	PAINT	1	J S
19		1			CLEAN UP & FINAL FITTING	1	J
20		2	4	3	MAKE & PRIME DOOR FRAME	1	J
21		9		2	CONCRETE FLOOR BASE	1	
22		9	10	1	LAY FLOOR SCREED	1	S
23		10	15		HANG DOORS	1	
24		2	5	2	MAKE WOODEN DOORS	1	S
25		5	10		PRIME DOORS	1	S
26	ADLO1	1	7		B		E
27	ADL	30-1-70				071270E	
28	ADL	H241270	2			110171L	
29	ADL	H010171	1				
30	ADL	L			SKILLED LABOURER		
31	ADL	L			UNSKILLED LABOURER		
32	ADLS1S	301170					E
33	ADLS1L	301170	2				E
34	ADLS1S	301170	2				
35	ADLS2L	301170	2				E
36	ADLS2L	301170	2				E
37	ADL	1	5 7	130 1170	2 WORKSHOP PROJECT FOR DENNIS LOCK BOOK		1

FORM 1/42400,888   © International Computers Limited 1982   Printed in Great Britain

FIGURE 9:1 INPUT DATA FOR THE WORKSHOP PROJECT

This coding sheet contains information necessary for the keypunch operators to produce punched cards from which the computer can calculate all the reports described in this chapter. It does not include any control cards for the stopping, starting and printing actions of the computer but control cards can be prepared by the computer department or bureau.

The project planner, at least in the first instance, need only concern himself with writing the data lines.

4 to 5 Sub-project code. This code is allocated by the project planner. It serves to identify one project from another when the company has more than one project on the computer file. In this case, the workshop project is the only work being scheduled, so that the sub-project code is strictly unnecessary.

Note. The data contained in the first five columns is relevant to all activities, and it is permissible to copy this group of characters down the columns on the coding sheet, as shown in Figure 9:1, in order to save clerical time. Care is taken to avoid the introduction of any ambiguity, and the width of any such group must always be clearly indicated by a bracket or underline.

6 to 9 Preceding event name of the activity being input. Either letters or figures can be used, but they must be written to the right of the field (right justified).

10 to 13 Succeeding event name, again right justified.

14 This is a space allowed for an activity identifier. It is used when the network contains two or more parallel activities which share the same preceding and succeeding event names. A letter can be given to each activity, in order that it can have a unique identity within the computer. Other programs do not allow parallel activities at all, and isolating dummies must be drawn on the network (Figure 7:1).

15 to 18 The estimated duration of the activity. This must be expressed in the units used throughout the project network, and it is written to the right-hand side of the field (right justified).

19 This column carries the letter N when an activity is non-splittable. If this letter is not included on the punched card, the computer is allowed to interrupt any activity, and then restart it, in order to achieve the best deployment of resources to obtain a smooth usage. Note that activities 3,4 and 4,9 have been considered as non-splittable in this project. Once concreting has started, it would obviously be unwise to have the work interrupted because the strength of the finished structure might be affected adversely.

20 to 43 Activity description.

Note the important use of this field for the input of dummy activities. This is seen in rows 5 and 6, where the two dummies required for this project network have been coded. The word "Dummy" must be writen in columns 20 to 24, as shown.

44 to 56 Not used in this simple example.

47 to 48 A letter code chosen to identify one type of resource.

49 to 62   The number of resource units (men in this case) needed for the activity throughout its entire duration. This refers to the resource type specified in columns 47 to 48, and must be right justified.

63 to 64   A letter code chosen to identify a second type of resource.

65 to 68   The number of resource units required for the duration of this activity from the second resource type. Again, this data must be written to the right of the field.

69 to 78   These columns can be used to input third and fourth types of resource needed for the activity. They are not required for this project.

79   A letter S is written in this column to signify that the card is a type S card, intended for the input of data relating to an activity.

80   Not used in this project.

The twenty-five cards punched from the first twenty-five rows of the coding sheet correspond to the twenty-five activities which comprise the project network (Figure 6:1). They contain all the data necessary to describe the specific requirements of each activity. They do not, however, provide all the back-up information essential to define the overall project environment.

Event cards

In the ICL program, S type cards can also be used to input data relating to single events. The designation of card type instructs the computer to read data from the card, and interpret its relevance according to a particular arrangement of column groups. These groups have already been outlined, in the description of the first twenty-five rows of the coding sheet. When the S type card is used for single events, therefore, the same arrangement of columns must be used, although it is obvious that some of the data relating to activities, such as the use of resources, and the duration, cannot apply to single events. In these non-applicable cases, the appropriate columns are simply left blank.

In this project, it is necessary to specify two events, in addition to the listing of activities already accomplished. Consider first row 26 on the coding sheet. Here, the primary reason for adding event 1 to the computer file is to notify the computer that it is a start event. If this were not done, the event would be identified as a start dangle during the error search routine which is automatically performed by the program (see Figure 7:9). In this example, however, the same card has been used to provide a target start date for the event, which effectively sets the start date for the whole project.

Because the arrangement of columns is the same as that used for the first twenty-five cards, which input the activities, this start date could have been input on activity 1,2 (row 1 of the coding sheet). Columns 50 to 55 are used in each case. An explanation of the input for event 1 follows:

1   *A*, written in this column, means add the information contained on this card to the file, under the reference of the event named in columns 6 to 9.

2 to 3   Project code.

4 to 5   Sub-project code.

6 to 9   Event name (right justified).

10 to 18   Not used.

19   Event type. Letter *B* in this column signifies a "beginning" (or "start") event.

20 to 49   Not used.

50 to 55   Target date, if required.

56   Target date type. Letter *E*, in this case, indicates that the date set is the earliest possible start date for the event.

57 to 78   Not used.

79   Card type, which in this case is again coded *S*.

80   Not used.

The second event which must be input specifically is event 17, because it is an end event. It appears on row 27 of the coding sheet, and its treatment is almost the same as that given to event 1. The only differences are to be found in columns 19 and 56. Because this is an end, and not a start event, the letter *E* is written in column 19. The target date for this event is, of course, the target date for completion of the whole project. This is, therefore, the latest date on which the event can be allowed to finish, and a letter *L* is written in column 56. Note that target dates can be imposed on any activity, and on events which are neither starts nor finishes. In each case it is necessary, on the *S* type card, to specify whether the date is an earliest or latest target. Other types of input card, not described in this project case study, allow both earliest and latest dates to be input for the same event or activity. When the earliest and latest dates are made to coincide, the computer is forced to schedule the relevant event or activity on the date given.

It is permissible for networks to be drawn with more than one start or finish event. Every single terminal event must, however, be specifically input as demonstrated in this example. In the ICL PERT 1900 program, any such events which are not included in the input card deck will be reported as dangles during the first error search by the computer. The allocation of target dates is not mandatory, and it is quite in order for a network to be input to the computer without any imposition of target dates whatever.

Time now

It is, however, essential to give the computer a date from which to start scheduling calculations. This is the so-called "time-now." A type 2 card is used solely for this purpose, and for the workshop project it will be seen that the time-now card appears at row 28 of the coding sheet. Notice that it is not necessary to use column 1, because a new time-now is set for every computer run, and the card can only have one purpose, which does not have to be qualified by the description "A" for "add" or any other command. It is also unnecessary to state the subproject code, because in cases where more than one subproject is being input for inclusion in the resource calculations the computer will start them all from the same time-now. When it is necessary to allocate priorities to different subprojects, or to start them at chosen times, this is achieved by the input of target dates to appropriate events. Naturally these target dates must be set at dates later than time-now. The coding arrangement of a type 2 card is obvious from examination of the coding sheet in Figure 9:1. The time-now date chosen for this project is 30 November 1970, and this is the date from which all printed schedules will start. The actual use of a target date to determine the start date of a project has been demonstrated by the choice of a target date on event 1 which is one week later than time-now. (See row 26 of the coding sheet.) The effect of this will be to produce printed reports starting at 30 November 1970 but with no activities scheduled during the first week. Notice that calendar dates are written in numerical form, and that one pair of digits is always used to signify the day, the month and the year.

At this point it would, perhaps, be wise to pause in order to reassure the reader. One is apparently faced with the need to write data onto coding sheets in a complicated arrangement, which must be varied according to the type of information being input. This, of course, is the approximate truth, but in practice visual aids exist which make the task far simpler than it would at first appear. One method would involve the printing of special coding sheets, with columns headed with printed instructions, giving precise details of the use to which the form should be put. There would be one type of coding sheet corresponding to each type of punched card that the program demands. However, some types of punched card are only input singly for each computer run. The time-now card is one example because, obviously, only one time-now date can be declared for each schedule calculation. The use of special coding sheets in such circumstances would be wasteful, because only the first row could be used.

ICL have produced a very useful solution to this particular problem in the shape of header slips. These are available for users of the program, and they are laid along the top of the coding sheet according to the type of data being input. The example which is used to input a time-now card is shown in Figure 9:2. Compare this example with the data written on row 28 of the coding sheet. In fact, all data on this particular coding sheet was written with the aid of a series of such header sheets, full details of which appear in the *User's Guide*, published by ICL.

Bank holidays

Should any calendar days be unavailable for normal working owing to some predetermined event, then these can be input to the computer, which will not schedule any work for the periods specified. In the workshop project, both the Christmas and New Year holidays will interrupt the flow of work. Type 8 cards are used to specify holiday dates, and the arrangement of columns is given below.

1 Letter *A* in this column means that the information contained on this punched card is to be added to the computer file. The use of this column is identical to that described for type *S* cards.

2 to 3 Project code.

6 Write *H* for holiday in this column.

7 to 12 The date of the first day of the holiday. This must be expressed numerically, with a pair of digits representing the day, the month and the year.

13 to 16 The holiday duration, expressed in the time units which have been used throughout the network to describe activity durations. In the workshop project all estimates are given in calendar days, so that a bank holiday occupying one day would be indicated by the figure 1 in this column. This data is written to the right-hand side of the field (right justified). The day which starts the holiday, and whose date appears in columns 7 to 12, must be included in this duration.

79 A figure 8 is written in this column to signify that a type 8 card is being input to the computer.

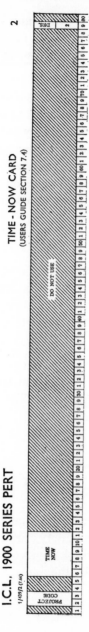

FIGURE 9:2   EXAMPLE OF AN ICL CODING SHEET HEADER CARD

When input data is being coded for any computer operation it is essential to observe the arrangement of columns on punched cards that the program demands. This arrangement is specific to each program, and to each card type used within the program. ICL PERT 1900 needs a number of different card types, each of which performs its own particular input function. Since each card type has a unique arrangement of columns, it is useful to have some visual aid which can be used as a guide when data is being entered onto coding sheets. ICL have printed header cards, to be laid along the top of the coding sheet. There is a header sheet available for every type of card, and the example shown here is for type 2 cards

All columns which are not included in this list are to be left blank. Two type 8 cards have been prepared for the workshop project, and their coding instructions will be found in rows 29 and 30 of the coding sheet reproduced in Figure 9:1. Notice that the subproject code is not included in the data. Type 8 cards, in common with the remainder of cards on this coding sheet, carry data which is common to the complete schedule, affecting all subprojects alike. If the building company wanted to build some other project, they could input it at the same time, and allocate the code 02 to identify that subproject. It could be started at any time after time-now, according to some target date imposed on its start event, and it would compete for the same resources as subproject 01 (the workshop project) according to priorities calculated automatically by the computer from network data. This "multiproject" scheduling is discussed in more detail in Chapter 10.

Project resource identities

In rows 31 and 32 of the coding sheet, two type 9 cards have been specified. These cards are necessary in order to provide a description of the resources denoted by the letter codes used on other punched cards, for example on the type S cards in columns 57 and 63. The arrangement of columns on type 9 cards will be obvious from examination of the coding sheet. If required, the description can be allowed to extend over columns 10 to 75, inclusive. The description written on these type 9 cards is that which the computer will print in the appropriate headings on resource usage tables and other output reports.

Normal resource level cards

It is necessary to "inform" the computer of the resources that are normally available in each trade or category. This is the level to which the computer will try and allocate work on a smooth usage pattern. The punched cards used for this purpose are designated type E cards. Since the workshop project is going to be scheduled twice, in order to test the effects of using either one labourer and one skilled man or two labourers and two skilled men, two corresponding sets of type E cards have been coded. The first set appears in rows 33 and 34, whilst the second set is coded in rows 35 and 36. Coding of type E cards can allow very complex resource availability patterns to be set up, but in this simple example their use has been restricted to the following arrangement.

1   The letter *A* in this column tells the computer to add the information contained in this punched card to the file. For a fuller description of the use of this column, please refer to the type *S* activity cards, which share the same arrangements.

2 to 3   Project code.

4 to 5   Resource set. This facility is only used when, as in the workshop project, it is desired to run the schedule with more than one set of resource availabilities, in order to test the effects of setting availabilities at different levels. Here, the one man, one labourer set has been coded *S*1 and the two men, two labourer option *S*2. Separate control cards, provided by the computer bureau, will instruct the computer which set to use and which to ignore in any one scheduling run. Thus, in the workshop project, one run will be performed using the two cards coded in rows 33 and 34, whilst another will use instead the cards coded in rows 35 and 36.

6 to 9   Resource code. This is the code used throughout the input data to designate each different category of resource. Thus, this is the same code as that used on the activity cards in columns 63 to 64. It will be seen that this code also appears on the project resource identity cards. In this project the letter *S* has been chosen to represent skilled men and the letter *L* denotes labourers. This entry must always be left justified.

10 to 15   This part of the punched card is used to input the calendar date from which the resource will become available for scheduling, at the rate of availability specified elsewhere on this same card. In simple projects, such as this workshop project, these resources will become available from the start date of the project, or before.

16 to 19   The rate of availability of the resource is written in these columns, right justified. It can be seen from the four cards specified on rows 33 to 36 of the coding sheet that the *S*1 resource set has been input with an availability of one man from each resource type, and the *S*2 set has been coded at two men from each trade.

With the exception of column 79, the remainder of this *E* type card is not needed for the simple workshop project. Facilities do exist, however, for using other fields on these cards to specify any planned changes which will occur in the resource levels. Such changes could arise, for example, as a result of planned expansion or contraction of a department. If it is known in advance that a substantial proportion of a group of tradesmen will be away on holiday at the same time, then the level for that type of resource can be reduced from the start date of the holiday, and changed back on the return date. Any number of changes can be input for each type of resource, using continuation cards wherever necessary, For each change in level, the new availability quantity is input, together with the date from which it becomes effective.

79   The letter *E* must be written in this column to signal the computer that an *E* type card is being input.

Project heading card

The final line of the coding sheet in Figure 9:1 has been used to specify the data to be punched in the project heading card. This card serves several purposes, each of which plays some overall part in directing the project scheduling process. Once again only a selection of the features that the ICL PERT 1900 program provides have been used in this example.

1   As with most other card types used in the ICL PERT 1900 program, this column is used to instruct the computer to add, delete, change or make a partial addition to data on the project file. Full details of the coding have already been listed in the section which described activity cards. Here, the letter *A* has been written. The computer has been instructed to add all the information contained on this punched card to the project file.

2 to 3   The project code letters.

4 to 5   Leave blank.

6   A figure *0* written in this column would mean that the computer is not required to convert calculated dates into calendar dates, but is allowed to print them out simply as day numbers. If calendar dates are wanted in the printed reports, then a figure 1 must be written in column 6.

It is obviously convenient to arrange all printed reports with calendar dates. Readers who have used networks without the assistance of a computer will know that conversion of time analysis results from network numbers to calendar dates can be a very tedious undertaking. Not all computer programs, however, have the ability to carry out this conversion. It is a factor which should be taken into account when the choice of a suitable program is being made.

7 to 22   When the original network was drawn, the planner used units of his own choice in order to express the estimated duration of each activity. The only inviolate rule which governed his use of units was that once chosen, the same units had to be used throughout. These units might have been in hours, shifts, days, half shifts, or any other period convenient to the planner.

The number of days in any working week could be five, six, or even seven. Each company has its own specific requirements. The computer program has to cater for all tastes, and columns 7 to 22 are used to specify the exact relationships that the planner needs.

Unfortunately, the versatility of the ICL program in respect of its acceptance of many combinations of time units has led to some complexity in the coding process. The ICL *User's Guide* carries a full explanation, together with some actual examples. However, the reader would be well advised to consult his bureau, or ICL direct, before committing his data to the computer operator for an actual run. Otherwise an expensive mistake could occur.

In the workshop project, each unit of duration is intended to indicate one calendar day. There are five working days in each week. These facts are signalled to the computer by punching the figures 5, 7, 1 and 1 in columns 10, 14, 18 and 22, respectively.

23 to 28   This field is used for the input of the calendar date from which all printed reports and graphs are to be generated. ICL call it the project base date. It is not necessarily the same date as time-now. In this project, time-now has been set approximately one week later than the base date. All that this means is that the printed reports will have no activities scheduled on them from their start until time-now is reached. When a single project, such as this workshop project, is being input for an initial schedule calculation, it would in fact be customary to use the same date for time-now and project base date. The only reason for doing otherwise in this example has been to demonstrate the action of these input dates.

29   Not used in this simple project. It is used for specifying a particular checking routine that the computer can apply during any schedule updates. If a figure 1 is entered, then the computer will not accept any progress data for an activity that has been started unless the activity has otherwise been reported as started. This facility is entirely optional.

30   This column is also used for a code which determines the way in which the computer will deal with progress information during subsequent, updating runs. Unlike the use of column 29, however, it is not optional and must not be left blank. Several codes can be used, each of which specifies the degree of detail necessary when reporting progress. Although no update will be carried out on the workshop project schedule, this column has to be filled in.

In this example the figure 2 has been input. This instructs the computer to regard as incomplete any activities not reported as complete. This may sound like a statement of the obvious, but will become clearer by reference to the project network (Figure 6:1). If, during updating, activity 6,8 (fit door lintel) is reported as finished, but no mention is made of activity 4,6, then the computer must recognise that the network logic does not allow completion of the door lintel unless it can assume completion of all previous activities. Code 2 in column 30 specifically denies the computer the priviledge of such assumptions, and would in this case result in the print-out of an error message.

31 to 78   This field is used to input the project description. Whatever the planner decides to write here will be printed at the top of each report that the computer produces.

79   This, as with all punched cards used in the input to the ICL PERT 1900 program, is the column reserved for a code which tells the computer the primary function of the card. Project heading cards are coded type 1.

80   Not used.

Summary of data preparation

All data necessary for scheduling the workshop project resources by computer has now been described. This example can only be regarded as a demonstration, intended to illustrate the nature of coding rather than to give actual instruction. Once the planner has chosen a particular program that suits his needs, he must obtain a copy of the appropriate instruction manual, and he would also be well advised to seek practical guidance from the computer company or bureau. One must allow that, to the newcomer, data coding might seem to be a perplexing procedure which involves a number of bewildering steps. But in reality the problem is soon overcome by a combination of practice and direct instruction. The use of a checklist is strongly recommended, so that each time a new set of data is prepared no major item of input is forgotten.

The complete deck of punched cards that the computer needs for each schedule calculation might be classified into three basic parts.

Control cards. These cards carry all information necessary to operate those parts of the program which are required by the planner. They include instructions to the computer that define the page layouts of printed reports. They also contain commands that start or stop calculations. In fact, they perform an overall control function which should ensure that the computer does the calculations and operations that will result in a set of reports according to the planner's exact requirements. Control cards are best prepared by the computer department, and not by the project planning team, because they usually demand some knowledge of computer operation. Once a set of control cards has been prepared for a planning department, they should remain useful for inclusion with subsequent schedule runs, and will only need changing when the planners decide that they would prefer some other type of output reports than those which the control cards were punched to organise.

Semi-permanent data. Many cards contained in the input deck will contain data that is not specific to the project itself, but is instead more directly concerned with specifying the overall environment within which the schedule must be calculated. These are the conditions which are dependant upon the capacity and working rules of the company carrying out the project. They include such items as resource levels, statutory holiday dates, and the names and codes of resources. Once coded and punched, these cards will be used for more than one computer run, and do not have to be rewritten at each new schedule attempt. In this example, the cards which are coded on rows 29 to 36 (inclusive) fall into this category.

Network data. Justification for incurring the expense of a computer calculation will usually arise from the need to schedule a new project, or to update the schedule for an existing project in order to allow for the effects of actual progress as work proceeds. Update cards will not be demonstrated until the next chapter, but the activity cards, event cards, project title card, and the time-now card all represent examples of card types that must be input afresh whenever a new project is introduced to the computer. These are the cards which form the bulk of clerical and punching work whenever a new computer schedule has to be prepared.

When all data has been coded it is essential to carry out a thorough check for clerical errors. This is best achieved by reading back from the coding sheets onto the network, ticking off each activity or event as it is verified. Incorrect copying of numbers, the omission of activities or the duplication of activities in the input lists can be checked and corrected by this method.

Once a checked set of coding sheets has been prepared, they can be sent to a card punching department or agency. The sequence in which the card deck is assembled is not important at this stage, because the different card types within the pack will be sorted into a particular arrangement of card type groups by the computer staff later. It is therefore not necessary to write the coding sheets in any particular sequence. It is wise to prepare written instructions for the computer department or bureau, in order that they are left in no doubt regarding the type of calculations that are to be performed, and the manner in which the results are to be sorted, edited and printed out. This letter, together with the completed card deck is taken or sent to the computer where the cards are sorted into a predetermined sequence, combined with control cards, and fed into the computer.

OUPUT REPORTS FOR THE WORKSHOP PROJECT

After receiving all the data described in the first part of this chapter, the computer has prepared a set of project schedules in accordance with the instructions set out in the project specification. But before any of these schedules could be calculated, the computer had to carry out a check on the network data in order to discover any input errors. In this simple project there were no errors, and the computer then proceeded to calculate the critical path through the network, and it also completed the time analysis by finding the amount of float available on non-critical activities. No output reports were requested from the computer for the time analysis calculations, but the results must form the basis from which resources will be allocated to activities when the smooth schedules are produced. Therefore, although no output need be printed, the time analysis results will be placed automatically in the computer files.

Before proceeding to an examination of the detailed, practical project schedules that the computer has printed, it is useful to take a brief look at one report generated by the computer as a direct result of time analysis. This is the resource aggregation table, shown in Figure 9:3. A resource aggregation table results from a project schedule where there is no restriction imposed on the loading of resources. Infinite capacities are assumed; the only constraints being imposed by the network logic and its time analysis. Every activity is scheduled at its earliest start date, and a simple summation of the resources required is made on a day-by-day basis.

The resource aggregation table has been included here because it allows direct comparison between the manually produced example in Chapter 6. Any reader who wishes to compare Figures 6:2 and 9:3 on a day by day

I C L 1900 SERIES PERT   01/07/70   OUTPUT SHEET NUMBER 9

PROJECT DL   WORKSHOP PROJECT FOR DENNIS LOCK BOOK   RUN 0   TIME-NOW 30NOV70   PAGE 1

RESOURCE AGGREGATION TABLES

DATE	L /UNSKILLED LABOURER S			/SKILLED			DATE
	REQ	AV	REM	REQ	AV	REM	
30NOV70	0	1	1	0	1	1	0
1DEC70	0	1	1	0	1	1	0
2DEC70	0	1	1	0	1	1	0
3DEC70	0	1	1	0	1	1	0
4DEC70	0	1	1	0	1	1	0
7DEC70	1	1	0	1	1	1	1
8DEC70	2	1	1	3	1	0	1
9DEC70	2	1	1	2	1	1	1
10DEC70	2	1	1	3	1	1	1
11DEC70	2	1	1	0	1	1	1
14DEC70	2	1	1	0	1	1	2
15DEC70	1	1	0	0	1	1	2
16DEC70	2	1	0	1	1	0	2
17DEC70	2	1	1	1	1	1	2
18DEC70	1	1	0	2	1	0	2
21DEC70	1	1	0	1	1	0	3
22DEC70	1	1	0	1	1	0	3
23DEC70	1	1	0	1	1	0	3
28DEC70	1	1	0	1	1	0	4
29DEC70	1	1	0	1	1	0	4
30DEC70	1	1	0	1	1	0	4
31DEC70	1	1	0	1	1	0	4
4JAN71	1	1	0	2	1	1	5
5JAN71	2	1	1	2	1	1	5
6JAN71	2	1	1	2	1	1	5
7JAN71	2	1	1	2	1	1	5
8JAN71	1	1	0	2	1	1	5
11JAN71	1	1	0	1	1	1	6
12JAN71	1	1	0	1	1	0	6
13JAN71	1	1	0	0	1	1	6
14JAN71	0	1	0	0	1	1	6

FIGURE 9:3   WORKSHOP PROJECT RESOURCE AGGREGATION TABLE

This table has been calculated by the computer before any attempt to smooth resource usage. It is based solely on the results of time analysis and represents the manpower requirements which would be needed to start every activity at its earliest possible start time. It is an unacceptable schedule because it completely disregards the limited number of men available. Even if there were no limit to the manpower which could be assigned to the project, the schedule is too uneven, with too many peaks and troughs to allow efficient working

basis will discover that they are identical, although the computer version has the advantage of being calendar-dated. The use of simple day numbers, rather than calendar dates, is an aid to the preparation of manual schedules, because greater flexibility to change is achieved. As soon as any schedule is expressed in calendar dates, non-working days such as weekend and holidays must be allowed for whenever a recalculation is made. The computer is not so inhibited, because it can be programmed to make the recalculation before printing out its reports.

Notice that the load requirements have been calculated for each resource type, starting from 30 November 1970. This is the "time-now" date that was specified in the input data. But the actual schedule does not start until 7 December 1970, because this was the scheduled earliest start date imposed on the beginning event (row 26 of the coding sheet, Figure 9:1). For every day, three results are printed out for each resource type. These are arranged in tabulated columns, which have the following headings:

AV   This is an abbreviation for "available," and is a re-statement of the quantity of the resource that the planner has input as being normally available. For the purpose of resource aggregation, this quantity is, in fact, ignored.
REQ   The level of resources required on each day to meet the demands of the computed schedule.
REM   This column shows the level of resources that remains each day, from those available, after deduction of the number required to perform all project activities according to schedule requirements. If, as in this case, more resources have been scheduled than are totally available, then the remainder must be negative.

Report 1. Resource limited, using resource set number one. Using the results of time analysis, the computer has calculated a practical working schedule in which the arrangement of activities never calls for the use of more men than actually exist in the work situation. For the workshop project, the contractor only has one skilled man plus one labourer who can readily be made available. These resources constitute the quantities input as "resource set number one."

The detailed schedule is shown in Figure 9:4. All activities have been included except dummies. The exclusion of dummies is a matter of choice for the planner, and it is usually better to have them out of the practical

```
I C L  1900 SERIES PERT                      08/07/70                    OUTPUT SHEET NUMBER 2
                  PROJECT  DL   WORKSHOP PROJECT FOR DENNIS LOCK BOOK        RUN      TIME NOW 30NOV70  PAGE
   ALL ACTS EX DUMMIES IN SCHED START AFTER RESOURCE LIMITED ANALYSIS=RES SET S1
```

S/P	PREC EVENT	SUCC EVENT	U I	REPORT CODE	DESCRIPTION	DUR	EARLIEST START	SCHED START	SCHED FINISH	LATEST FINISH	REM FLOAT	R1		R2	
01	1	2			CLEAR SITE AND MARK OUT	1	7DEC70	7DEC70	8DEC70	3DEC70	-3	1L	1	1S	
01	2	3			DIG FOUNDATIONS	4	8DEC70	8DEC70	14DEC70	9DEC70	-3	1L	4		
01	2	4			MAKE & PRIME DOOR FRAME	3	8DEC70	8DEC70	11DEC70	11DEC70	0	1S	3		
01	2	8			CUT ROOF TIMBERS	1	8DEC70	11DEC70	14DEC70	30DEC70	10	1S	1		
01	2	5			MAKE WOODEN DOORS	2	8DEC70	14DEC70	16DEC70	4JAN71	10	1S	2		
01 N	3	4			CONCRETE FOUNDATIONS	2	14DEC70	14DEC70	16DEC70	11DEC70	-3	1L	2		
01	4	6			FIT DOOR FRM & LAY BRIX	10	16DEC70	16DEC70	4JAN71	29DEC70	-3	1L	10	1S	1
01	6	8			FIT DOOR LINTEL IRSJ>	1	4JAN71	4JAN71	5JAN71	30DEC70	-3	1L	1	1S	
01	2	7			DIG SOAKAWAY AND TRENCH	2	8DEC70	5JAN71	7JAN71	4JAN71	-3	1L	2		
01	5	10			PRIME DOORS	1	10DEC70	5JAN71	6JAN71	5JAN71	-1	1S	1		
01 N	4	9			CONCRETE FLOOR BASE	2	16DEC70	7JAN71	11JAN71	4JAN71	-5	1L	2		
01	8	11			FIT ROOF TIMBERS	2	5JAN71	11JAN71	13JAN71	4JAN71	-7	1L	2	1S	
01	7	12			LAY RUBBLE AND DRAIN	1	10DEC70	13JAN71	14JAN71	5JAN71	-7	1L	1	1S	
01	9	10			LAY FLOOR SCREED	1	18DEC70	14JAN71	15JAN71	5JAN71	-8	1S	1		
01	12	16			FILL TRENCH AND CONCRETE	2	11DEC70	14JAN71	18JAN71	8JAN71	-6	1L	2		
01	11	13			FIT FASCIA BOARDS	1	7JAN71	15JAN71	18JAN71	5JAN71	-9	1S	1		
01	10	15			HANG DOORS	1	4JAN71	18JAN71	19JAN71	6JAN71	-9	1L	1	1S	
01	13	15			FIT GUTTERS AND PIPES	1	8JAN71	19JAN71	20JAN71	6JAN71	-10	1S	1		
01	11	14			FIT ROOF SHEETS & LIGHTS	2	7JAN71	20JAN71	22JAN71	7JAN71	-11	1L	2	1S	
01	8	14			CASE LINTEL & BUILD PPET	2	5JAN71	22JAN71	26JAN71	7JAN71	-13	1L	2	1S	
01	14	16			SEAL ROOF JOINTS	1	11JAN71	26JAN71	27JAN71	8JAN71	-13	1S	1		
01	15	16			PAINT	2	11JAN71	27JAN71	29JAN71	8JAN71	-15	1L	2	1S	
01	16	17			CLEAN UP & FINAL FITTING	1	13JAN71	29JAN71	1FEB71	11JAN71	-15	1L	1	1S	1

FIGURE 9:4 WORKSHOP PROJECT RESOURCE LIMITED SCHEDULE

The computer has calculated the plan shown here in a sequence of activities permitted by the logic of the network diagram, and at a rate which does not cause available resources to be exceeded. The order in which activities are listed can be chosen from several possibilities according to the requirements of the project manager. In this example they are arranged in order of scheduled start date. The letter *N*, which appears in the first column twice, indicates activities that have been specified as non-splittable in the input. All other features of the schedule are fully explained in the text

working lists. Activities have been listed in order of their scheduled starting dates. They could, however, have been arranged in many other ways, according to the needs of the individual project manager. The page layout is not fixed, but can be chosen by the planner in advance. His wishes are translated into instructions for the computer in the form of control cards, which are added to his own input data by the computer staff. The actual arrangement of columns chosen for this example will be found useful for most project applications. The headings are not all obvious and need explanation.

S/P   The subproject code, allocated to distinguish this project from any others which may be on the computer file.

PREC EVENT   This is the event number of the start event of the activity being listed. (Preceding event.)

SUCC EVENT   The finishing event of the activity being listed. (Succeeding event.)

UI   When two or more activities are drawn in parallel on the network, so that they share the same preceding and succeeding event numbers, a unique identifying letter can be input in the ICL program which allows the computer to distinguish between them. This was explained in Figure 7:1(*c*). If an identifying letter does ever have to be input, it is repeated in the output in this column.

REPORT CODE   If necessary, a code can be allocated to each activity, according to the wishes of the project manager, in order to place it in some classification that will assist the management of the project. The most customary form of report coding is to use an abbreviation for the name of the department which is going to be primarily responsible for carrying out the activity. Another possibility, often used, is to use the initials of the manager responsible for the activity. Once allocated, these codes can be used for sorting the output reports, or for editing them. Thus it would be practicable to print out a separate report for each department, because the computer would select activities for reporting according to each code in turn, as instructed on a specially prepared set of control cards. When report codes are used, they are input on the activity, or *S* type punched cards. A three-letter code can be used, and columns 44 to 46 are reserved for this purpose. No report codes were allocated in the workshop project because the situation was too simple. Departmental codes are, however, demonstrated in the next chapter.

DESCRIPTION   The description of each activity is printed in this column. Some project managers are disappointed when they first attempt to use a computer for scheduling, because the descriptions that appear in the printed reports are too ambiguous, or have been abbreviated without due care and attention. When an activity is viewed on the network diagram, its purpose is apparent both from the written description, and from the surrounding activities. If, for example, an activity "lay drains" were to be followed by another described as "make good concrete," then the position of this second activity on the network effectively adds information to its written description. There is no doubt that the concrete to be made good is that which lies over the drain trench. But when this same activity is printed out in a computer listing, there is no guarantee that it will have any direct relationship with its neighbouring activities. No one can know which concrete has to be made good, unless the description is more sensibly worded. A better description in this case would have been, "make good concrete over drain."

Whenever a project schedule contains a large number of similar activity descriptions, it is often useful to include a cost code or job number in the description. This enables recipients of the schedule to identify each activity positively, without the need to refer back to the event numbers on the network diagram. Planners who take a pride in their work will learn, in fact, to write their activity descriptions so that each occupies exactly one line in the printed column. In effect, they anticipate the appearance of the finished reports. They write their descriptions accordingly, because the neat and tidy reports that result are easier to read and use.

EARLIEST START   The dates listed in this column are derived solely from time analysis. They are included in the schedule only for information in the event of resources becoming available for work unexpectedly. If it were necessary to find a man a job, ahead of schedule, then the dates in this column would be consulted. Otherwise, although these dates may be feasible from network logic and time analysis, they do not allow for the effects of resource limitations.

DUR   The original estimate for the duration of each activity, expressed in the units of time used throughout the network.

SCHED START and SCHED FINISH   These two columns contain the dates which the computer has calculated for the scheduled start and finish of each activity. Not only do these dates take into account the constraints of network logic and subsequent time analysis, but they also respect the availability of resources. In fact, since this report is a resource limited schedule, no activity will have been scheduled on a date when resources are already fully occupied, even though the resulting delay in starting the activity must mean an extension to the total project duration. These scheduled dates represent the solution to the project planning problem, as calculated by the computer within the confines of the program, and all the other rules that have been set by the planner.

LATEST FINISH   The latest permissible dates for activity completions, resulting from network time analysis, are printed out in this column. If any activity is not completed by the date shown in this column, then the total project completion will inevitably be late unless some emergency action can be taken. Although the project manager should aim to work within scheduled completion dates, there will be occasions when the latest permissible dates assume prime significance. If, for example, an activity does run beyond its schedule, then the planner can use the latest date as a sort of "backstop," not to be exceeded at any cost.

Sometimes a target date has been imposed on a project which is earlier than the network duration allows, even using infinite resources. The workshop project is, in fact, saddled with a target date that is three days too soon, and can never be achieved. Another cause for project schedules exceeding their targets is the imposition of a resource limited calculation, as in this particular report. Any extension of a schedule beyond its target date must mean that some activities become "super critical." Not only do they have no float, but indeed their float becomes a negative quantity. Critical activities, with zero float, will have their latest permissible completion dates coincident with their scheduled completion dates. Activities scheduled late will possess negative float, and their latest permissible completion dates will be *earlier* than their scheduled completion dates. The schedule attempts to show a practical solution, where the targets are impossible to meet.

REM FLOAT   Many classifications of float exist, and some of these have been identified in Chapter 6. However, for practical purposes most project planners are concerned with the total float possessed by any particular activity. After the process of resource smoothing, some of this total float may have been used up owing to the need to delay activities in order to avoid undue work peaks. The amount of float that remains to each activity after the computer has completed its scheduling task is called the remaining float. It is printed out in this column, and expressed in working days, the same units used to estimate durations throughout the original network.

RESOURCES   The final columns of the printed schedule are devoted to

RESOURCE LIMITED RESOURCE TABLES

DATE	/UNSKILLED LABOURER S AV	REQ	REM	/SKILLED S AV	REQ	REM	DATE
30NOV70	1	0	1	1	0	1	0
1DEC70	1	0	1	1	0	1	0
2DEC70	1	0	1	1	0	1	0
3DEC70	1	0	1	1	0	1	0
4DEC70	1	1	0	1	1	0	0
7DEC70	1	1	0	1	1	0	1
8DEC70	1	1	0	1	1	0	1
9DEC70	1	1	0	1	1	0	1
10DEC70	1	1	0	1	1	0	1
11DEC70	1	1	0	1	1	0	1
14DEC70	1	1	0	1	1	0	2
15DEC70	1	1	0	1	1	0	2
16DEC70	1	1	0	1	1	0	2
17DEC70	1	1	0	1	1	0	2
18DEC70	1	1	0	1	1	0	2
21DEC70	1	1	0	1	1	0	3
22DEC70	1	1	0	1	0	1	3
23DEC70	1	1	0	1	0	1	3
28DEC70	1	1	0	1	1	0	4
29DEC70	1	1	0	1	1	0	4
30DEC70	1	1	0	1	1	0	4
31DEC70	1	1	0	1	1	0	5
4JAN71	1	1	0	1	1	1	5
5JAN71	1	1	0	1	1	1	5
6JAN71	1	1	0	1	1	0	5
7JAN71	1	1	0	1	1	0	5
8JAN71	1	1	0	1	1	1	6
11JAN71	1	1	0	1	1	0	6
12JAN71	1	1	0	1	1	0	6
13JAN71	1	1	0	1	1	0	6
14JAN71	1	1	0	1	1	0	7
15JAN71	1	1	0	1	1	0	7
18JAN71	1	1	0	1	1	0	7
19JAN71	1	0	1	1	1	0	7
20JAN71	1	1	0	1	1	0	8
21JAN71	1	1	0	1	1	0	8
22JAN71	1	1	0	1	1	0	8
25JAN71	1	0	1	1	1	0	8
26JAN71	1	1	0	1	1	0	8
27JAN71	1	1	0	1	1	0	9
28JAN71	1	1	0	1	1	0	9
29JAN71	1	0	1	1	1	0	9
1FEB71	1	0	1	1	1	0	9

FIGURE 9:5 RESOURCE LIMITED WORK LOAD TABLES FOR WORKSHOP PROJECT

When the computer calculated the schedule of activities printed in Figure 9:4, it was instructed not to exceed the resource capacities available. Whenever this rule is applied it must be recognised that the project duration may have to be allowed to run out beyond the ... completion time forecast from time analysis of the network. Shortest possible duration for the workshop project is ...

a restatement of the resource requirements that the planner specified for each activity in his original input data. In the first activity printed, for example, one labourer will be employed for one day, together with one skilled man, also for one day. The next activity is going to need one labourer for four days, without any skilled men. These estimates are simply repeated here for reference. They might prove very useful to a departmental manager who has no access to the original network diagram, or who does not wish to have his schedule data in network form. If desired, these columns can be omitted from the printed reports altogether.

A close study of the schedule in Figure 9:4 reveals that project completion is not planned until 1 February 1971. This result is seen in the activity "clean up and final fitting," which appears as the last entry on the list. The latest permissible completion date for this activity, and therefore for the project is seen to be 11 January 1971. This latest date results from the input of a target date on event 17 (see row 27 of the coding sheet, Figure 9:1). If the customer insists that his workshop must be finished by 11 January, this schedule is quite obviously unacceptable. Planned completion of the project on time has been thwarted because insufficient resource levels have been specified for the work. The actual daily manpower usage associated with this schedule has been reported by the computer in the table which is reproduced here as Figure 9:5. This table has the same format as that already described for Figure 9:3, the resource aggregation table. But this time a very smooth usage of men has been achieved. Starting from "time-now" on 7 December 1970, the rate of working is almost constant at one man per day for each resource type. There are, however, one or two gaps.

Notice that the resource usage table does not indicate the need for any men at all on the scheduled project completion date of 1 February 1971. This results from a particular characteristic of the ICL program, which arranges the run of each activity to start at the beginning of one day and finish at the beginning of another. The final activity on the list in Figure 9:4, for example, is scheduled to start at the beginning of 29 January, and to occupy all of that day. There follow two weekend days, which the computer has automatically excluded from those days available for working. The activity is scheduled to complete on 1 February 1971, but this in fact means completion at the opening of work on that day. Had another activity followed activity 16,17, then it would have been possible for it to start on 1 February. It will be seen that all of the activities in the list have been scheduled according to this rule. True completion date for the project could, therefore, be regarded as close of work on Friday, 29 January 1971.

A resource limited schedule for the workshop project was among those produced by manual methods to illustrate Chapter 6. Since the imposed conditions were identical for both the manual and computer calculations, it is possible to make a direct comparison between both sets of results. Reference to Figure 6:3 will show that a very smooth schedule was arranged by the use of charts and graphs. Apart from a single idle day for the skilled man, which occurred on day number 27, ideal resource usage was achieved over a total working duration of thirty-five weekdays. The solution represented by Figure 9:5, however, is not so perfect. It is seen that there are gaps in the usage of both skilled and unskilled labour. Project duration is not easy to compare directly, because one version is defined by day numbers whilst the computer schedule is given calendar dates. If the total number of working days is added up from the table in Figure 9:5, a duration of thirty-seven days will be discovered; two days longer than the same project needs when scheduled manually.

Unfortunately, it has been shown that schedules produced by the computer, therefore, may be less than perfect. The so-called "optimum solution" may not be achieved. One does not have to search far for the basic reason. It has to be remembered that the computer is not a thinking animal. When the manual schedule was produced, a mixture of logic and intuition was applied in order to get at the smoothest load chart. The planner was able to use his judgement, vary any rules as he went along, and scan the overall chart from time to time in order to jog his intuition. The computer has no intuition. It can only work within rules that are fixed by the program and the input data. Some of these rules are the "priority rules" that govern the priorities which determine the claim that activities have when competing for common resources. Some experiments can be performed with different priority options, but the results are not likely to be worth the effort and expense. All of the schedules produced for this book are calculated with highest priority given to activities which have the least amount of remaining float.

Should, therefore, the computer be dismissed as a useless planning tool? Or should efforts be made instead to improve the results in order to achieve optimum resource schedules? These problems have to be placed in their true perspective against the practical conditions likely to be met in an actual industrial project. The schedule produced for the workshop project, although not as perfect as it might have been, would nevertheless have been a feasible working plan. If the project had contained thousands of activities, and not just a few, then a comparison between manual and computer methods would have been impossible in any case, because no chart could have contained all the necessary data conveniently. Even supposing that the computer could produce a perfect solution, in which all activities dovetailed neatly to give a smooth resource pattern, real-life situations must intervene to disrupt the ideal plan and cause some unexpected hiccups in the day to day work load. Illness, bad weather, trade disputes, scrapped work and a host of other events can give rise to the need for on-the-spot management corrections to the project schedule. However the plan is to be produced, it only has to approximate to a perfectly smooth load. The computer is well able to calculate schedules which, although not always the optimum solutions, will be entirely adequate for all practical purposes.

The remaining schedules to be demonstrated in this chapter will show that the computer possesses the great and overriding advantage of flexibility, when it is compared to manual methods. Once the input data has been prepared, it can be used in a variety of ways to test different project conditions. Estimates, resource levels, target dates and network logic can all be changed at the discretion of the project manager, and a fresh schedule prepared in an orderly printed report. All of this takes only minutes, but would be entirely out of the question if no computer were available.

Report 2. Time limited, using resource set number one. In Figure 9:6, another schedule has been produced by the computer. This plan has attempted to meet the project scheduled end date with the resources specified by resource set number one. This resource set is that which only provides for the use of normally available men; in this case one skilled man and one labourer. Under no circumstances, however, may any critical activity be delayed to avoid planned resource overloads, because the schedule has been calculated with the time limited option imposed, unlike the previous schedule which was resource limited.

Once again it is seen that the project target completion date of 11 January 1971 has not been satisfied by the plan. But on this occasion resource restrictions cannot be held responsible, because the imposition of a time limit rule must mean that project completion on time takes precedence over the need to keep within resource limits. The answer to this particular problem stems from the network itself. The duration of the network critical path is simply longer than the time allowed between the target start

I C L 1900 SERIES PERT   08/07/70   OUTPUT SHEET NUMBER 223

PROJECT DL WORKSHOP PROJECT FOR DENNIS LOCK BOOK   RUN   TIME NOW 30NOV70 PAGE 1

ALL ACTS EX DUMMIES IN SCHED START AFTER TIME LIMITED ANALYSIS-RES SET S1

S/P	PREC EVENT	SUCC EVENT	U I	REPORT CODE	DESCRIPTION	DUR	EARLIEST START	SCHED START	SCHED FINISH	LATEST FINISH	REM FLOAT	RESOURCES R1		R2	
01	1	2			CLEAR SITE AND MARK OUT	1	7DEC70	7DEC70	8DEC70	3DEC70	-3	1L	1	1S	1
01	2	3			DIG FOUNDATIONS	4	8DEC70	8DEC70	14DEC70	9DEC70	-3	1L	4		
01	2	4			MAKE & PRIME DOOR FRAME	3	8DEC70	8DEC70	11DEC70	11DEC70	0	1S	3		
01	2	8			CUT ROOF TIMBERS	1	8DEC70	11DEC70	14DEC70	30DEC70	10	1S	1		
01	2	5			MAKE WOODEN DOORS	2	8DEC70	14DEC70	16DEC70	4JAN71	10	1S	2		
01 N	3	4			CONCRETE FOUNDATIONS	2	14DEC70	14DEC70	16DEC70	11DEC70	-3	1L	2		
01	4	6			FIT DOOR FRM & LAY BRIX	10	16DEC70	16DEC70	4JAN71	29DEC70	-3	1L	10	1S	1
01	2	7			DIG SOAKAWAY AND TRENCH	2	8DEC70	30DEC70	4JAN71	4JAN71	0	1L	2		
01 N	4	9			CONCRETE FLOOR BASE	2	16DEC70	30DEC70	4JAN71	4JAN71	0	1L	2		
01	5	10			PRIME DOORS	1	10DEC70	4JAN71	5JAN71	5JAN71	0	1S	1		
01	6	8			FIT DOOR LINTEL 1RSJS	1	4JAN71	4JAN71	5JAN71	30DEC70	-3	1L	1	1S	
01	7	12			LAY RUBBLE AND DRAIN	1	10DEC70	4JAN71	5JAN71	5JAN71	0	1L	1	1S	
01	9	10			LAY FLOOR SCREED	1	18DEC70	4JAN71	5JAN71	5JAN71	0	1S	1		
01	8	11			FIT ROOF TIMBERS	2	5JAN71	5JAN71	7JAN71	4JAN71	-3	1L	2	1S	
01	8	14			CASE LINTEL & BUILD PPET	2	5JAN71	5JAN71	7JAN71	7JAN71	0	1L	2	1S	
01	10	13			HANG DOORS	1	4JAN71	5JAN71	6JAN71	6JAN71	0	1L	1	1S	
01	12	16			FILL TRENCH AND CONCRETE	2	11DEC70	6JAN71	8JAN71	8JAN71	0	1L	2		
01	11	13			FIT FASCIA BOARDS	1	7JAN71	7JAN71	8JAN71	5JAN71	-3	1S	1		
01	11	14			FIT ROOF SHEETS & LIGHTS	2	7JAN71	7JAN71	11JAN71	7JAN71		1L	2	1S	
01	13	15			FIT GUTTERS AND PIPES	1	8JAN71	8JAN71	11JAN71	6JAN71		1S	1		
01	14	16			SEAL ROOF JOINTS	1	11JAN71	11JAN71	12JAN71	8JAN71	-2	1S	1		
01	15	16			PAINT	2	11JAN71	11JAN71	13JAN71	8JAN71	-3	1L	2	1S	
01	16	17			CLEAN UP & FINAL FITTING	1	13JAN71	13JAN71	14JAN71	11JAN71	-3	1L	1	1S	

FIGURE 9:6   TIME LIMITED SCHEDULE FOR THE WORKSHOP PROJECT

The schedule shown here has been produced by the computer with a mandatory target completion date of 11 January 1971 imposed. The overall time allowed between the target start and finish dates for the project is insufficient, and less than the critical path duration of the network. The computer has therefore done the best that it can, and contained the project within the critical network duration, although completion must be planned a few days late. This schedule looks workable until the associated manpower requirements, shown in Figure 9:7, are studied

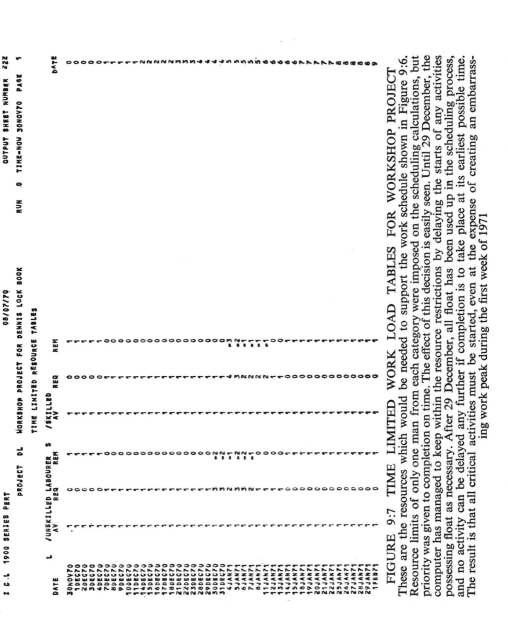

FIGURE 9:7 TIME LIMITED WORK LOAD TABLES FOR WORKSHOP PROJECT

These are the resources which would be needed to support the work schedule shown in Figure 9:6. Resource limits of only one man from each category were imposed on the scheduling calculations, but priority was given to completion on time. The effect of this decision is easily seen. Until 29 December, the computer has managed to keep within the resource restrictions by delaying the starts of any activities possessing float as necessary. After 29 December, all float has been used up in the scheduling process, and no activity can be delayed any further if completion is to take place at its earliest possible time. The result is that all critical activities must be started, even at the expense of creating an embarrassing work peak during the first week of 1971

date of 7 December 1970, for event 1, and the target completion date of 11 January 1971 for event 17. In effect, the target completion date was too optimistic. The computer cannot schedule the impossible. Fortunately the error was small, amounting only to three days. The schedule must, therefore, be acceptable on a purely timescale basis.

If Figure 9:6 does display a schedule which meets the approximate timescale requirements of the workshop project, it certainly falls far short of a practical resource allocation plan. A table of the resources necessary to carry out the plan, on a day by day basis, is shown in the report of Figure 9:7. Smoothing has been carried out very effectively until 30 December, when the demands of critical activities have suddenly resulted in serious overloads. The computer has delayed some non-critical activities in the early part of the schedule, in order to keep within resource limits. Eventually, however, too many activities have been forced into one period with all their float used up by the scheduling process. The time limiting rule has left the computer no choice except to schedule all critical activities on or before their latest permissible start dates. At this point in the schedule, time priorities have completely taken over, and resource allocation has collapsed. Resource limits have had to be exceeded disastrously.

Report 3. Time limited, using resource set number two. It is obvious from a study of the first two reports that the workshop project must either be allowed to run late, or it must be provided with additional labour. The computer has therefore been instructed to carry out a second time limited schedule run, using resource set number two. This resource set was specified in the input data (Figure 9:1) as having availability levels of two men in each trade, instead of only one. The effect of this change is that the computer is not now forced to delay non-critical activities in the early part of the schedule to the same extent as before. These early activities do not, therefore, become delayed to the extent where they clash with later, critical activities. There is less competition for resources, and the computer is able to contain the whole project schedule within its critical limits without having to exceed planned resources.

The schedule which results from these higher resource capacities is shown in Figure 9:8, and its daily manpower needs are displayed in Figure 9:9. Project completion, as in Report 2, has been planned within the critical duration of the network. The time limiting rule has therefore been observed by the computer, although the target completion date of 11 January 1971

L ACTS EX DUMMIES IN SCHED START AFTER TIME LIMITED ANALYSIS=RES SET 52

PREC EVENT	SUCC EVENT	U I	REPORT CODE	DESCRIPTION	DUR	EARLIEST START	SCHED START	SCHED FINISH	LATEST FINISH	REM FLOAT	R1 RESOURCES		R2	
1	2			CLEAR SITE AND MARK OUT	1	7DEC70	7DEC70	8DEC70	3DEC70	-3	1L	1	1S	1
2	3			DIG FOUNDATIONS	4	8DEC70	8DEC70	14DEC70	9DEC70	-3	1L	4		
2	4			MAKE & PRIME DOOR FRAME	3	8DEC70	8DEC70	11DEC70	11DEC70	0	1S	3		
2	7			DIG SOAKAWAY AND TRENCH	2	8DEC70	8DEC70	10DEC70	4JAN71	14	1L	2		
2	8			CUT ROOF TIMBERS	1	8DEC70	8DEC70	9DEC70	30DEC70	13	1S	1		
2	5			MAKE WOODEN DOORS	2	8DEC70	9DEC70	11DEC70	4JAN71	13	1S	2		
5	10			PRIME DOORS	1	10DEC70	11DEC70	14DEC70	5JAN71	13	1S	1		
7	12			LAY RUBBLE AND DRAIN	1	10DEC70	11DEC70	14DEC70	5JAN71	13	1L	1	1S	1
3	4			CONCRETE FOUNDATIONS	2	14DEC70	14DEC70	16DEC70	11DEC70	-3	1L	2		
12	10			FILL TRENCH AND CONCRETE	2	11DEC70	14DEC70	16DEC70	8JAN71	14	1L	2		
4	6			FIT DOOR FRM & LAY BRIX	10	16DEC70	16DEC70	4JAN71	29DEC70	-3	1L	10	1S	10
4	9			CONCRETE FLOOR BASE	2	16DEC70	16DEC70	18DEC70	4JAN71	8	1L	2		
9	10			LAY FLOOR SCREED	1	18DEC70	18DEC70	21DEC70	5JAN71	8	1S	1		
6	8			FIT DOOR LINTEL 1RSJ>	1	4JAN71	4JAN71	5JAN71	30DEC70	-3	1L	1	1S	1
10	15			HANG DOORS	1	4JAN71	4JAN71	5JAN71	6JAN71	1	1L	1	1S	1
8	11			FIT ROOF TIMBERS	2	5JAN71	5JAN71	7JAN71	4JAN71	-3	1L	2	1S	2
8	14			CASE LINTEL & BUILD PPET	2	5JAN71	5JAN71	7JAN71	7JAN71	0	1L	2	1S	2
11	13			FIT FASCIA BOARDS	1	7JAN71	7JAN71	8JAN71	5JAN71	-3	1S	1		
11	14			FIT ROOF SHEETS & LIGHTS	2	7JAN71	7JAN71	11JAN71	7JAN71	-2	1L	2	1S	2
13	15			FIT GUTTERS AND PIPES	1	8JAN71	8JAN71	11JAN71	6JAN71	-3	1S	1		
14	16			SEAL ROOF JOINTS	1	11JAN71	11JAN71	12JAN71	8JAN71	-2	1S	1		
15	16			PAINT	2	11JAN71	11JAN71	13JAN71	8JAN71	-3	1L	2	1S	2
16	17			CLEAN UP & FINAL FITTING	1	13JAN71	13JAN71	14JAN71	11JAN71	-3	1L	1	1S	1

FIGURE 9:8   TIME LIMITED SCHEDULE FOR THE WORKSHOP PROJECT USING ADDITIONAL RESOURCES

If the schedule shown here is compared with that of Figure 9:6, very little difference can be discerned. Both allow for work to start on 7 December 1970 and both show the project completion date as 14 January 1971. In this schedule, however, the computer has been given higher resource limits, with two men for each trade category normally available. This was the option called "resource set 2" in the input data. The result is seen when the smoother work load table of Figure 9:9 is examined. Sufficient resources now exist to allow some early activities to start before they become critical. Bunching of critical activities around the first week of 1971, which was an undesirable feature of the previous schedule, has been avoided

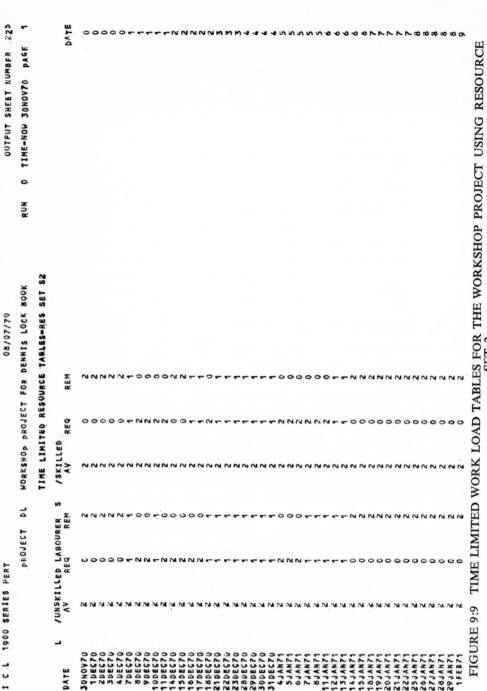

FIGURE 9:9 TIME LIMITED WORK LOAD TABLES FOR THE WORKSHOP PROJECT USING RESOURCE
SET 2

This table shows the manpower usage needed for each day of the workshop project if the plan shown in Figure 9:8 is to be followed. It is not a perfect plan, because some idle days exist during the working period. However, the project is

has again been exceeded owing to the duration of the critical path amounting to three days longer than the time interval sandwiched between the target start and finish dates. But, unlike the schedule in Report 2, the computer has managed to keep within the resource limits set. The previous impossible work peaks of three, and even four men have been avoided. To the extent that the computer has made a plan which satisfies both time and resource limits, this solution can be regarded as successful.

Now compare these computer results with those obtained manually for the same project, with the same time limit imposed. The original manual solution was shown in Figure 6:4, but comparison is simplified when both the manual and computer versions are plotted as load histograms on a common scale. Figure 9:10 has been drawn for this purpose. It is apparent that the resource allocation plan from the computer is not as ideal as its manual counterpart. Whereas the mentally produced schedule has arranged continuous employment of each resource category, the computer has allowed the introduction of some gaps in the smooth load pattern. There are a few days when the planned manpower usage is reduced from two men to only one, and then jumps back to two again. This discontinuity leaves a question mark over the useful employment of one man from each of the two trades during the slack days.

The computer, being without the human capacity for seeing ahead, has only been able to consider the situation, working forward through the plan on a day by day basis. If, on the day being examined, any activity can be started without exceeding time or resource limits, then it will be started even though it might have been better to delay the scheduled start in order to close up gaps occurring later in the plan. When the schedule was produced by a human brain, many earlier activities which possessed float were delayed, even though they could have been started within stated resource limits, until the resulting load was reasonably continuous. Nevertheless, the computer schedule is practicable, and could be used successfully for the control of this project. It embraces all the benefits of a network-based plan, so that the sequence of activities observes all priorities necessary for completion of the project on time. The resource requirements, if not perfect, are sensibly planned.

The computer stands its best chance of planning smooth workloads for time limited schedules when resources are available at approximately the strengths which the project demands. If resource limits are set too low, activities with zero or negative float will claim priority over the inadequate

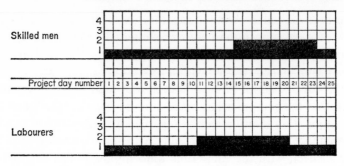

(*a*) Manual resource schedule

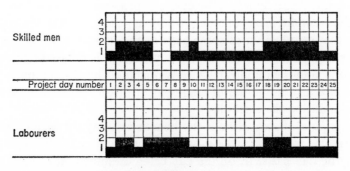

(*b*) Computer resource schedule

FIGURE 9:10 TIME LIMITED RESOURCE TABLE COM-
PARISONS FOR THE WORKSHOP PROJECT

Diagram (*a*) is a copy of the resource histogram for the workshop
project which was first shown in Figure 6:4. It was derived from a
schedule of activities whose main objective was to secure project completion in the shortest possible duration, and with the smoothest possible
deployment of manpower. When the same task was given to the computer, the table of Figure 9:9 was generated. The computer result has
been plotted here in diagram (*b*) to allow direct comparison with the
solution obtained manually

resources, the limits set must be breached, and the computer will then
proceed to ignore resource limits completely. When, on the other hand,
resources are set too high, the computer finds itself able to schedule all or
most activities at their earliest possible start dates, without any need for
delays. The resulting schedule then becomes virtually a resource aggregation, without effective smoothing.

When only one or two resource categories have to be scheduled, it is possible to test different resource levels in a series of computer runs. This has been demonstrated here for the workshop project in Reports 2 and 3. But such test runs can prove very expensive when projects assume the size and complexity likely to be encountered in real life. If several trades or resource categories have to be included in the plan, the number of possible permutations in level changes could be formidable, and far too expensive to allow testing for the best solution. These problems may appear very serious at first, but paradoxically they become easier to surmount as the scale and complexity of projects approach dimensions which are more in accord with actual projects than the simple workshop project illustrated here.

A company engaged in the fulfilment of industrial projects will most probably be controlling several projects simultaneously. These will be in various stages of completion, and all will compete for the common resources owned by the company. Each project must have been estimated for pricing purposes, and production budgets are necessary in order to safeguard planned profit margins. It is to be expected also that the company will have calculated a long-range financial plan, within which orders for new work can be accepted up to predetermined sales forecasts which, in turn, relate to budgeted overall plant and labour capacities. From these plans and budgets, therefore, the company must be in possession of reasonably accurate knowledge of the total resource capacities needed to fulfil the total work program for each year.

Any attempt to extract a single project from the total work load, and to schedule its resources in isolation, immediately raises problems of priority conflicts between projects. It also demands that a decision is made on the apportionment of resources which must be deployed from the total pool in order to satisfy the single project. This situation would meet all the difficulties that have been discussed in this chapter because the timing and average usage levels of each resource would be difficult to assess with sufficient accuracy. It is unlikely that any project would consume resources in a neat block pattern, and much more likely that resources would switch gradually from one project to the next. The answer lies in the use of a computer to carry out a comprehensive schedule of total company resources, where networks are produced for all projects and processed together as one large, company network. This is called multiproject scheduling, and it represents one of the most rewarding applications of the modern business computer. Multiproject scheduling is introduced and demonstrated in the next chapter.

10 MULTIPROJECT SCHEDULING: A CASE STUDY

Multiproject scheduling must, by its very nature, involve the consideration of many activities. Even when the method is used to schedule the resources in one department only, the resulting combination of all project networks can lead to computer input of several thousand activities. In practice, the amount of effort needed to operate the system is less frightening than one would expect, and once plans have been established they are far easier to reschedule than by any comparable manual method. However, it is very difficult within the limited scope of a book to represent a real-life situation as a case study, and it becomes essential to scale the problem down to something less than life size in order to preserve clarity.

True multiproject scheduling usually involves many departments throughout a company, so that all key project resources are considered. The number of projects being handled at any time could approach twenty or more, depending, of course, on the nature of the industry and size of company. In this chapter it has been necessary to consider only two projects, and limit scheduling to a small design office that only needs to consider two grades of skill. Nevertheless, the examples which do follow have been derived from actual experience and are truly representative of the industry from which they are taken. Although the two projects demonstrated are sufficiently small to allow scheduling by simple manual techniques, they are not artificial and would lead in real life to finished machinery valued at something between £50 000 and £100 000.

Computer facilities

All of the data preparation and computer reports in this chapter were specially prepared by *K* and *H* Business Consultants Limited. They used an IBM 360/40 computer, and the program was the *K* and *H* CPM/RPSM package. Like the ICL program demonstrated in the previous chapter, the *K* and *H* program is also powerful and flexible. It is capable of carrying out multiproject resource scheduling for projects containing many thousands of activities. Either the ICL or the K and H program could have been used for calculating the schedule in this case study.

PROJECT ENVIRONMENT—THE INGERDALE MACHINE TOOL COMPANY LIMITED

The Ingerdale Machine Tool Company is in business for the purpose of designing and manufacturing complex transfer machinery. These machines are specially built for each customer, and no two machines are ever alike. A typical project might involve the design and construction of several special machines for drilling and milling operations, together with a mechanism for transferring the workpiece from each operation to the next. Such machines are widely used, for example, by the motor car manu-facturers for the production of precision engine components such as cylinder heads and blocks. Because each machine has to be designed specially, the design costs can account for up to 20 per cent of total factory cost. Delivery time from order to machine installation is also largely influenced by the amount of time that the design office needs to produce manufacturing drawings and specifications for purchased components. The selling price for one project can range from around £20 000 to over £1 million.

The total number of staff employed in the design departments amounts to over one hundred, and these are supplemented, when necessary, by extensive use of outside subcontract drawing office personnel. Companies which carry out a small number of large projects are very dependent upon market conditions, and need to be capable of flexibility in adjusting their staffing levels in order to cope with unavoidable fluctuations in workload. Use of subcontract draughtsmen does not, however, remove the need to schedule work and produce manpower forecasts. Subcontract staff are not a commodity that can be turned on and off at will. Most subcontracting drawing offices demand adequate notice for the provision of people in substantial numbers. Time must also be allowed for the controlling design department to arrange for specific training and supervision of temporary staff, in order that the quality and standards of their product do not become diluted by external influences.

For the purposes of this simple case study it has to be assumed that a design department exists within the Ingerdale Machine Tool Company that contains about thirty permanent employees. It will be advantageous to consider the composition of this department in some detail before going on to discuss the actual projects, because this will show the reasons behind some of the decisions made in the scheduling process. The design department is made up as follows:

Management and indirect

Manager, design engineering	1
Supervisor, mechanical engineering	1
Supervisor, control engineering	1
Supervisor, subcontract engineering	1
Manufacturing liaison engineers	2
Print room and clerical staff, messengers, etc	10
Total management and indirect staff	16

Direct design staff

Mechanical design engineers	6
Mechanical design draughtsmen	3
Control design engineers, electrical and hydraulic	3
Control design draughtsmen	2
Total direct design staff	14
Total direct and indirect staff	30

Temporary staff (subcontract)

Mechanical design draughtsmen	As required (maximum 10)

Note: Company policy does not allow the employment of subcontract staff to carry out design engineering. This rule is enforced in order to safeguard the company's hard-won reputation for design quality and reliability.

The engineering design department can call upon the services of a small planning department for their project planning if they wish. In the past, simple manual bar charting methods have been used, and owing to a natural resistance to any change from familiar practices the design staff have not used the services of the planning office. This case study starts with the assumption that an experiment is being conducted by the planning department in order to demonstrate the use of the computer for resource scheduling to the design manager. An order for a small transfer machine has provided the material for the experiment, and the design manager has specified a number of engineers from his total team that could be expected to form the project design team. This project has the works order number 75001.

This single project situation is very similar to the case study in the previous chapter, and the only real differences lie in the arrangements on the coding sheets for card punching, which have to be adapted to suit the needs of the *K* and *H* program instead of the ICL 1900 PERT program. Following the description of this experiment, however, a more complex situation will be described, caused by the unexpected receipt of a new order for a second, and larger transfer machine. This additional order will throw a strain on design resources. Instead of an experiment in single resource planning, the department has to progress into multiproject scheduling for both projects, so that all available resources can be planned to their best advantage.

The discussions in this chapter are not restricted to the actual techniques associated with the networks and their input to the computer. Effective scheduling of departmental resources depends upon the careful setting of several parameters, each of which demands the application of common sense. It is well known that the term "common sense" is itself a paradoxical one, and that in reality common sense is a comparatively rare commodity. Many attempts at resource scheduling fail because simple, but necessary rules are not observed. In particular, these rules govern the choice of resource grades that need scheduling and the rejection of those trades or skills that do not. Setting of available levels for each class of manpower is also a problem that does not always receive the attention it deserves.

PROJECT DEFINITION: SINGLE TRANSFER MACHINE—WORKS ORDER 75001

The machine selected by Ingerdale for their first planning experiment had to perform a rough boring operation in all four main bores of a cast-iron cylinder block. It was to form part of a major transfer line complex, comprising many other machines. However, all of the other machines except the finish boring machines were to be supplied by other manufacturers. The Ingerdale machine, therefore, had to be capable of picking the blocks up from the previous transfer section, and offloading them onto the following machine. This transfer process involved turning the block upside down on completion of boring, in order to present it in the correct attitude for the next machining operation.

The starting date for design was set at 1 February 1971. This date was, therefore, chosen as the "Time-now" date for the computer schedule. It was decided to give design engineers the distinguishing letter code *L*, and their work was valued at a cost, inclusive of overheads, of £20 per working day. Draughtsmen were coded *D*, and cost £16 each day, per man. The network diagram that was developed for this project is shown in Figure 10:1.

Computer input for single project experiment

Computer input for the experimental schedule of the single transfer machine was to be by means of punched cards. The coding sheet for all the data input cards is shown in Figure 10:2, whilst the control cards were prepared by the bureau from information supplied in a letter to them. The input arrangements on the *K* and *H* coding sheets are probably the most simple of all available programs. It is only necessary to write the data for activities (corresponding to the *S* type cards in the previous chapter, for the ICL program). *K* and *H* regard all other input as their responsibility, to be coded from the user's written instructions.

It is seen, therefore, that only one type of card has been specified on the coding sheets in Figure 10:2. This is the *P* card, and column 1 is used to carry this command to the computer. There follow the preceding and succeeding event numbers for each activity, called the *I* and *J* nodes by *K* and *H*. In columns 12 to 15, the activity duration is written. Working days have been used in this example. A report code can be entered in columns 17 to 22, and this can be used to arrange output reports that are edited or sorted to suit particular departments. Ingerdale chose three such codes in order that separate reports could be printed out for the design engineers, for the draughtsmen, and for the general office.

The description for each activity is written in columns 23 to 52. Notice that the works order number has been included for every activity, and that it has been neatly tabulated in the same columns. Although only one project is being considered at present, Ingerdale have made provision for the possible introduction of other projects by including the works order number, 75001, with every activity description. If this were not done, there would exist a real possibility of confusion with activities carrying similar descriptions, but belonging to different projects. It also provides the computer with a basis for sorting the output reports into different machines, if necessary. The *K* and *H* program, like several others, has the capability of being able to sort the output reports into lists that are dependent on the information appearing in almost any column.

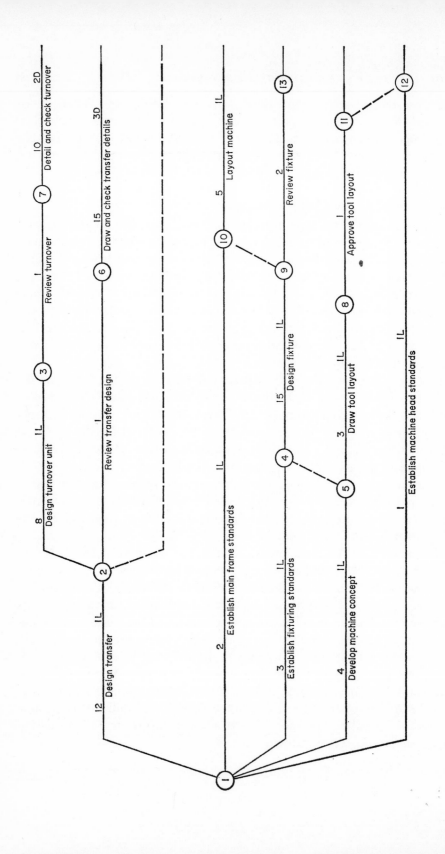

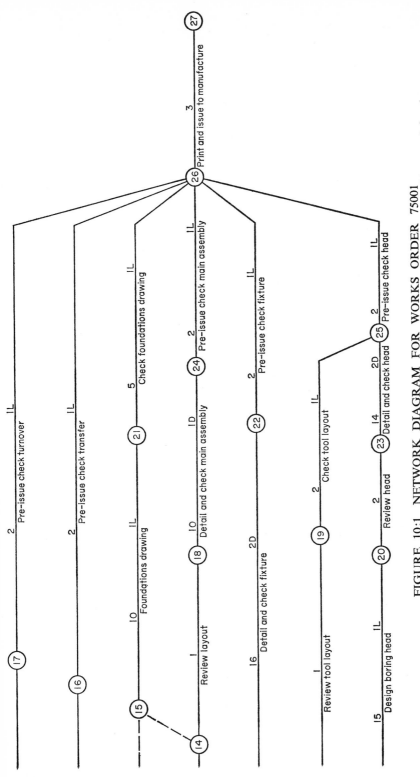

FIGURE 10:1 NETWORK DIAGRAM FOR WORKS ORDER 75001

This network diagram shows all the mechanical design activities for a single station transfer line machine, used for the purpose of boring cylinders in cast-iron cylinder blocks for a motor car engine production plant. It is introduced here to provide the first of two projects that will be used to demonstrate the application of a computer for scheduling resources for more than one project at the same time

PROJECT	CODED	DATE	PAGE
INGERDALE MACHINE TOOL COY LTD	Dennis Lock	1 FEB 71	1 OF 2
		VERIFIED	CHECKED

CARDS	I	J	D	REPORT CODE	DESCRIPTION	C T	AC	A B	TIME C	R1	R2	R3	R4
P01001	01002	02	12	DESIGN7500 1	DESIGN TRANSFER LAYOUT								
	02	03	8		DESIGN TURNOVER LAYOUT								
	03	07	1		REVIEW TURNOVER DESIGN								
	02	06	1		REVIEW TRANSFER DESIGN				L	I			
	17	26	2		PRE-ISSUE CHECK TURNOVER				L	I			
	16	26	2		PRE-ISSUE CHECK TRANSFER				L	I			
	15	21	10		MAKE FOUNDATIONS DRAWING				L	I			
	21	26	5		CHECK FOUNDATION DRAWING				L	I			
	01	02	2		ESTABLISH FRAME STANDARD				L	I			
	08	14	5		DESIGN MACHINE LAYOUT				L	I			
	14	18	1		REVIEW MACHINE LAYOUT								
	24	26	2		PRE-ISSUE CHECK ASSEMBLY				L	I			
	01	04	3		ESTABLISH FIXTURE STDS.				L	I			
	01	05	4		DEVELOP MACHINE CONCEPT				L	I			
	02	12	15		ESTABLISH HEAD STANDARDS				L	I			
	04	09	2		DESIGN FIXTURE LAYOUT				L	I			
	09	13	2		REVIEW FIXTURE LAYOUT				L	I			
	22	26	3		PRE-ISSUE CHECK FIXTURE				L	I			
	05	05			DRAW TOOL LAYOUT				L	I			
	08	11	1		APPROVE TOOL LAYOUT								
P01	01019		1	DESIGN7500 1	REVIEW TOOL LAYOUT								

K & H business consultants limited, SYSTEM 360/30 SUB PROJECT Ø1 RUN 1

PROJECT INGERDALE MACHINE TOOL COY LTD	CODED Dennis Lock	DATE 1 FEB 71	PAGE 2 OF 2
CARDS	PUNCHED	VERIFIED	CHECKED

I (1–6)	J (7–11)	D (12–15)	16	REPORT CODE (17–22)	23–27	DESCRIPTION (28–52)	CT (53)	AC (54–57)	AB (58)	TIME (59–61)	C (62)	R1 (63–67)	R2 (68–72)	R3 (73–76)	R4 (77–80)
PØ1Ø19	Ø1Ø25	2		DESIGN	75ØØ1	CHECK TOOL LAYOUT						L 1			
26	27	3		OFFICE		PRINT & ISSUE TO PRODUCN									
12	2Ø	15		DESIGN		DESIGN BORE HEAD LAYOUT						L 1			
2Ø	23	2		DESIGN		REVIEW BORE HEAD LAYOUT									
25	26	2		DESIGN		PRE-ISSUE CHECK HEAD						L 1			
Ø7	17	1Ø		DRAWIN		DETAIL & CHECK TURNOVER						D 2			
Ø6	16	15		DRAWIN		DETAIL & CHECK TRANSFER						D 3			
18	24	1Ø		DRAWIN		DET. & CHECK MACHINE ASSY						D 1			
13	22	16		DRAWIN		DET. & CHECK FIXTURE						D 2			
23	25	14		DRAWIN	75ØØ1	DET. & CHECK BORING HEAD						D 2			
Ø2	15		D												
14	15		D												
Ø9	1Ø		D												
Ø5	Ø4		D												
PØ1Ø11	Ø1Ø12		D												

FIGURE 10:2 COMPUTER INPUT DATA FOR WORKS ORDER 75001

The two coding sheets shown here contain card punching instructions for every activity in the network of Figure 10:1. They fulfill the same function as the coding sheets used in Chapter 9, but this time their format is suitable for the *K* and *H* CPM/RPSM program. Each program has its own input requirements, and this one is particularly praiseworthy for its simplicity. Some other programs need more than one punched card to describe each activity and its associated resources. This degree of simplicity becomes very important when very large networks are being prepared

Column 53 can be used to signal the use of a continuation card to the computer, should the space provided by a single card be insufficient to carry an adequate description of any activity. It is not necessary to describe the exact use of this feature, or of the columns from 54 to 62. In fact, columns 54 to 57 are available for the input of activity cost estimates. Costs can be input in this way for materials, for example. However, Ingerdale have chosen to input their labour costs in terms of a rate for each man day. Cost rates are input by means of control cards, and only require written instructions to the computer bureau, who will themselves arrange for card coding and punching.

Columns 58 to 62 provide the user with an opportunity to express slightly more complex interrelationships between different activities than those allowed by basic network logic. It is, for example, possible to say that one activity may not start before the lapse of some specified period following completion of the preceding activity. Alternatively, instead of a gap between activities, the user can specify overlaps, so that an activity is scheduled to start before its predecessor activity has been completed. This arrangement avoids the use of ladder networks (see Chapter 5), and anticipates the development of precedence networking (see Chapter 11).

Up to four resource types can be input for any one activity, and the data is written in the fields headed $R1$, $R2$, $R3$ and $R4$. In this case study no activity needs more than one resource type at a time. It is only necessary, therefore, to make use of the $R1$ field. The resource code is written to the left-hand side of the space available, and the quantity to the right.

One or two points of interest remain before the subject of coding sheets can be left. Dummies are input by entering data in columns 1 to 11 as if they were real activities. Then it is only necessary to write a letter D in column 16. When a character, or a group of characters is repeated in the same columns for all activities, it is permissible to use a bracket and carry them down the page. The punch operators recognise this instruction, and will punch the characters out in full each time. But ambiguity must be avoided if this short-cut approach is used. Notice, in Figure 10:2, that each group of characters treated in this way has been heavily underlined in order to leave no room for doubt.

In this example, each figure zero has been crossed out with a diagonal stroke. This has been done in order that the punch operators can distinguish between the figure zero and the letter O. The convention is reversed from that used in Chapter 9, where the letter was crossed. Choice of convention depends upon the custom of the particular punching department employed. The reader will notice that the figures ∅1∅ have been added in front of every event number. This anticipates the introduction of other projects later on, for subsequent runs. If every event number on future projects is similarly prefixed, but with different groups of numbers, there will be no possibility of having the same event number occur twice in different networks. It is also possible to prevent this duplication by assigning a subproject code number to each separate project, but this has not been done in this example.

Supporting data for single project experiment

When the punch coding sheets of Figure 10:2 were sent off to the computer for processing, they were accompanied by various instructions contained in a letter. These instructions supplied the computer bureau with all the information necessary to punch up the control cards for the run, although they were written in everyday English, and the bureau staff were left to translate the data into the exact form required by the program. Some of this supporting information was straightforward, but other items had to be decided, as management decisions.

It was necessary to tell the bureau that all estimates of activity durations were expressed in days, and that there were to be five days worked in every week. Bank holidays were listed as 9 and 12 April 1971; 31 May and 1 June. Time-now was stated as 1 February 1971. From all this data, the computer would be able to calculate a calendar of dates on which work could be scheduled.

As this was to be the first run on the computer for Ingerdale, the bureau had no previous knowledge of this company's particular wishes in respect of report arrangements. A request was therefore made in the letter for the actual page formats and column headings that are shown later in this chapter. The instructions included the name of the project, the arrangement of columns on each page, the order in which activities were to be printed, and a request for resource usage tables with cost reports included. Each detail of these reports was finally agreed by discussion with the bureau over the telephone.

Resource codes were specified. *L* indicated "layout," and stood for design engineers who produced layout drawings. *D* was to represent draughtsmen. These letters were chosen by Ingerdale, and they were free to choose any letters from the alphabet. Obviously, this arrangement would limit the total number of resources that could be separately scheduled to twenty-six.

However, since only two trades were to be considered, this presented no problem.

A slightly more difficult decision had to be made concerning the number of engineers and draughtsmen available to work on the project. It would not be possible to specify the total department as being free, because other work was still being carried out from previous projects. It was finally decided to state that two designers and four draughtsmen could be allocated to the project. These were the levels input to the computer. Cost rates were given as £20 per man-day for each engineer and £16 per man-day for a draughtsman.

The *K* and *H* program prints out all start events and all end events, whether they are errors or legitimate "dangles." It is therefore essential that the planner tells the bureau which events are expected to appear on the list of dangles printed out. The print-out can then be compared to the expected list, and any events that are on the print-out but do not appear on the prediction list can be regarded as dangling errors. For this project there was only one start event, Ø1ØØ1, and one end event, Ø1Ø27. The output reports requested were:

1   Resource usage necessary to achieve shortest possible project duration
2   Resource usage table for a resource limited schedule calculation
3   List of all activities, printed out separately for each department and listed in sequence of their scheduled start dates. The dates calculated on this report to be in accord with the resource usage of report 1, or in other words to show the shortest possible project duration
4   Another activity list, similar to report 3, but scheduled within available resource limits. This schedule, therefore, would be associated with the resource table of report 2

Notes on the choice of resource categories

When the data supplied to the computer is compared with the actual department, it appears that only a fraction of the total available resources are being considered. There are thirty permanent employees in the team, and yet only six are being scheduled. Of course, one reason for this is that the company has not yet achieved true multiproject scheduling, and all work cannot be put onto the computer. That situation will be delayed until the second project is added to the computer schedule, later in this chapter.

But there are sound reasons for not including the total department, even in the final multiproject calculations. The arguments which lead to these decisions are important, and must be understood if multiproject scheduling is to be achieved as a practical solution. It is highly probable that it is these particular decisions which determine whether or not any attempt at multiproject scheduling will succeed. Indeed, a mistaken belief that every individual and every item of work must be considered within the framework of the computer schedule must deter any planner from taking the multiproject plunge.

The answer lies in a careful choice of activities that should be given resource estimates, and a realisation that some activities do not employ men for a sufficient part of their duration to be included in the resource allocation process. As a very general rule, direct staff should be scheduled, and indirect staff should not. But there are exceptions to this rule, and it is necessary to retrace the decision-making process that was followed at Ingerdale.

It would not have been feasible, for example, to make any attempt at scheduling the activities of design management and supervision staff. Their time is always spread too widely over a large number of different jobs, and cannot be tied down. It is not even possible to define their activities by including them on the network diagram. The same arguments can be applied without difficulty to all clerical staff. They are best regarded as being available to provide a regular service, and their numbers are best established by deciding upon some reasonable proportion of clerical workers to the total departmental strength. It may also become necessary, in larger organisations, to apply work measurement techniques in order to achieve maximum efficiency. But resource allocation from networks would certainly not be the correct technique to apply.

It becomes apparent, therefore, that any decision on whether or not to include a particular trade or category of skill in the computer scheduling process depends largely upon whether or not it can be sensibly depicted by activities on the network diagram. Any activity on the network that does not demand the use of resources for an appreciable part of its duration may have to be considered as one which does not need any resources at all. Sometimes these activities are worth splitting up into two, so that the first part might show no resources and the second would have some resource usage specified. There are computer techniques available which allow the user to vary the rate of resource usage throughout the duration of any activity according to a number of stepped levels. These techniques may become necessary in certain cases, but they are usually more trouble than they are worth, and best left alone.

In production departments, similar decisions must be faced. A good example can be given if inspection activities are considered. When complex assemblies are being made that must be subjected to a long period of inspection, definable inspection activities can be shown on a network, and it is usually reasonable to assign resources full time to these activities. If the type of production being scheduled consists, however, of a large number of operations, each of which is inspected in very small stages, then it may be far more difficult to schedule inspection as separate activities. "On-line" inspection particularly is to be regarded as a continuous service, and not a series of network activities.

All of these principles were well understood by the planning team at Ingerdale. They had already learned from previous mistakes. When the experiment was conducted in the design engineering department, the planning team made an analysis of the way in which work was normally carried out, and then recommended to the design management which resources should be included in the scheduling calculations. Whilst the arguments put forward were accepted by the management as common sense in general, considerable difficulty was experienced by the planning team in getting agreement to whittle down the total number of resource categories from the possible number of about twelve, as shown in the list given earlier in this chapter, to the two actually used. In particular, the management displayed extreme reluctance when it was suggested to them that the control design engineers and draughtsmen should be omitted from any detailed resource calculations.

But it would not have been sensible to include control design in the planning and scheduling process. The work of that small group of people depended upon a continuous flow of information from the mechanical designers and draughtsmen. It was virtually impossible to identify any controllable activity in advance. One control engineer might work on several different projects in one day, according to the information available to him. Much of his work would involve discussions with outside suppliers, and visits, so that he would prefer to schedule his own work to suit the day by day situation. It made more sense to regard the control designers as a service group who had to be employed in sufficient strength to support the level of mechanical design staff used, on a strictly proportional basis.

Effective project control depended on ensuring that the mechanical designers were correctly scheduled. It then became essential to see that the mechanical designers passed over the information needed by the control engineers, but this was a matter for supervision rather than scheduling.

Management remained unconvinced of this policy for a considerable time. They were only finally convinced after scheduling had been operated successfully for several months, and the first major project had been completed on target. Indeed, at management's request, control engineering activities were added to one network for a later project (after the period covered by this case study). The results led to their prompt removal, because the resource allocation figures were meaningless, and the difficulty in expressing accurate relationships between the mechanical and control engineering tasks on the networks soon made nonsense of the logic and subsequent time analysis.

Although the whole of the case study presented in this chapter is centred upon the fictitious company of Ingerdale, all the situations are drawn from actual episodes in real companies. In order to make a success of any multi-project scheduling, it is necessary to cut the problem down to its simplest proportions. When the choice is made about which activities to include on the networks and which resources to schedule, one should seek to establish a "backbone" schedule of key resources. Any resources that can be regarded as providing a continuous service to the key resources can then be allowed to fit to the "backbone" as the project proceeds. Provided that the man-power levels have been correctly established from reliable bulk estimates, the smooth work schedules for key resources produced by the computer should automatically allow for a controlled and manageable flow of work into the groups of supporting resources. Any project team unable to accept this statement would at least be well advised to make their first attempts at multiproject scheduling on this basis.

Computer output reports for single project experiment

By most modern industrial project standards the single transfer machine network is very small. Consequently, it was simple to handle on the computer. There were no errors at all on the input coding sheets, and all the punched cards were accurately punched. Within one day of the coding sheets being sent to the bureau, all punched cards had been input to the computer, the data processed and all output reports printed according to Ingerdale's requirements. All the output reports prepared for this case study

INGERDALE MACHINE TOOL COMPANY LIMITED

DATE	DESIGN — AVAIL	USAGE	REM.G	COST	SUB-CONTR. — AVAIL	USAGE	REM.G	COST	RES ACC.COST
1FEB71	2	3	−1	60	4		4		60
2FEB71	2	3	−1	60	4		4		120
3FEB71	2	3	−1	60	4		4		180
4FEB71	2	3	−1	60	4		4		240
5FEB71	2	3	−1	60	4		4		300
8FEB71	2	3	−1	60	4		4		360
9FEB71	2	3	−1	60	4		4		420
10FEB71	2	2		40	4		4		460
11FEB71	2	3	−1	60	4		4		520
12FEB71	2	3	−1	60	4		4		580
15FEB71	2	3	−1	60	4		4		640
16FEB71	2	3	−1	60	4		4		700
17FEB71	2	3	−1	60	4		4		760
18FEB71	2	3	−1	60	4	3	1	48	868
19FEB71	2	2		40	4	3	1	48	956
22FEB71	2	2		40	4	3	1	48	1,044
23FEB71	2	2		40	4	3	1	48	1,132
24FEB71	2	2		40	4	3	1	48	1,220
25FEB71	2	2		40	4	3	1	48	1,308
26FEB71	2	3	−1	60	4	3	1	48	1,416
1MAR71	2	3	−1	60	4	3	1	48	1,524
2MAR71	2	3	−1	60	4	5	−1	80	1,664
3MAR71	2	3	−1	60	4	5	−1	80	1,804
4MAR71	2	2		40	4	5	−1	80	1,924
5MAR71	2	2		40	4	5	−1	80	2,044
8MAR71	2	2		40	4	7	−3	112	2,196
9MAR71	2	2		40	4	7	−3	112	2,348
10MAR71	2	1	1	20	4	7	−3	112	2,480
11MAR71	2	2		40	4	7	−3	112	2,632
12MAR71	2	2		40	4	7	−3	112	2,784
15MAR71	2	2		40	4	7	−3	112	2,936
16MAR71	2	2		40	4	7	−3	112	3,088
17MAR71	2	1	1	20	4	7	−3	112	3,220
18MAR71	2	1	1	20	4	7	−3	112	3,352
19MAR71	2	1	1	20	4	7	−3	112	3,484
22MAR71	2	1	1	20	4	7	−3	112	3,616
23MAR71	2	1	1	20	4	7	−3	112	3,748
24MAR71	2	2		40	4	5	−1	80	3,868
25MAR71	2	3	−1	60	4	2	2	32	3,960
26MAR71	2	3	−1	60	4		4		4,020
29MAR71	2	2		40	4		4		4,060
30MAR71	2		2		4		4		4,060
31MAR71	2		2		4		4		4,060
1APR71	2		2		4		4		4,060

are similar in their general arrangement of page layout to those demonstrated for Chapter 9. The only significant difference is that in this chapter resource costs have been estimated and related to the schedules on a day by day basis.

It will be remembered that Ingerdale asked the bureau to make two sets of reports, one based on completion of the project within available resource limits, and the other showing the arrangements necessary to finish all work within the shortest possible time possible, as defined from the critical path duration. For purposes of comparison, the tables of resources that would be needed for each of these two alternative solutions are reproduced here in Figures 10:3 and 10:4. In Figure 10:3, the daily resource usage requirements are calculated according to a schedule that would complete the project on the last date shown—1 April 1971. (The computer has been specially programmed to stop printing after the last date on which activities appear in the schedule, including those activities which do not need resources.)

Notice that several overload periods have been predicted, both for designers and for subcontract draughtsmen. The day by day cost of each grade of staff is printed in the cost columns, and the cumulative project cost is shown in the column at the extreme right-hand side of the report. It is seen that the estimated cost of all design work reaches £4060. It is possible to make use of this cost information by plotting it as a graph, against which actual expenditure can be measured and checked as the project proceeds.

Now turn to Figure 10:4. This time the computer has produced a table that relates to a schedule which is resource limited. At no time are the daily resource needs of the project allowed to exceed capacity. Both designers and subcontract draughtsmen have been kept within the limits specified by

---

FIGURE 10:3   TIME LIMITED RESOURCE USAGE TABLE FOR
WORKS ORDER 75001

This table lists the resources needed each day in order to achieve project completion in the earliest possible time. The computer has attempted to arrange all the activities within the available resource capacities. In satisfying the time limit imposed, the computer has been forced to schedule critical activities to start whether resources are free or not, and overloads have therefore become necessary. A particular point of interest is the appearance of cost estimates. These have been calculated from the daily usage rate for each resource, multiplied by the cost rate supplied by the planning team to the computer bureau. Daily totals have been added up in the extreme right-hand column to give cumulative costs, so that the total estimated cost for the design of this project appears in the entries at the foot of this column. This estimate is seen to be £4060. This table of resources applies to the actual work schedules shown in Figure 10:5

INGERDALE MACHINE TOOL COMPANY LIMITED

DATE	DESIGN - AVAIL	USAGE	REM.G	COST	SUB-CONTR. - AVAIL	USAGE	REM.G	COST	RES ACC.COST
1FEB71	2	2		40	4		4		40
2FEB71	2	2		40	4		4		80
3FEB71	2	2		40	4		4		120
4FEB71	2	2		40	4		4		160
5FEB71	2	2		40	4		4		200
8FEB71	2	2		40	4		4		240
9FEB71	2	2		40	4		4		280
10FEB71	2	1	1	20	4		4		300
11FEB71	2	2		40	4		4		340
12FEB71	2	2		40	4		4		380
15FEB71	2	2		40	4		4		420
16FEB71	2	2		40	4		4		460
17FEB71	2	2		40	4		4		500
18FEB71	2	2		40	4		4		540
19FEB71	2	2		40	4		4		580
22FEB71	2	2		40	4		4		620
23FEB71	2	2		40	4		4		660
24FEB71	2	2		40	4		4		700
25FEB71	2	2		40	4		4		740
26FEB71	2	2		40	4		4		780
1MAR71	2	2		40	4		4		820
2MAR71	2	2		40	4	2	2	32	892
3MAR71	2	2		40	4	2	2	32	964
4MAR71	2	2		40	4	2	2	32	1,036
5MAR71	2	2		40	4	2	2	32	1,108
8MAR71	2	2		40	4	4		64	1,212
9MAR71	2	2		40	4	4		64	1,316
10MAR71	2	2		40	4	4		64	1,420
11MAR71	2	2		40	4	4		64	1,524
12MAR71	2	2		40	4	4		64	1,628
15MAR71	2	2		40	4	4		64	1,732
16MAR71	2	2		40	4	4		64	1,836
17MAR71	2	1	1	20	4	4		64	1,920
18MAR71	2	1	1	20	4	4		64	2,004
19MAR71	2	1	1	20	4	4		64	2,088
22MAR71	2	1	1	20	4	4		64	2,172
23MAR71	2	1	1	20	4	4		64	2,256
24MAR71	2	2		40	4	3	1	48	2,344
25MAR71	2	2		40	4	3	1	48	2,432
26MAR71	2	2		40	4	1	3	16	2,488
29MAR71	2	2		40	4	3	1	48	2,576
30MAR71	2	1	1	20	4	3	1	48	2,644
31MAR71	2	1	1	20	4	3	1	48	2,712
1APR71	2	1	1	20	4	3	1	48	2,780
2APR71	2	1	1	20	4	3	1	48	2,848
5APR71	2	1	1	20	4	3	1	48	2,916
6APR71	2	1	1	20	4	3	1	48	2,984
7APR71	2	2		40	4	2	2	32	3,056
8APR71	2	2		40	4	2	2	32	3,128
13APR71	2	1	1	20	4	2	2	32	3,180

DATE	DESIGN - AVAIL	USAGE	REM.G	COST	SUB-CONTR. - AVAIL	USAGE	REM.G	COST	RES ACC.COST
14APR71	2	2		40	4	3	1	48	3,268
15APR71	2	2		40	4	3	1	48	3,356
16APR71	2	1	1	20	4	3	1	48	3,424
19APR71	2	1	1	20	4	3	1	48	3,492
20APR71	2		2		4	3	1	48	3,540
21APR71	2		2		4	3	1	48	3,588
22APR71	2		2		4	3	1	48	3,636
23APR71	2		2		4	3	1	48	3,684
26APR71	2		2		4	3	1	48	3,732
27APR71	2		2		4	3	1	48	3,780
28APR71	2		2		4	3	1	48	3,828
29APR71	2		2		4	3	1	48	3,876
30APR71	2		2		4	3	1	48	3,924
3MAY71	2		2		4	3	1	48	3,972
4MAY71	2		2		4	3	1	48	4,020
5MAY71	2	1	1	20	4		4		4,040
6MAY71	2	1	1	20	4		4		4,060
7MAY71	2		2		4		4		4,060
10MAY71	2		2		4		4		4,060
11MAY71	2		2		4		4		4,060

FIGURE 10:4 RESOURCE LIMITED TABLE OF RESOURCES FOR WORKS ORDER 75001

Here, the project planner has exercised his option to instruct the computer that resource limits must, on no account, be exceeded. This has meant an extension beyond the shortest possible project duration indicated from time analysis of the network diagram. When this table is compared with that of Figure 10:3, it is seen that the imposition of resource limits has delayed scheduled completion from 1 April, to 11 May 1971

Ingerdale. Once again the cumulative costs are seen to reach £4060. But the project completion date has been extended from 1 April 1971 to 11 May 1971. As in the example of the workshop project in Chapter 9, this project is really too small to give the computer an adequate chance of producing a very smooth pattern of resource usage, if one considers day by day fluctuations as a percentage amount from the totals available. However, the results are practicable in this case. The plan could be used.

As a direct result of this experiment, Ingerdale's design engineering department have been given several specific facts about their project on which they can base management decisions. They know:

1   That the predicted total design costs are expected to amount to £4060
2   The earliest possible completion date is 1 April 1971
3   The completion date, using available men, will be 11 May 1971
4   If the earlier date is to be met, they will have to provide an additional design engineer during February and early March, and three additional subcontract draughtsmen for the first two weeks in March 1971

Not all reports have been included in this book, because they are not all significant to the discussions. However, for each of the two schedule possibilities so far attempted, there will be a corresponding list of activities, complete with their scheduled starting and finishing dates. One of these schedules is printed in Figure 10:5. Advantage has been taken of the facilities provided in the program for sorting reports into different departments. By means of the codes written on the input sheets in Figure 10:2, it has been possible to produce a separate report for the design engineers, the subcontract draughtsmen and the general office. Within each of these activity lists, each entry appears in sequence according to its scheduled starting date. All other activity schedules used in this case study will follow the same pattern.

PROJECT DEFINITION: MULTIPROJECT SCHEDULE

At the same time that the single machine schedule experiment was carried out, Ingerdale received an order for another new transfer machine. But this second order was for a larger machine than that being carried out under

INGERDALE MACHINE TOOL COMPANY LIMITED

DEPARTMENT — DESIGN

RESOURCE SCHEDULE ALL ACTIVITIES — SINGLE TRANSFER MACHINE, W/ORDER 75001

PREC EVENT	SUCC EVENT	DURN	WORKS ORDER	..ACTIVITY DESCRIPTION..	EARLIEST START	SCHEDULED TIMES START	FINISH	LATEST FINISH	REM.G FLOAT	RESOURCES
1001	1002	12	75001	DESIGN TRANSFER LAYOUT	01FEB71	01FEB71	16FEB71	26FEB71	8	L 1 1
1001	1004	3	75001	ESTABLISH FIXTURE STDS.	01FEB71	01FEB71	03FEB71	08FEB71	3	L 1 1
1001	1005	4	75001	DEVELOP MACHINE CONCEPT	01FEB71	01FEB71	04FEB71	04FEB71		L 1 1
1001	1012	1	75001	ESTABLISH HEAD STANDARDS	01FEB71	04FEB71	04FEB71	10FEB71	4	L 1 1
1004	1009	15	75001	DESIGN FIXTURE LAYOUT	04FEB71	05FEB71	25FEB71	01MAR71	2	L 1 1
1005	1008	3	75001	DRAW TOOL LAYOUT	05FEB71	05FEB71	09FEB71	09FEB71		L 1 1
1008	1011	1	75001	APPROVE TOOL LAYOUT	10FEB71	10FEB71	10FEB71	10FEB71		L 1 1
1011	1019	1	75001	REVIEW TOOL LAYOUT	11FEB71	11FEB71	11FEB71	23MAR71	28	L 1 1
1012	1020	15	75001	DESIGN BORE HEAD LAYOUT	11FEB71	11FEB71	03MAR71	03MAR71		L 1 1
1001	1010	2	75001	ESTABLISH FRAME STANDARD	01FEB71	17FEB71	18FEB71	01MAR71	7	L 1 1
1002	1006	1	75001	REVIEW TRANSFER DESIGN	17FEB71	17FEB71	17FEB71	04MAR71	11	L 1 1
1002	1003	8	75001	DESIGN TURNOVER LAYOUT	17FEB71	26FEB71	09MAR71	10MAR71	1	L 1 1
1009	1013	2	75001	REVIEW FIXTURE LAYOUT	26FEB71	26FEB71	01MAR71	03MAR71	2	L 1 1
1010	1014	5	75001	DESIGN MACHINE LAYOUT	26FEB71	26FEB71	04MAR71	08MAR71	2	L 1 1
1020	1023	1	75001	REVIEW BORE HEAD LAYOUT	04MAR71	04MAR71	05MAR71	05MAR71		L 1 1
1014	1018	2	75001	REVIEW MACHINE LAYOUT	05MAR71	05MAR71	05MAR71	11MAR71	4	L 1 1
1015	1021	10	75001	MAKE FOUNDATIONS DRAWING	05MAR71	05MAR71	18MAR71	22MAR71	2	L 1 1
1003	1007	2	75001	REVIEW TURNOVER DESIGN	01MAR71	10MAR71	11MAR71	11MAR71	1	L 1 1
1016	1026	2	75001	PRE-ISSUE CHECK TRANSFER	11MAR71	11MAR71	12MAR71	29MAR71	11	L 1 1
1019	1025	5	75001	CHECK TOOL-LAYOUT	12FEB71	15MAR71	16MAR71	25MAR71	7	L 1 1
1021	1026	2	75001	CHECK FOUNDATION DRAWING	19MAR71	19MAR71	25MAR71	29MAR71	2	L 1 1
1022	1026	2	75001	PRE-ISSUE CHECK FIXTURE	24MAR71	24MAR71	25MAR71	29MAR71	2	L 1 1
1011	1026	2	75001	PRE-ISSUE CHECK TURNOVER	16MAR71	25MAR71	26MAR71	29MAR71	1	L 1 1
1024	1026	2	75001	PRE-ISSUE CHECK ASSEMBLY	22MAR71	26MAR71	29MAR71	29MAR71		L 1 1
1025	1026	2	75001	PRE-ISSUE CHECK HEAD	26MAR71	26MAR71	29MAR71	29MAR71		L 1 1

FIGURE 10:5   WORKING SCHEDULE FOR WORKS ORDER 75001

The three reports reproduced here contain all the activities from the network diagram for the single-station transfer machine. They are printed out in order of their scheduled starting dates. These dates have been calculated by the computer so that the project will |be completed in the shortest possible time, even though this means planning for resource levels higher than those normally available. The associated day by day resource needs are dispayed in Figure 10:3

continued on next page

INGERDALE MACHINE TOOL COMPANY LIMITED

DEPARTMENT — DRAWING   RESOURCE SCHEDULE ALL ACTIVITIES — SINGLE TRANSFER MACHINE, W/ORDER 75001

PREC EVENT	SUCC EVENT	DURN	WORKS ORDER	..ACTIVITY DESCRIPTION..	EARLIEST START	SCHEDULED TIMES START	FINISH	LATEST FINISH	REM.G FLOAT	RESOURCES	
1006	1016	15	75001	DETAIL & CHECK TRANSFER	18FEB71	18FEB71	10MAR71	25MAR71	11	D	3
1013	1022	16	75001	DET.& CHECK FIXTURE	02MAR71	02MAR71	23MAR71	25MAR71	2	D	2
1023	1025	14	75001	DET.& CHECK BORING HEAD	08MAR71	08MAR71	25MAR71	25MAR71		D	2
1007	1017	10	75001	DETAIL & CHECK TURNOVER	02MAR71	11MAR71	24MAR71	25MAR71	1	D	2
1018	1024	10	75001	DET.& CHECK MACHINE ASSY	08MAR71	11MAR71	24MAR71	25MAR71	1	D	1

INGERDALE MACHINE TOOL COMPANY LIMITED

DEPARTMENT — OFFICE   RESOURCE SCHEDULE ALL ACTIVITIES — SINGLE TRANSFER MACHINE, W/ORDER 75001

PREC EVENT	SUCC EVENT	DURN	WORKS ORDER	..ACTIVITY DESCRIPTION..	EARLIEST START	SCHEDULED TIMES START	FINISH	LATEST FINISH	REM.G FLOAT	RESOURCES
1026	1027	3	75001	PRINT & ISSUE TO PRODUCN	30MAR71	30MAR71	01APR71	01APR71		

FIGURE 10:5 continued

works order 75001. In fact, it imposed a real strain on their design resources and led to a decision to implement computer scheduling forthwith, and progress from the experimental stage to actual multiproject scheduling.

The second project was allocated the works orders 75011 and 75012. It was to be a two-station transfer line, or in other words a transfer line containing two separate machining stations. This project, like the first, was for the machining of parts of a cylinder block. However, the component was entirely different, intended for the motor car of a different customer. The first station had to carry out milling operations on two faces of the cylinder block simultaneously. This machine was numbered 75011. The second machine in the line, 75012, had to drill a small group of holes, and then insert probes into the holes to check that they were clear of any obstructions such as broken pieces of drill. A network was drawn for this project, and it is shown in full at Figure 10:6. Starting date for this new project was to be 22 February 1971.

Computer input for multiproject schedule

Conversion of the network in Figure 10:6 into card punching instructions was once again carried out using coding sheets. There is no need to examine these in detail, since they follow exactly the same process as that employed for the first project, 75001. Only the top of the first sheet has been reproduced here, and it appears in Figure 10:7. There is one point worthy of mention. The prefix "020" has been added to each event number, so that all the events in this new project are distinguishable from those in project 75001, which were prefixed "010."

Another method for distinguishing between both projects would have been to allocate a subproject code to each, and arrange with the computer bureau to have this code input along with each activity. Thus all activities from the first project could, for example, have been given the subproject code "01" in some prearranged columns on their coding sheets, and a different code could have been used for the second project. These subproject codes become very important when separate reports have to be printed out for each subproject. Indeed, they ought really to have been used in this case study, and their omission led to some difficulty at the computer bureau.

Now consider the first project, works order 75001. It started its design phase early in February, according to a plan prepared by hand. The computer schedule resulting from the first experiment was then implemented,

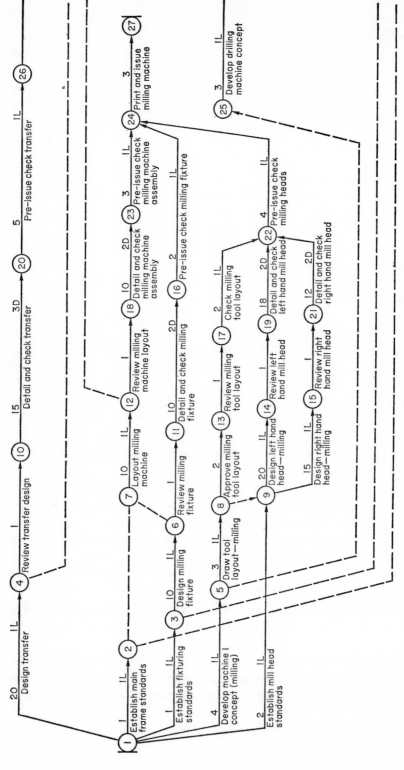

FIRST STATION. WORKS ORDER 70011

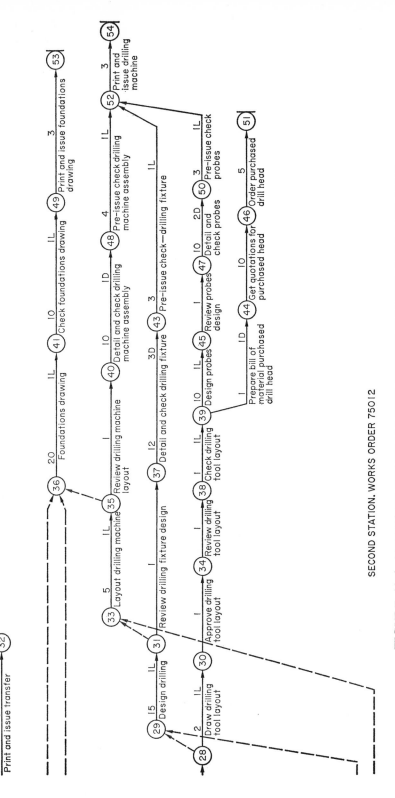

SECOND STATION. WORKS ORDER 75012

FIGURE 10:6   NETWORK DIAGRAM FOR WORKS ORDERS 75011 AND 75012

This network diagram was drawn as a result of a second machine tool order at Ingerdale. The new project will compete with works order 75001 for available design staff and both projects must be scheduled together

k & h business consultants limited,   SYSTEM 360/30

PROJECT	CODED	DATE	PAGE 1 OF 5
INGERDALE MACHINE TOOL COY LTD	Dennis Lock	22 FEB 71	
	PUNCHED	VERIFIED	CHECKED

CARDS	I	J	D	DESCRIPTION	C T	AC	A B	TIME C	R1	R2	R3	R4
P0200102000			20	DESIGN7Ø11 DESIGN TRANSFER LAYOUT					/ /			
P0200402010			1	DESIGN7Ø11 REVIEW TRANSFER DESIGN								
P0200202020			5	DESIGN7Ø11 PRE-ISSUE CHECK TRANSFER					/ /			
P0200102002			1	DESIGN7Ø11 ESTABLISH FRAME STANDARD					/ /			
P0200102003			1	DESIGN7Ø11 ESTABLISH FIXTURE STDS					/ /			
P0202502040				DESIGN7Ø11 DRILLING CONCEPT					/ /			

and work was rearranged to conform to the resource limited option. However, before much progress could be made, this new project for a two-station transfer line came along and destroyed the schedule for the first project. Although it was fairly easy to prepare the input to the computer for the two-machine project, it would be useless to attempt a resource schedule without considering the interaction from the current work of works order 75001. It is therefore necessary to include data for both projects, representing the total work in the design department, if resources are to be realistically treated.

The network in Figure 10:1, and the input data resulting from it (Figure 10:2) all relate to a "time-now" of 1 February 1971. If this data is to be included in a new calculation at the computer where the time-now has been set at 22 February 1971, it is obvious that it must be modified in some way to take account of progress already achieved. Otherwise all the activities from the original data will be rescheduled from 22 February. This process of adapting data to bring it into line with the current project situation is called "updating." It is a feature of all computer scheduling, whether multiproject resources are being calculated or not, since almost every schedule has to be revised at some time during the life of a project to take account of unavoidable changes.

The significance of "time-now" must be fully understood. This is the date from which all work will be scheduled. It is the date that the computer will use as a start for all networks being input, unless a later scheduled date has been specified for the start event of one or more networks. It is not necessary to choose "time-now" to correspond with the actual date of a computer run, and indeed it may be advantageous to adopt a date that is about a week ahead of the date when input preparation is started. If this is done, progress information for current projects must be made in part as advance forecasts. One has to ask the question "What will have been achieved on Monday next?" or something similar instead of simply looking at the current state of achievement. Although this policy must introduce

---

FIGURE 10:7 COMPUTER INPUT FOR WORKS ORDERS
75011 AND 75012

Only a small portion of the total input is shown here because the method is identical with that shown in Figure 10:2. However, in this case the prefix "020" has been added to every event number to avoid any possibility of duplicating event numbers already held in the computer files from works order 75001

small errors into the schedule, since no prediction can ever be completely correct, the resulting schedules will at least bear a date that is not one week late, and they should be sufficiently accurate to be acceptable to their recipients.

The complete set of update data for project 75001 is shown in Figure 10:8. Notice that only activities that have experienced progress or change have to be considered. All data previously input is retained by the computer, so that the update process is really aimed at correcting the computer files before new calculations start. It is not necessary to input all the data afresh. The first group of activities reported on the coding sheet in Figure 10:8 are those which are either completed, or are expected to be completed before 22 February is reached. The letter A is written in column 1 to inform the computer that completion data is being fed in. It is then only necessary to write in the two event numbers for the activity, and write a letter C in column 16. At the same time, it is wise to mark off the activities on a print of the network diagram, in order that a record is kept of the state of the network as it is now retained within the computer.

Activities that are started, but will not be complete when time-now is reached, can be reported as being in progress by using Q type cards. Two entries are seen in the example. The letter R has been entered in column 16 to signify that these activities are being reported as started. The duration shown in column 15 is the estimated number of days remaining to activity completion after the time-now date of 22 February. Thus, it has been estimated, for example, that activity $\emptyset1\emptyset\emptyset4, \emptyset1\emptyset\emptyset9$ has five days to run after time-now before it can be considered complete. Again, it is necessary to keep a record of the file content produced by these changes, and this is done once more by marking up the network diagram print.

Any activity that has been reported started on a Q type card must, obviously, be picked up on the new schedule from time-now. It would be undesirable if, for example, one of the activities shown on the coding sheet of Figure 10:8 were to be rescheduled as a result of the new calculations to start from a date later than 22 February. This would imply an interruption to work in progress. The computer program, therefore, will not interrupt work reported as started. One can confidently expect to see the two activities on this coding sheet scheduled to continue in progress from 22 February 1971.

The updating process also allows the planner to make any other changes to the computer file that he needs. He can, for example, change the dura-

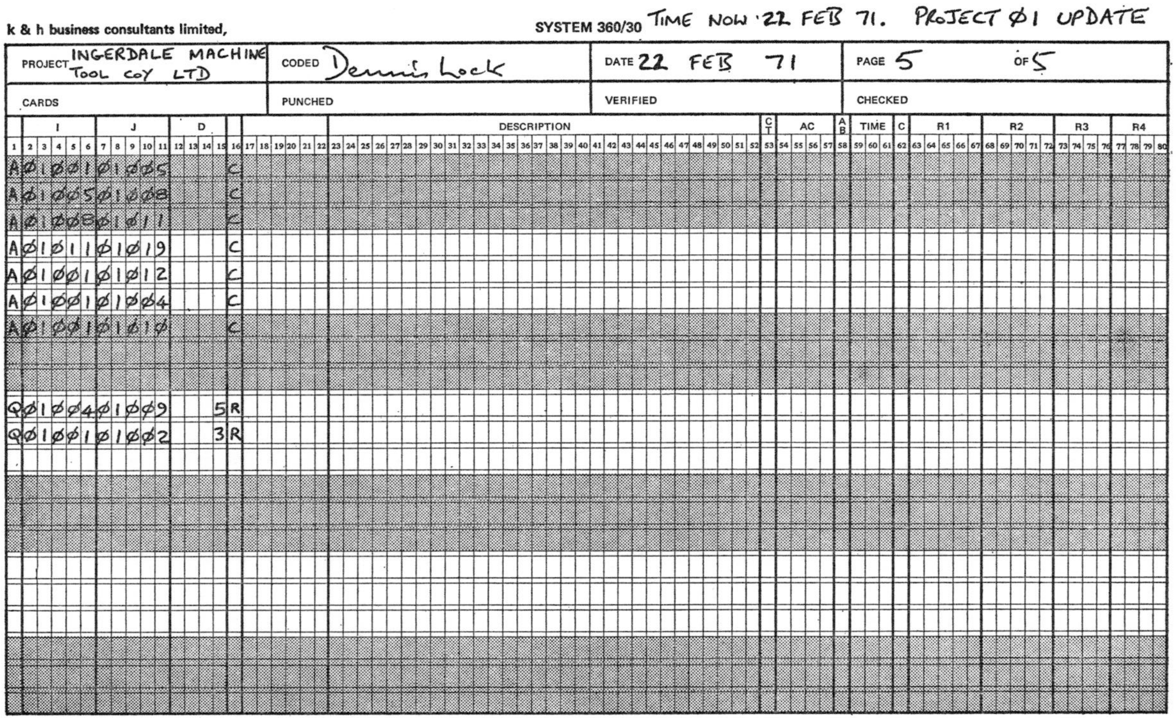
k & h business consultants limited, SYSTEM 360/30 TIME NOW 22 FEB 71. PROJECT Ø1 UPDATE

PROJECT INGERDALE MACHINE TOOL COY LTD — CODED Dennis Lock — DATE 22 FEB 71 — PAGE 5 OF 5

CARDS — PUNCHED — VERIFIED — CHECKED

1	I (2–6)	J (7–11)	D (12–15)	16
A	Ø1ØØ1	Ø1ØØ5		C
A	Ø1ØØ5	Ø1ØØ8		C
A	Ø1ØØ8	Ø1Ø11		C
A	Ø1Ø11	Ø1Ø19		C
A	Ø1ØØ1	Ø1Ø12		C
A	Ø1ØØ1	Ø1ØØ4		C
A	Ø1ØØ1	Ø1Ø1Ø		C
Q	Ø1ØØ4	Ø1ØØ9	5	R
Q	Ø1ØØ1	Ø1ØØ2	3	R

FIGURE 10:8 COMPUTER INPUT FOR UPDATING WORKS ORDER 75001 SCHEDULE
Two types of punched cards will result from the instructions given on this coding sheet. *A* type cards are used to report activities that have been completely finished, or will be by the time-now date. *Q* cards can either be used to make changes to information previously supplied to the computer, and stored in its file, or they are used to report activities which have started. In this case they have been used to report activities in progress

tions of activities that are not in progress. He can also make alterations to the network logic by adding or deleting activities. The actual methods for making these, and any other possible changes, will not be discussed here. The methods depend entirely upon the program being used, and the reader is referred to the manual issued by *K* and *H* Business Consultants Limited for the actual details that would apply to the projects in this chapter.

Supporting data for the multiproject schedule

When the single project was input to the computer at the start of this chapter, it was necessary to supply the computer bureau with facts and figures from which they subsequently prepared a set of control cards. This has to be repeated for every run, so that every new item of information is considered during the calculations. The two most obvious bits of information that had to be supplied for this example were that the new time now has been set at 22 February 1971, and the new project title is to be "Double transfer machine, w/order 75011/75012."

A close look had to be taken at the levels of resources which could be declared as being available for both projects together. In fact, these resources amounted to the total net capacity of the department. By "net" capacity, it should be understood that it would be unwise to declare that the total strength available for both projects was identical to the departmental strength. Some men must be held back in reserve for such work as modifications arising from previous projects, and other unexpected work. Illness and absenteeism from annual holidays is also allowed for by making a slight reduction in the resources definitely assigned. The levels input to the computer were therefore decided as:

Mechanical design engineers (L)   4
(From a total departmental strength of 6)
Mechanical design draughtsmen (D)   6
(From a total subcontract possibility of ten, and three permanent staff. This level of six was acknowledged to be very conservative, and was based on a desire to keep the subcontract level as low as possible.)

The total list of expected start and finish dangling events had to be repeated, and now amounted to:

Start dangles, $\emptyset1\emptyset\emptyset1$ and $\bar{\emptyset}2\emptyset\emptyset1$
End dangles, $\emptyset1\emptyset27$ and $\emptyset2\emptyset54$

There was no change in resource code letters, cost rates, statutory holiday dates or page layouts for reports. It was decided, however, to impose a scheduled latest completion date for event Ø1Ø27, in order that the first project would claim priority for resources in all calculations. 27 April 1971 was chosen as the scheduled completion date because this agreed with production needs for the first project. The experimental runs had already indicated that this date would be feasible without undue resource overload. Two computer calculations were requested, one with the timescale limited to the critical path duration of the double transfer machine project, and the other allowed to run out on a resource limited basis, except that the scheduled date for the single transfer machine project must be maintained.

A usage table of resources was requested for each project, for each different scheduling option imposed on the calculations. For each of these two options, that is the resource limited and time limited calculations, there would be a list of activities for each project, again split into departmental reports. And finally, a total resource usage table for the complete department, showing the effect of both projects combined, was requested.

Computer output reports for multiproject schedules

One of the less desirable features of the computer is that it has the ability, through its line printing machine, to print out data at something over 1000 lines per minute. To the computer operator, and from the point of view of saving expense in computer time, perhaps this degree of speed is necessary. However, it is an undoubted fact that the results of about ten minutes' computing time can sometimes be a wad of reports several inches thick. This case study, simple though it was, did, in fact, result in a fat pile of paper.

The first duty of the planning team, therefore, was to sift through the pages and pages of print-out to remove all irrelevant items. There were lists of input data, summaries of all the data input on the control cards, time analysis results, resource aggregation tables and a good deal of other associated information of no particular use for project management. The reports that were finally chosen as necessary for the purposes of control and management decision boiled down to only a few sheets. This procedure of editing the total output before it is sent to management is vital. Nothing can be calculated to cause scepticism or downright hostility more than reports that are about four times more bulky than they need to be.

Figure 10:9 shows the total departmental manpower scheduled for both projects, based on the first project meeting its scheduled date of 27 April, and the second project being completed at its earliest possible date. Final completion of both projects, on this basis, would take place on 14 May 1971. However, this would involve a fairly high degree of resource overload, right through from the start of the schedule until the end of April. Figure 10:10, on the other hand, also shows the overall departmental load, but this time arranged to conform to a schedule which would allow the second project to run out and avoid overloads.

Although the resource limited schedule of Figure 10:10 does achieve a very level pattern of resource usage for the design engineers, it has not been so successful for the subcontract draughtsmen. Indeed, the limit has been exceeded during the second two weeks of March. One may wonder how this could possibly happen, since the computer was operating on the basis of resource limit rules. However, it must be remembered that a scheduled date had been imposed on the completion event for the first project, demanding that it should not be delayed beyond 27 April. It is the priority claim created by this scheduled date that has caused the computer to schedule above available resource limits.

The degree of smoothing achieved in the resource limited schedule is remarkable. One should expect to see a better result than that encountered in previous examples in this book, because the number of activities is far higher, and the computer is given a greater chance to pick and choose between different activities. Fluctuations are now reduced to a smaller proportion of the total men available. And this example is still very small by most industrial standards, so that the reader can imagine the possibilities for projects which contain many thousands of activities.

When the time limited and resource limited usage tables are compared, one finds that the total completion time predicted for both projects has shifted from 18 May to 29 June 1971, as a direct result of the resource limitation. Now suppose that the completion date of 29 June 1971 is acceptable to Ingerdale. The first project will still be scheduled to complete on 27 April, as a direct result of the scheduled date imposed. The table of Figure 10:10 acts as a very good indicator of the time when more work will be wanted in the department. There is a sharp fall off in the usage of design engineers from 12 May onwards.

It has been found that schedules set up in this way have a habit of being accurate in their predictions to an uncanny degree. In another multiproject situation, where three projects together contained some 2500 activities, a

INGERDALE MACHINE TOOL COMPANY LIMITED   INGERDALE2 PAGE   1

TE	DESIGN – AVAIL	USAGE	REM.G	SUB-CONTR. – AVAIL	USAGE	REM.G
FEB71	4	6	-2	6		6
FEB71	4	6	-2	6		6
FEB71	4	6	-2	6		6
EB71	4	5	-1	6		6
EB71	4	6	-2	6		6
MAR71	4	6	-2	6		6
AR71	4	6	-2	6		6
AR71	4	6	-2	6		6
AR71	4	6	-2	6		6
AR71	4	6	-2	6		6
AR71	4	6	-2	6		6
AR71	4	6	-2	6	2	4
AR71	4	6	-2	6	5	1
AR71	4	6	-2	6	5	1
AR71	4	6	-2	6	5	1
AR71	4	6	-2	6	7	-1
AR71	4	6	-2	6	7	-1
AR71	4	5	-1	6	7	-1
AR71	4	5	-1	6	9	-3
AR71	4	5	-1	6	7	-1
AR71	4	5	-1	6	7	-1
AR71	4	5	-1	6	9	-3
AR71	4	5	-1	6	9	-3
AR71	4	4		6	11	-5
R71	4	5	-1	6	11	-5
R71	4	5	-1	6	9	-3
R71	4	5	-1	6	9	-3
R71	4	5	-1	6	9	-3
R71	4	5	-1	6	9	-3
R71	4	5	-1	6	11	-5
R71	4	5	-1	6	11	-5
R71	4	4		6	11	-5
R71	4	4		6	9	-3
R71	4	3	1	6	9	-3
R71	4	4		6	9	-3
R71	4	4		6	8	-2
R71	4	4		6	9	-3
R71	4	4		6	10	-4
R71	4	4		6	12	-6
R71	4	4		6	12	-6
R71	4	4		6	12	-6
R71	4	2	2	6	12	-6
R71	4	2	2	6	9	-3
R71	4	2	2	6	9	-3
71	4	2	2	6	9	-3
71	4	2	2	6	9	-3
71	4	1	3	6	7	-1
71	4	3	1	6	7	-1
71	4	4		6	2	4
71	4	4		6		6
71	4	2	2	6		6
71	4	2	2	6		6
71	4	4		6		6
71	4	4		6		6

FIGURE 10:9 TIME LIMITED TOTAL RESOURCE USAGE
TABLE

If works order 75001 is to finish by its target completion date of 27 April, and the other project is to be completed within its shortest possible duration, then the resources necessary will be those shown in these tables

I.S.T.—H

similar table of resource usage predicted that design engineers would become available on 15 October. The schedule was produced at the beginning of August, in that year. Management were given this information, and this helped them to time a new order delivery date. The resulting design work actually started on the 15 October, just coinciding with the release of engineers from the previous projects. This degree of accuracy was achieved by a combination of detailed scheduling, good estimates, an effective computer program (ICL 1900 in that case), and close attention to project control to keep the program on schedule.

Industrial projects seldom have time to spare in real life. If 29 June proves too late for the completion of the double transfer machine project, and 18 May has to be the target date for finishing all work and issuing the drawings, then the engineering department have no option other than to accept the schedule of manpower shown in Figure 10:9. At least they do have some reserve capacity, and they have got a clear picture of the actual number of men needed. The pattern remains reasonably smooth for the design engineers, although the schedule for the draughtsmen leaves something to be desired. Whichever option the management finally chooses, the time limited or resource limited schedule, there will be a corresponding detailed list of activities from which the two projects can be carried out and monitored on a very close, day to day basis.

It is only necessary to show the schedules of activities for one of these options, because the two sets of reports have the same format. The time limited option has been chosen, and the first list of activities appears in Figure 10:11. Once again it has been broken down into the three departmental areas, and all activities have been listed in order of their scheduled starting dates. This report contains all the activities remaining to complete the first project, for a single transfer machine. Associated directly with this report is a usage table for the single project, showing the proportion of resources from the total usage table of Figure 10:9 that have been allocated to this single project.

The resource table in Figure 10:12 shows that the costs remaining for the single transfer machine project, works order 75001, now amount to £3800. It will be remembered that the original cost estimate for this project, as shown in Figure 10:3, was £4060. It follows that the cost of this project to date should not exceed the difference between these two figures. In other words, the computer has evaluated the amount of work achieved on the project, and enabled it to be expressed in pounds sterling. If the costs have

FIGURE 10:10 RESOURCE LIMITED TOTAL RESOURCE TABLE

These are the resources needed to complete the first project, works order 75001, by its target completion date of 27 April, whilst allowing the second project to be subject to resource limitations. The effect of these management decisions has been to delay completion of the second project from 18 May until 7 July 1971

continued on next page

INGERDALE MACHINE TOOL COMPANY LIMITED

DATE	DESIGN - AVAIL	USAGE	REM.G	SUB-CONTR. - AVAIL	USAGE	REM.G
5MAY71	4	3		6	4	2
6MAY71	4	4	1	6	3	3
7MAY71	4	4		6	3	3
10MAY71	4	4		6	3	1
11MAY71	4	1		6	5	1
12MAY71	4	2	3	6	5	
13MAY71	4	2	2	6	6	
14MAY71	4	2	2	6	6	
17MAY71	4	2	2	6	7	
18MAY71	4	1	2	6	6	
19MAY71	4	1	3	6	6	
20MAY71	4	1	3	6	6	
21MAY71	4	1	3	6	6	
24MAY71	4	1	3	6	6	
25MAY71	4	2	2	6	6	
26MAY71	4	2	2	6	4	2
27MAY71	4	1	2	6	4	2
28MAY71	4	1	3	6	5	1
2JUN71	4	1	3	6	5	1
3JUN71	4	2	2	6	5	1
4JUN71	4	2	2	6	5	1
7JUN71	4	2	2	6	5	1
8JUN71	4	1	3	6	5	1
9JUN71	4	1	3	6	5	1
10JUN71	4	1	3	6	5	1
11JUN71	4	1	3	6	5	1
14JUN71	4	1	3	6	5	1
15JUN71	4	1	2	6	2	1
16JUN71	4	2	3	6	2	1
17JUN71	4	1	3			4
18JUN71	4	1	3			4
21JUN71	4	2	3			6
22JUN71	4	1	2			6
23JUN71	4	1	3			6
24JUN71	4		4			6
25JUN71	4		4			6
28JUN71	4		4			6
29JUN71	4		4			6
30JUN71	4		4			6
1JUL71	4		4			6
2JUL71	4		4			6
5JUL71	4		4			6
6JUL71	4		4			6
7JUL71	4		4			6

FIGURE 10:10 continued

een recorded, one should expect to find that they amounted to no more han £340. Any result in excess of this figure would lead to an investigation, ecause an adverse trend must be assumed. The significance of this type of eport for cost control can therefore be imagined, especially when long-term rojects of high value are considered. Effective cost control demands that osts are measured, compared against budgets, and then also analysed with eference to the value of the work actually achieved. This scheduling ystem, and in particular the report of Figure 10:11, possesses all the ecessary ingredients.

In Figure 10:13, the activity lists for the double transfer machine project re shown. These are, as usual, divided up into their separate departments. he resources necessary to sustain this schedule appear in the table of igure 10:14, which concludes the examples produced for this case study. he predicted cost for works orders 75011 and 75012 together, as shown in he resource table, amount to £6952. Since this schedule is the first calculated or this particular project, it contains all the activities needed from start to nish, and the estimated cost is the total for the whole design. Thus, a basis as been set for the cost control of this project, and when the next update is arried out it will become possible to evaluate the work done, and compare he results against actual expenditure using the same techniques just de-cribed for the single transfer machine project.

Multiproject scheduling by computer can be seen, therefore, as a very owerful technique, provided always that it is sensibly used. Some of its otentialities have been described in this chapter. Programs are being eveloped and improved all the time, and those which already exist have not et been fully exploited. The total range of possibilities available to future lanners must lead to more effective project management and control. But e must be prepared to use the techniques available to us. It is somewhat isheartening to learn from several major computer bureaux that the bulk f their network analysis time is spent on pure time analysis, and that only a ery small proportion of customers even carry out resource scheduling for ingle projects.

Here is the working schedule for works order 75001 that would result if management were satisfied with the resource usage pattern shown in Figure 10:9

continued on next page

I N G E R D A L E   M A C H I N E   T O O L   C O M P A N Y   L I M I T E D

D E P A R T M E N T --- D E S I G N

RESOURCE SCHEDULE ALL ACTIVITIES -- SINGLE TRANSFER MACHINE, W/ORDER 75001

PREC EVENT	SUCC EVENT	WORKS ORDER	DURN	..ACTIVITY DESCRIPTION..	EARLIEST START	SCHEDULED TIMES START	FINISH	LATEST FINISH	REM.G FLOAT	RESOURCES
1001	1002	75001	12	DESIGN TRANSFER LAYOUT	22FEB71	22FEB71	09MAR71	22MAR71	9	L 2
1012	1020	75001	15	DESIGN BORE HEAD LAYOUT	22FEB71	22FEB71	12MAR71	25MAR71	9	L 1
1004	1009	75001	15	DESIGN FIXTURE LAYOUT	22FEB71	03MAR71	23MAR71	23MAR71		L 1
1002	1003	75001	8	DESIGN TURNOVER LAYOUT	10MAR71	10MAR71	19MAR71	01APR71	9	L 1
1002	1006	75001	1	REVIEW TRANSFER DESIGN	10MAR71	10MAR71	10MAR71	26MAR71	12	
1020	1023	75001	2	REVIEW BORE HEAD LAYOUT	15MAR71	15MAR71	16MAR71	29MAR71	9	
1003	1007	75001	1	REVIEW TURNOVER DESIGN	22MAR71	22MAR71	22MAR71	02APR71	9	
1019	1025	75001	2	CHECK TOOL LAYOUT	22FEB71	22FEB71	23MAR71	20APR71	18	L 1
1009	1013	75001	2	REVIEW FIXTURE LAYOUT	15MAR71	24MAR71	25MAR71	25MAR71		
1010	1014	75001	5	REVIEW MACHINE LAYOUT	15MAR71	24MAR71	31MAR71	30MAR71		
1014	1018	75001	1	REVIEW MACHINE LAYOUT	22MAR71	31MAR71	31MAR71	02APR71	2	L 1
1015	1021	75001	10	MAKE FOUNDATIONS DRAWING	22MAR71	31MAR71	15APR71	15APR71		
1016	1026	75001	2	PRE-ISSUE CHECK TRANSFER	01APR71	01APR71	02APR71	22APR71	12	L 1
1017	1026	75001	2	PRE-ISSUE CHECK TURNOVER	06APR71	06APR71	07APR71	22APR71	9	L 1
1025	1026	75001	2	PRE-ISSUE CHECK HEAD	06APR71	08APR71	13APR71	22APR71	7	L 1
1021	1026	75001	5	CHECK FOUNDATION DRAWING	05APR71	16APR71	22APR71	22APR71		L 1
1024	1026	75001	2	PRE-ISSUE CHECK ASSEMBLY	06APR71	19APR71	20APR71	22APR71	2	L 1
1022	1026	75001	2	PRE-ISSUE CHECK FIXTURE	08APR71	21APR71	22APR71	22APR71		L 1

FIGURE 10:11   UPDATED SCHEDULE FOR WORKS ORDER 75001, TIME LIMITED TO A TARGET COMPLETION DATE

INGERDALE MACHINE TOOL COMPANY LIMITED

RESOURCE SCHEDULE ALL ACTIVITIES – SINGLE TRANSFER MACHINE, W/ORDER 75001

DEPARTMENT —— DRAWING

PREC EVENT	SUCC EVENT	WORKS ORDER ..ACTIVITY DESCRIPTION..	DURN	EARLIEST START	SCHEDULED TIMES START	FINISH	LATEST FINISH	REM.G FLOAT	RESOURCES	
1006	1016	75001 DETAIL & CHECK TRANSFER	15	11MAR71	11MAR71	31MAR71	20APR71	12	D	3
1023	1025	75001 DET.& CHECK BORING HEAD	14	17MAR71	17MAR71	05APR71	20APR71	9	D	2
1007	1017	75001 DETAIL & CHECK TURNOVER	10	23MAR71	23MAR71	05APR71	20APR71	9	D	2
1013	1022	75001 DET.& CHECK FIXTURE	16	17MAR71	26MAR71	20APR71	20APR71		D	2
1018	1024	75001 DET.& CHECK MACHINE ASSY	10	23MAR71	01APR71	16APR71	20APR71	2	D	1

INGERDALE MACHINE TOOL COMPANY LIMITED

RESOURCE SCHEDULE ALL ACTIVITIES – SINGLE TRANSFER MACHINE, W/ORDER 75001

DEPARTMENT —— OFFICE

PREC EVENT	SUCC EVENT	WORKS ORDER ..ACTIVITY DESCRIPTION..	DURN	EARLIEST START	SCHEDULED TIMES START	FINISH	LATEST FINISH	REM.G FLOAT	RESOURCES
1026	1027	75001 PRINT & ISSUE TO PRODUCN	3	14APR71	23APR71	27APR71	27APR71		

FIGURE 10:11 continued

0 SINGLE TRANSFER MACHINE, W/ORDER 75001

DATE	DESIGN – USAGE	COST	SUB-CONTR. – USAGE	COST	RES ACC.COST
22FEB71	2	40			40
23FEB71	2	40			80
24FEB71	2	40			120
25FEB71	2	40			160
26FEB71	2	40			200
1MAR71	2	40			240
2MAR71	2	40			280
3MAR71	3	60			340
4MAR71	3	60			400
5MAR71	3	60			460
8MAR71	3	60			520
9MAR71	3	60			580
10MAR71	3	60			640
11MAR71	3	60	3	48	748
12MAR71	3	60	3	48	856
15MAR71	2	40	3	48	944
16MAR71	2	40	3	48	1,032
17MAR71	2	40	5	80	1,152
18MAR71	2	40	5	80	1,272
19MAR71	2	40	5	80	1,392
22MAR71	2	40	5	80	1,512
23MAR71	2	40	7	112	1,664
24MAR71	1	20	7	112	1,796
25MAR71	1	20	7	112	1,928
26MAR71	1	20	9	144	2,092
29MAR71	1	20	9	144	2,256
30MAR71	1	20	9	144	2,420
31MAR71	1	20	9	144	2,584
1APR71	2	40	7	112	2,736
2APR71	2	40	7	112	2,888
5APR71	1	20	7	112	3,020
6APR71	2	40	3	48	3,108
7APR71	2	40	3	48	3,196
8APR71	2	40	3	48	3,284
13APR71	2	40	3	48	3,372
14APR71	1	20	3	48	3,440
15APR71	1	20	3	48	3,508
16APR71	1	20	3	48	3,576
19APR71	2	40	2	32	3,648
20APR71	2	40	2	32	3,720
21APR71	2	40			3,760
22APR71	2	40			3,800
23APR71					3,800
26APR71					3,800
27APR71					3,800
28APR71					3,800
29APR71					3,800
30APR71					3,800
3MAY71					3,800
4MAY71					3,800

FIGURE 10:12 TIME LIMITED RESOURCE USAGE TABLE FOR THE MEN NEEDED TO COMPLETE WORKS ORDER 75001 BY ITS TARGET DATE

This table is interesting because, apart from showing the resources needed to finish the design of this single-station [...] It can therefore be used to provide a basis for cost

INGERDALE MACHINE TOOL COMPANY LIMITED

DEPARTMENT --- DESIGN RESOURCE SCHEDULE ALL ACTIVITIES - DOUBLE TRANSFER MACHINE, W/ORDER 75011/75012

PREC EVENT	SUCC EVENT	DURN	WORKS ORDER	..ACTIVITY DESCRIPTION..	EARLIEST START	SCHEDULED TIMES START	FINISH	LATEST FINISH	REM.G FLOAT	RESOURCES
2001	2003	1	75011	ESTABLISH FIXTURE STDS	22FEB71	22FEB71	22FEB71	02MAR71	6	L 1
2001	2004	20	75011	DESIGN TRANSFER LAYOUT	22FEB71	22FEB71	19MAR71	30MAR71	7	L 1
2001	2005	4	75011	MILLING MACHINE CONCEPT	22FEB71	22FEB71	25FEB71	25FEB71		L 1
2001	2009	2	75011	ESTAB MILL HEAD STANDARD	22FEB71	22FEB71	23FEB71	11MAR71	12	L 1
2003	2006	10	75011	DESIGN MILLING FIXTURE	23FEB71	23FEB71	08MAR71	16MAR71	6	L 1
2001	2007	10	75011	ESTABLISH FRAME STANDARD	22FEB71	22FEB71	24FEB71	16MAR71	14	L 1
2005	2008	3	75011	DRAW MILLING TOOL LAYOUT	26FEB71	26FEB71	02MAR71	11MAR71	7	L 1
2025	2028	3	75012	DRILLING MACHINE CONCEPT	26FEB71	26FEB71	02MAR71	02MAR71		L 1
2008	2013	2	75011	APPROVE MILLING TOOL LYT	03MAR71	03MAR71	04MAR71	04MAY71	41	L 1
2029	2031	15	75012	DESIGN DRILLING FIXTURE	03MAR71	03MAR71	23MAR71	23MAR71		L 1
2013	2017	1	75011	REVIEW MILLING TOOL LYT	05MAR71	05MAR71	05MAR71	05MAY71	41	L 1
2006	2011	20	75011	REVIEW MILL FIXTR DESIGN	09MAR71	09MAR71	05APR71	27APR71	33	L 1
2009	2014	20	75011	DESIGN LEFTHAND MILLHEAD	03MAR71	03MAR71	05APR71	08APR71	2	L 1
2007	2012	10	75011	LAYOUT MILLING MACHINE	09MAR71	09MAR71	26MAR71	30MAR71	2	L 1
2004	2010	1	75011	REVIEW TRANSFER DESIGN	22MAR71	22MAR71	22MAR71	15APR71	16	L 1
2009	2015	15	75011	DESIGN RIGHT-HD MILLHEAD	03MAR71	03MAR71	15APR71	20APR71	3	L 1
2031	2037	1	75012	REVIEW DRILL FIXTURE DES	24MAR71	24MAR71	24MAR71	22APR71	19	L 1
2033	2035	5	75012	DRILLING MACHINE LAYOUT	24MAR71	24MAR71	30MAR71	30MAR71		L 1
2012	2018	5	75011	REVIEW MILL MACHINE LYT	23MAR71	23MAR71	29MAR71	26APR71	18	L 1
2028	2030	2	75012	DRAW DRILL TOOL LAYOUT	03MAR71	03MAR71	30MAR71	02APR71	3	L 1
2030	2034	1	75012	APPROVE DRIL TOOL LAYOUT	05MAR71	05MAR71	31MAR71	23APR71	15	L 1
2035	2040	1	75012	REVIEW DRILL MACHINE LYT	31MAR71	31MAR71	31MAR71	29APR71		L 1
2036	2041	20	75011	FOUNDATIONS DRAWING	08MAR71	08MAR71	01APR71	06APR71	3	L 1
2034	2038	1	75012	REVIEW DRILL TOOL LAYOUT	09MAR71	09MAR71	05APR71	07APR71	2	L 1
2038	2039	1	75012	CHECK DRILL TOOL LAYOUT	31MAR71	31MAR71	21APR71	13APR71	3	L 1
2014	2019	10	75011	REVIEW L MILLHEAD DESIGN	31MAR71	31MAR71	21APR71	23APR71	3	L 1
2039	2045	1	75012	DESIGN PROBES LAYOUT	10MAR71	10MAR71	16APR71	21APR71	2	L 1
2015	2021	1	75011	REVIEW R MILLHEAD DESIGN	24MAR71	24MAR71	03MAY71	11MAY71	6	L 1
2044	2046	10	75012	GET QUOTATION-DRILL HEAD	11MAR71	11MAR71	22APR71	26APR71	2	L 1
2045	2047	1	75012	REVIEW PROBES DESIGN	24MAR71	24MAR71	27APR71	13MAY71	12	L 1
2048	2052	4	75012	PRE-ISS CHK DRILLMACHINE	19APR71	19APR71	26APR71	13MAY71	13	L 1
2016	2024	3	75011	PRE-ISS CHK MILL FIXTURE	24MAR71	24MAR71	27APR71	13MAY71	12	L 1
2023	2024	3	75011	PRE-ISS CHK MILL W/C ASY	07APR71	07APR71	28APR71	07MAY71	7	L 1
2017	2022	5	75011	CHECK MILLING TOOL LYT	08MAR71	08MAR71	05MAY71	13MAY71	6	L 1
2041	2026	10	75011	PRE-ISSUE CHECK TRANSFER	15APR71	15APR71	13MAY71	13MAY71		L 1
2050	2049	10	75011	CHECK FOUNDATION DRAWING	30APR71	30APR71	11MAY71	13MAY71	2	L 1
2043	2052	3	75012	PRE-ISS CHK DRILLFIXTURE	14APR71	14APR71	11MAY71	13MAY71	2	L 1
2050	2052	3	75012	PRE-ISSUE CHECK PROBES	08APR71	08APR71	11MAY71	13MAY71	2	L 1
2022	2024	4	75011	PRE-ISSUE CHK MILLHEADS	29APR71	29APR71	13MAY71	13MAY71		L 1

FIGURE 10:13 TIME LIMITED ACTIVITY SCHEDULES FOR WORKS ORDERS 75011 AND 75012
The working schedule shown here is particularly interesting because it was prepared by the computer with due regard to the resources needed not only for this project, but also for works order 75001

INGERDALE MACHINE TOOL COMPANY LIMITED

DEPARTMENT ---- DRAWING — RESOURCE SCHEDULE ALL ACTIVITIES - DOUBLE TRANSFER MACHINE, W/ORDER 75011/75012

PREC EVENT	SUCC EVENT	WORKS ORDER	..ACTIVITY DESCRIPTION..	DURN	EARLIEST START	SCHEDULED TIMES START	FINISH	LATEST FINISH	REM.G FLOAT	RESOURCES	
2011	2016	75011	DET & CHK MILLING FIXTUR	10	10MAR71	10MAR71	23MAR71	11MAY71	33	D	2
2018	2023	75011	DET & CHK MILL M/C ASSY	10	24MAR71	30MAR71	14APR71	10MAY71	18	D	2
2010	2020	75011	DETAIL & CHECK TRANSFER	15	23MAR71	06APR71	28APR71	06MAY71	6	D	3
2040	2048	75012	DET & CHK DRILL M/C ASSY	10	01APR71	06APR71	21APR71	07MAY71	12	D	1
2019	2022	75011	DET & CHK LEFT MILHEAD	18	01APR71	07APR71	04MAY71	07MAY71	3	D	2
2039	2044	75012	PREPARE DRILL HEAD B D M	1	10MAR71	19APR71	19APR71	27APR71	6	D	1
2037	2043	75012	DET & CHK DRILL FIXTURE	12	25MAR71	21APR71	06MAY71	10MAY71	2	D	3
2021	2022	75011	DET & CHK RIGHT MILLHEAD	12	22APR71	22APR71	07MAY71	07MAY71		D	2
2047	2050	75012	DET & CHK DRILL PROBES	10	25MAR71	23APR71	06MAY71	10MAY71	2	D	2

INGERDALE MACHINE TOOL COMPANY LIMITED

DEPARTMENT ---- OFFICE — RESOURCE SCHEDULE ALL ACTIVITIES - DOUBLE TRANSFER MACHINE, W/ORDER 75011/75012

PREC EVENT	SUCC EVENT	WORKS ORDER	..ACTIVITY DESCRIPTION..	DURN	EARLIEST START	SCHEDULED TIMES START	FINISH	LATEST FINISH	REM.G FLOAT	RESOURCES
2046	2051	75012	ORDER BOUGHT DRILL HEAD	5	25MAR71	04MAY71	10MAY71	18MAY71	6	
2026	2032	75011	PRINT & ISSUE TRANSFER	3	22APR71	06MAY71	10MAY71	18MAY71	6	
2052	2054	75012	PRINT & ISSUE DRILL M/C	3	23APR71	12MAY71	14MAY71	18MAY71	2	
2024	2027	75011	PRINT & ISSUE MILL M/C	3	05MAY71	14MAY71	18MAY71	18MAY71		
2049	2053	75011	PRINT & ISSUE FOUNDATION	3	14MAY71	14MAY71	18MAY71	18MAY71		

INGERDALE MACHINE TOOL COMPANY LIMITED

DESIGN - 1			SUB-CONTR. - DOUBLE TRANSFER MACHINE, W/ORDER 75011/75012 1		
DATE	USAGE	COST	USAGE	COST	RES. ACC. COST
22FEB71	4	80			80
23FEB71	4	80			160
24FEB71	4	80			240
25FEB71	3	60			300
26FEB71	4	80			380
1MAR71	4	80			460
2MAR71	4	80			540
3MAR71	3	60			600
4MAR71	3	60			660
5MAR71	3	60			720
8MAR71	3	60			780
9MAR71	3	60			840
10MAR71	3	60	2	32	932
11MAR71	3	60	2	32	1,024
12MAR71	3	60	2	32	1,116
15MAR71	4	80	2	32	1,228
16MAR71	4	80	2	32	1,340
17MAR71	4	80	2	32	1,452
18MAR71	4	80	2	32	1,564
19MAR71	4	80	2	32	1,676
22MAR71	3	60	2	32	1,768
23MAR71	3	60	2	32	1,860
24MAR71	4	80			1,940
25MAR71	4	80			2,020
26MAR71	4	80			2,100
29MAR71	4	80			2,180
30MAR71	4	80	2	32	2,292
31MAR71	3	60	2	32	2,384
1APR71	3	60	2	32	2,476
2APR71	3	60	2	32	2,568
5APR71	4	80	2	32	2,680
6APR71	3	60	6	96	2,836
7APR71	3	60	8	128	3,024
8APR71	3	60	8	128	3,212
13APR71	3	60	8	128	3,400
14APR71	3	60	8	128	3,588
15APR71	3	60	6	96	3,744
16APR71	2	40	6	96	3,880
19APR71	2	40	7	112	4,032
20APR71	2	40	6	96	4,168
21APR71	2	40	9	144	4,352
22APR71	2	40	10	160	4,552
23APR71	4	80	12	192	4,824
26APR71	4	80	12	192	5,096
27APR71	4	80	12	192	5,368
28APR71	2	40	12	192	5,600
29APR71	2	40	9	144	5,784
30APR71	2	40	9	144	5,968
3MAY71	2	40	9	144	6,152
4MAY71	2	40	9	144	6,336

	DESIGN -			SUB-CONTR. -		
	USAGE	COST		USAGE	COST	RES ACC.COST
	1			DOUBLE TRANSFER MACHINE, W/ORDER 75011/75012		
DATE						
5MAY71	2	40		7	112	6,488
6MAY71	1	20		7	112	6,620
7MAY71	3	60		2	32	6,712
10MAY71	4	80				6,792
11MAY71	4	80				6,872
12MAY71	2	40				6,912
13MAY71	2	40				6,952
14MAY71						6,952
17MAY71						6,952
18MAY71						6,952

FIGURE 10:14 TIME LIMITED RESOURCE USAGE TABLE FOR WORKS ORDERS 75011 AND 75012
If both projects described in this case study are to be run within their own respective time targets, then this table shows the numbers of men that must be allocated to the double transfer line machine. For this second project, this is the initial schedule, based upon the fact that no activities have been started. The cost predictions printed out in the extreme right-hand column therefore reach the cumulative total for the whole design costs attributable to the grades of men being scheduled

11

PRECEDENCE NETWORKS

Ever since the evolution of network analysis techniques, the basic notation has undergone a virtually continuous process of adaptation. In many cases, particular users have been unable to carry out scheduling of their projects to the degree of proficiency that they would have wished, and the existing networking methods were declared as being wholly or partially unsuitable. Sometimes these users would have been better advised to persevere with their attempts, because many of the failures in project scheduling are the fault of the planners themselves rather than the systems available to them. Failure, therefore, sometimes results from the user's lack of understanding of the existing techniques rather than any fault inherent in the techniques themselves. In some cases, planners have been led to develop their own versions of network analysis, where the notation has been modified to a greater or lesser degree. Where the techniques previously available failed only because they were misapplied, the resulting variations cannot always be regarded as improvements upon an original theme.

There have been one or two notable exceptions to this rule. Outstanding among these has been the development of precedence networking, a method which is rapidly finding favour with a number of planners from different industries. Any individual who has mastered the art of producing correct network logic for arrow diagrams in the PERT or CPM forms already used throughout this book should have no difficulty in adapting to the precedence notation, if he wishes. In order to introduce this method here, it can be said that the notation allows the planner a far greater degree of freedom for expressing complex interdependencies between different activities than was possible with other methods previously. On the other hand, input to the computer is correspondingly more complex.

Already precedence notation itself has started undergoing the process of development, and precedence diagrams produced within one organisation may look very different from those produced by another. All of the examples in this chapter are based on a relatively unadulterated form of the original notation. In fact, most of the diagrams have been drawn from the system specified by Cementation Limited, and incorporated into a computer program for that company by K and H Business Consultants Limited. Perhaps the simplest way in which the precedence method can be demonstrated initially is to take a small CPM network diagram and redraw it in precedence notation. By this means the fundamental differences can be highlighted, although the precedence diagram which results will not carry any of the more complex activity interdependencies of which it is capable because these were not contained in the CPM source.

Figure 10:1 has been chosen as the source material from which the precedence diagram of Figure 11:1 has been derived. Both of these diagrams have exactly the same logic implications, and both would produce the same results from time analysis. Only the diagram notation is different in this particular example. Notice that the activity arrows of the CPM network have been replaced by boxes in the precedence version. In other words, the activities are placed on the junctions of all the interconnecting lines in the diagram. The interconnections, therefore, become nothing more than dummies, at least in this particular example. If the logic is followed through in the same way that an engineering flow chart would be followed, then it is easy to satisfy oneself that Figures 10:1 and 11:1 convey the same meaning.

The mere fact that one is able to trace through a precedence diagram as though it were an engineering flow chart or block diagram is regarded by many as one of the system's chief advantages. It is said to be more readily accepted by engineers and management because no instruction is needed in the interpretation of the diagrams. These arguments are not agreed by everyone, and the advantages or otherwise of precedence notation over arrow diagrams are a fairly frequent source of discussion in professional planning circles, with personal preferences playing quite a large part in any conclusions reached.

In the mathematical theory of networks, linkages are called "arcs," and all the meeting points "nodes." It follows that precedence networking is one example of an "activity on node" system, whereas the other networks used in this book are all examples of the "activity on arrow" method. In Figure 11:1, it is obvious that the description for each activity has been written in its box. Resource requirements have been added, where appropriate, immediately under each activity description. In the two divisions at the foot of each box, it is seen that the duration has been placed in the left-hand

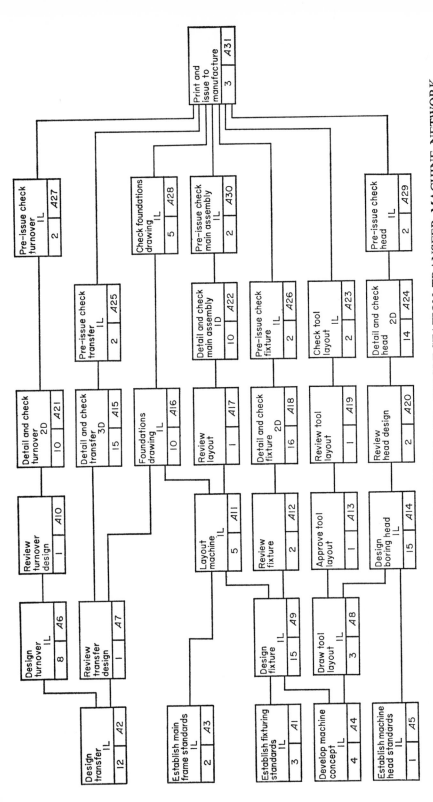

FIGURE 11:1 PRECEDENCE CONVERSION OF SINGLE-STATION TRANSFER MACHINE NETWORK
As an introduction to precedence notation, here is the network diagram that was first used in Chapter 10 (Figure 10:1) converted from CPM into precedence form

position whilst the number in the right-hand side is the activity code. Because each activity is self-contained within its own box, the code numbering system is simplified. The activity which was previously called 1,2 (Event 1 to Event 2) in the arrow diagram has been renamed simply *A*2 on the precedence diagram. It would have been possible simply to code this activity 2 instead of *A*2, but the addition of a letter is useful in preventing confusion between the duration entry and the activity code within the activity box on the network diagram.

But the principal advantages of the precedence system are discovered when one examines the possibilities that are opened up for the planner who has to manage complex interrelationships between different activities. Just as the arrow diagrams of PERT and CPM presented a new notation that was far more powerful that the older bar charts, so precedence notation has taken us all one step further. The remaining diagrams in this chapter will

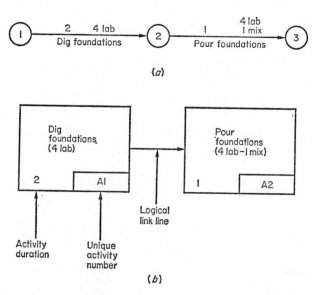

FIGURE 11:2 PRECEDENCE NOTATION—NORMAL
ACTIVITY CONSTRAINT

Here, a small part of an arrow diagram has been reproduced at (*a*), and its precedence counterpart is shown at (*b*). The connecting arrow in the precedence version is assumed to have no duration where none has been given. It is possible, however, to plan for delays that must occur between activities by adding a duration to the linking arrow. This could also be achieved in CPM notation by the insertion of a dummy between the two activities, and assigning a duration to the dummy

illustrate some of the possibilities afforded by the system. The range of activity constraints which can be depicted will become apparent from these examples, all of which have been taken from the K and H precedence system handbook.

In Figure 11:2, two fragments of network are shown together. In the figure at (a), two activities appear in CPM form, whilst the version at (b) represents their direct conversion to a precedence diagram. There are no events in precedence networks, but only activities. Although the schedule implications between both diagrams are identical, precedence cannot represent events 1, 2 or 3 from the diagram which appears at (a). It would be possible in the precedence diagram, however, to add a duration to the logical linking arrow. In some respects, precedence links are like dummies in CPM and PERT networks. Indeed, some computer programs allow the user to specify durations for dummies when they are planning by CPM and PERT. The effect of adding a duration estimate to the link in this precedence example would be to specify a minimum period that must elapse between completion of activity $A1$ and the start of activity $A2$.

These arguments are shown more clearly in Figure 11:3(a). All time units on this diagram are expressed in days. It is seen that the planner has added a duration of two days to the link arrow, so that activity B must wait for at least two days after completion of activity A before it can start. This is indicated in the small accompanying diagram, drawn to a simple timescale. At (b), a lag start relation is shown. In this case, activity B is allowed to start before activity A has been completely finished. In fact, it can start three days after the start of activity A, as indicated by the duration of three days assigned to the lag start constraint arrow. If this diagram had been drawn in CPM or PERT form, it would have been necessary to adopt one or other of the techniques previously described in Figures 5:8 and 5:9. Figure 11:3(c) shows yet another constraint type possible with precedence diagrams. This is the lag finish relationship. Here, it can be seen that the position of the linking arrow between both activities implies that the finish of the second is dependent upon the finish of the first. And, addition of the estimate of three days to the link has produced the interpretation drawn out to scale in the small timescaled version that also appears at (c). Completion of the second activity, B, must not be scheduled until three days after activity A's scheduled completion date.

The simple appearance of the network diagram of Figure 11:4 shows how a small construction project can easily be represented by a precedence

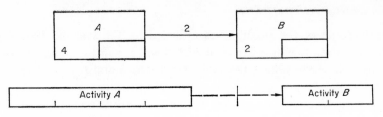

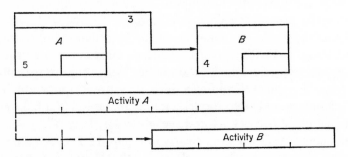

(*a*) Normal relation. With lag
Activity *B* cannot start until 2 days after the
completion of Activity *A*

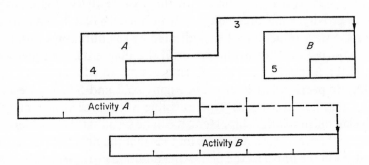

(*b*) Lag start relation
Activity *B* can start 3 days after
the start of Activity *A*

(*c*) Lag finish relation
Activity *B* cannot finish until 3 days after the
completion of Activity *A*

FIGURE 11:3 PRECEDENCE NOTATION—COMPLEX
CONSTRAINTS
At (*a*), (*b*) and (*c*), the three extensions provided by the use of precedence,
when compared with CPM notation, are illustrated

network. It will be seen that this example does contain one or two complex linkages between activities. One may, therefore, ask why precedence networks have not been universally adopted as a natural replacement for CPM or PERT. To seek the answer to this question, it is necessary to take a look at some disadvantages associated with the system. The first of these will become apparent from a glance at Figure 11:5. Here, two versions of the same network portion have been drawn, one in CPM form and the other in precedence notation. Notice how much more difficult it is to express the diagram at (*a*) in its precedence version at (*b*).

It must also be recognised that by no means all project planners need to make use of the facilities offered by precedence networks. In many cases the simpler arrow diagrams are sufficient to express all aspects of a project's activity constraints. Introduction of precedence notation would only be another system, and not necessarily a better one. Natural resistance to any change will prevent the use of precedence in such cases, and nothing will have been lost in the process. Indeed, once the entire staff of an organisation have been educated into accepting one form of network diagram, it would be unwise to embark upon a fresh course of persuasion if no real return could be expected for the investment.

Another disadvantage of precedence networks is encountered when the time comes to input them to the computer. In general, they need more than one punched card for every activity. For small networks this may not prove to be a serious drawback, but when networks are large, the use of more than one punched card for every activity becomes a considerable additional factor. Suppose, for example, that a network contains 10 000 activities. If the systems described in Chapters 9 or 10 were used, this network would result in the punching of 10 000 activity cards. The instructions for this card punching might involve the filling up of about 250 coding sheets. If the activities came from a precedence diagram, then at least two cards per activity would be expected with most computer programs. This must add a further 250 coding sheets to the clerical effort, with consequent risk of more mistakes. And 10 000 more punched cards will cost something like an additional £150 to produce, again with further risk of error.

It can be appreciated, therefore, that precedence networks have several factors that argue both for and against their adoption. In some project circumstances they will prove to be very practicable planning tools. Whether or not they are to be used often boils down to no more than the exercise of a

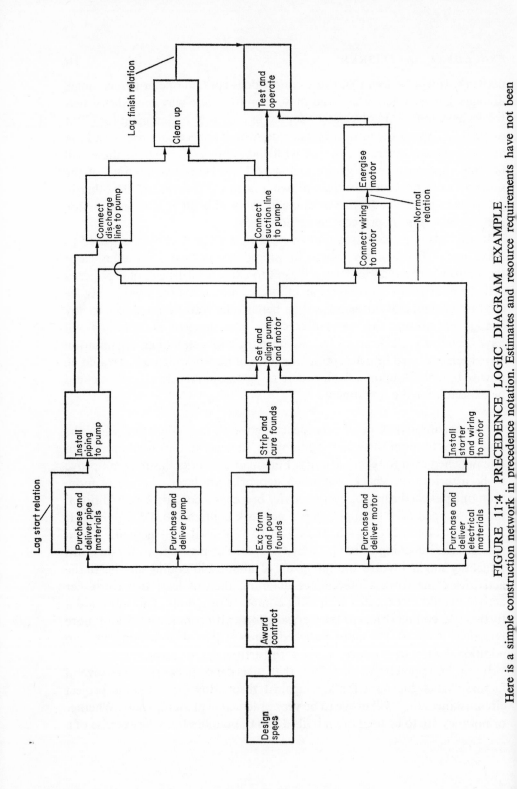

FIGURE 11:4 PRECEDENCE LOGIC DIAGRAM EXAMPLE

Here is a simple construction network in precedence notation. Estimates and resource requirements have not been

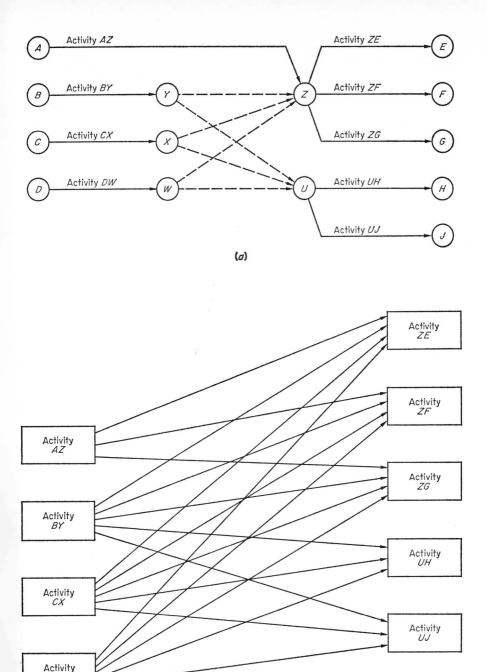

FIGURE 11:5 ONE DISADVANTAGE OF PRECEDENCE NOTATION

The complex constraints that can be depicted very simply by the adoption of predecence notation were demonstrated in Figure 11:3. However, this example takes a look at the other side of the coin. Although the CPM network in (*a*) is somewhat cluttered, it is made to look very clear by comparison with the clumsy attempt of precedence to show the same situation

planner's personal preference. Perhaps it would be unwise for beginners to attempt precedence networks before mastering the more simple critical path methods. The degree of complication added to computer input preparation is highly significant, and worthy of very careful consideration before the plunge is taken.

There would be no point in introducing another case study at this stage, because the reports generated by the computer for projects planned by precedence will look very like those produced from ordinary arrow diagrams. Only the input coding is changed, and that will vary very considerably from one program to another. It is true to say that fewer programs are available for the processing of precedence diagrams than those which can calculate schedules from CPM or PERT.

12 SHORT CUTS TO EFFECTIVE SCHEDULING

Any project schedule must demand some time, thought and effort if it is to become an effective tool for managing the project. Network diagrams have the notational power to express complex activity relationships, but this very advantage can mean the involvement of senior staff for protracted planning sessions when the logic is being evolved. It is not unusual for a network meeting to occupy departmental managers for a whole working day, during which they will draw the diagram, estimate the duration of each activity and specify the resources needed for each job. Most managers attend too many meetings. Any ideas which can reduce the time taken in network planning, or even eliminate the need for any meeting at all, must be worth investigating.

Some of the advanced techniques discussed later in this chapter can remove the need for any network drawing at all. But before any company can hope to reach a high degree of sophistication in its planning methods it must go through a learning period. This learning period has got to involve the preparation of several networks by orthodox means, and with as much input from senior management skill and experience as possible. When such planning meetings are held without any special time-reducing techniques, it is customary for a network specialist to conduct the proceedings. He will actually draw the network, step by step, as the working sequence for the project is worked out and discussed.

Most people have their own individual preference for drafting methods, but the outcome of a networking session is usually a fairly disreputable looking document. Every time the meeting changes its mind on a working sequence there will be a corresponding erasure on the original network, and it is more than probable that many activity arrows will cross over one another, making paths through the drawing difficult to follow. Of course, the network must be redrawn after the meeting, and generally tidied up. But the first time-saving step open to the planner is to use a stencil for drawing his event circles (or whatever shape he prefers) and to use a ruler for his straight lines. These simple steps do not add to drafting time, but they do help to keep down the size of the diagram and assist its subsequent interpretation.

STANDARD PROJECT NETWORKS

One of the simplest projects to plan is that which exactly duplicates a previous enterprise. The original network can be used again after suitable revision in the light of lessons learned from the first project. Estimates for the duration of each activity and for detailed resource requirements can be based on actual cost records. If a company is fortunate in receiving a series of repeat orders for the same basic project, then the network will eventually stabilise and become usable in a standard form. All the estimates will also stabilise, as the benefits of learning are felt, and manufacturing or construction times reduce to constant levels.

Not many industrial projects lend themselves to planning by complete standard networks. Very few projects can be expected to repeat exactly. Any construction project, for example, is dependent to some extent upon specific site conditions which may have to be taken into account at the planning stage, so that a repeat project at a different site must need a different plan. New industrial projects usually contain a high proportion of design activities which will be absent from any repeat order. Absolutely standard project networks are not, therefore, likely to form a big proportion of the total range of short cuts that can be taken towards effective scheduling.

Some examples of projects which do allow the application of completely standard networks can be cited. A company which supplies and installs pre-fabricated operating theatres to hospitals found that it was able to develop one single network that could be used to control the design, manufacture and installation of each contract. The standard network was comprehensive, and included activities for most of the optional extras likely to be ordered by customers. When each new project started, a print of the standard network was taken. This print was edited by the deletion of unwanted activities. Any additional work required was incorporated by the inclusion of new activities. Then estimates were added for the duration of all activities, and the network became a true representation of the specific project plan. These standard networks were used only for time analysis, but there was no basic reason why they should not have been extended for resource allocation.

A machine tool manufacturer built only special machines. No machine could be manufactured from a standard set of drawings because the requirements of each customer had to be studied in detail, and a machine designed and built accordingly. These were major projects, costing many hundreds of thousands of pounds to fulfil. Overall project durations typically reached about eighteen months. Although many of the machines were entirely different from each other in their basic conception, one particular range of machines could be isolated from the rest. These were very large plano-milling machines. Although the size, number of cutting heads and the power of drive motors varied considerably from one order to the next, it was found possible to develop a standard network that could be used to conduct resource allocation by computer, once each network had been suitably modified to suit the individual machine specification. These standard networks were integrated into an overall multiproject system, for which non-standard project networks were produced by another short-cut process, to be described later in this chapter.

STANDARD PART-PROJECT NETWORKS

Now consider the fairly typical case of a company which has contracted to plan and fulfil a range of projects for different customers. Even though each project is unique, and the design and execution completely different from all other projects, there will almost certainly be areas of working that can be identified as being common to at least two of the different projects. Every company develops its own working methods and rules, and the application of these does tend to impart some degree of uniformity among projects which appear at first sight to be completely alien in character.

Here is one example. Again the machine tool industry is the source, but the principle applies equally well to most other major projects undertaken for customers. A company engaged in the design, manufacture and installation of machine tool systems included within its range of products transfer lines for the precision machining of automobile components. Each fresh contract was as different from the last as one motor car's cylinder block is from another's gearbox case. Nevertheless, the company started to compare the networks produced for each contract in order to seek some common patterns of working. This search eventually proved very fruitful indeed, and led to a sophisticated system of multiproject resource scheduling which is outlined in the next section of this chapter.

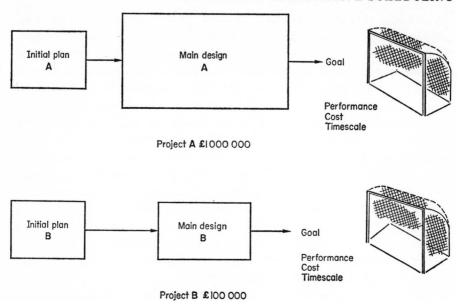

Project A £1 000 000

Project B £100 000

FIGURE 12:1 CONCEPT OF STANDARD PRELIMINARY
NETWORKS
Although two industrial projects handled by any company may differ
greatly in size, it is sometimes possible to find a great deal of similarity
in the planning steps which lead up to their full starts. A search for a
common standard network to cover the initial planning period for all
projects can often prove fruitful

One of the first discoveries made, however, was that no matter how
different any two projects might be from each other, both had to undergo
the same sequence of activities during the initial stages of planning and pre-
design. This concept is illustrated in Figure 12:1. Project *A* is expected to
cost all of £1 million, whilst project *B* is very much smaller and will cost
about £100 000 to complete. But both projects require the same amount of
preliminary activity before main design can be put in hand. The actual
network that evolved is shown in Figure 12:2. This network always has an
overall duration of about three weeks. It allows the project manager to plan
his own individual work during the initial setting up stages of the project.
No time estimates are made, but the network is regarded instead as a
detailed checklist which places all activities in a correct sequence. It serves
to get a new project started along the right lines, without having to wait for
the detailed project network to become available. In fact, it is seen that

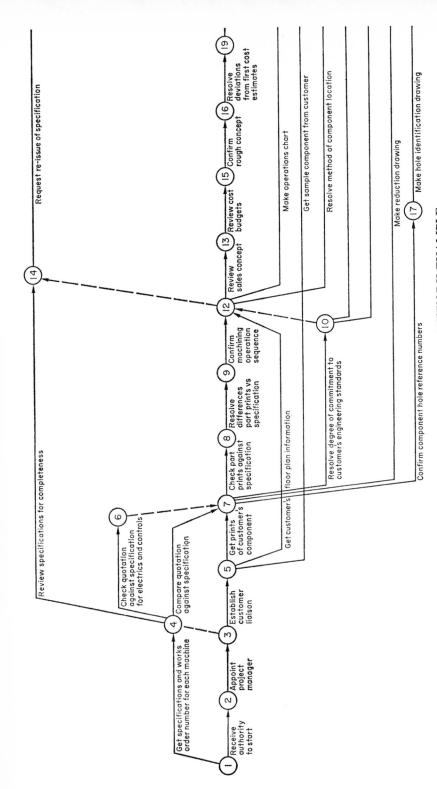

FIGURE 12:2 STANDARD PRELIMINARY NETWORK EXAMPLE

This network is used by a major American machine tool company for getting new machine tool projects off the ground. Notice that preparation of a main network for the project appears as one of the last activities in the preliminary plan. Not all projects need every activity, and the preliminary plan is edited as necessary

(Ingersoll Milling Machine Company, USA)

continued on next page

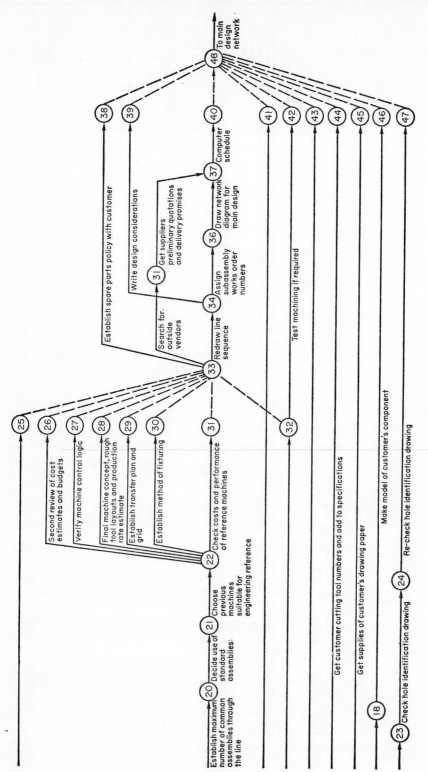

FIGURE 12:2 continued

preparation of the project network, and computer scheduling themselves form two of the final activities on this preliminary design network.

Incidentally, the preliminary design network has taken the place of a written procedure. Indeed, many studies by organisation and methods departments lend themselves to networking techniques. Of course, organisation and methods people have their own notation, which can show the flow of information or documents. Nevertheless, network diagrams can do this job adequately, and show up interdependencies very clearly. People do not willingly read lengthy procedures, but a network diagram, used as a wall-mounted checklist is very convenient. The machine tool company which supplied this example uses another standard network diagram for the "cleaning-up" activities at the end of each design project. These activities are largely concerned with getting all modifications included on original drawings, microfilming the drawings and sending off any drawings which are contractually the property of the customer. In many companies these activities would be described in written procedures, but one small network fulfils the same task.

STANDARD SUBNETWORKS
AN EXAMPLE OF A DESIGN DEPARTMENT PLANNING SYSTEM

Now compare the two networks which were used to provide the project examples used in Chapter 10. Each could be preceded by a standard start-up network, and each could equally well be followed by a standard clean-up network. In fact, both of these networks are derived from the type of project normally fulfilled by the same company which developed the two standard checklist networks already described in this chapter. At first sight there does not appear to be much scope for standardisation between these design networks. One project calls for the design and manufacture of a single transfer machine whilst the other needs two machines.

Nevertheless, these same projects yield a very good example of the way in which standard subnetworks can be evolved. This fact might seem even more remarkable when it is realised that the projects demonstrated in Chapter 10 were purposely over-simplified, in order that the planning steps could be shown with sufficient clarity in this book. In practice, projects for the design and supply of transfer line machinery can involve anything from one single machine to several sections of transfer line, each of which contains several machines to perform a varied set of cutting operations. Some large projects demand the provision of fifty machines, distributed along several sections of transfer. Not only are different machines often needed to perform a variety of operations, but sometimes single machines have to be fitted with cutting heads which carry out a mixture of operations at one machining station on the line.

Perhaps this situation looks hopeless as a candidate for any useful degree of standardisation. That, indeed, was the initial verdict of the actual machine tool manufacturer. The solution was discovered, by chance, when a very large order was received. The resulting network contained over 1500 activities for the control of the main design task alone. Seven sections of transfer contained, between them, some forty machines. But the network had a grouped appearance, with each machine standing out clearly from the logic. Analysis showed that it was possible to isolate small groups of design activities associated with the start of each section design, and further groups of activities which rounded off the design of the sections. Between these groups lay the designs of the machines themselves, and they still posed a serious problem.

The breakthrough came when it was realised that any machine, no matter what its function, could be classified into one which needed to be designed completely, or one which used purchased cutting heads. In general, the company policy was to design and manufacture its own milling heads, but to purchase heads for drilling and the associated operations of tapping, reaming and, in some cases, boring. It was found that, by developing one standard subnetwork for each of these machine types, any transfer line network could be synthesised from four basic subnetworks. Machines which needed a mixture of manufactured heads and purchased heads were accommodated by adding activities to one of the standard subnetworks.

Each of the four basic subnetworks is shown in Figure 12:3. In practice they are printed onto a material which has a self-adhesive backing. This allows them to be stuck onto a larger sheet very easily when the whole network is being built up. Translucent materials are used throughout, in order that dyeline prints can be taken from the whole network. For those interested, the material used for the subnetworks is "Ozakling," manufactured and supplied by Ozalid Limited.

The system uses four-digit event numbers, and it will be noticed that the last pair of numbers has already been printed onto the sheets for every event. Event numbers are converted into four figures by the addition of the last two digits from the works order number for each machine. This is made

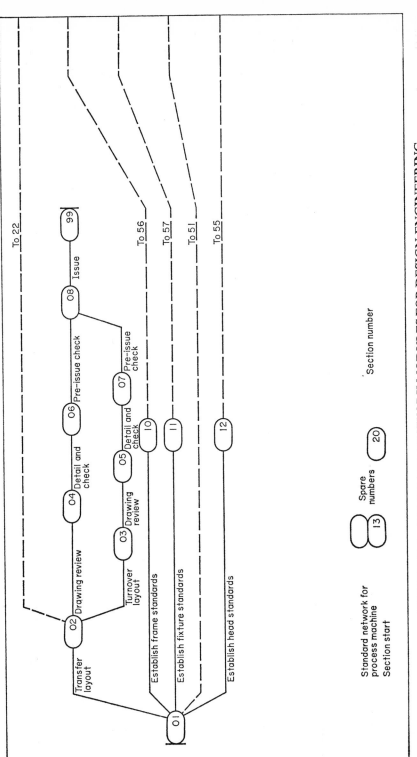

FIGURE 12:3 STANDARD NETWORK MODULES FOR DESIGN ENGINEERING
These four network sections can be used to build up complete network diagrams for controlling the design of large, special-purpose machine tool systems. Their use is illustrated in Figures 12:4 and 12:5

continued on next page

FIGURE 12:3 continued

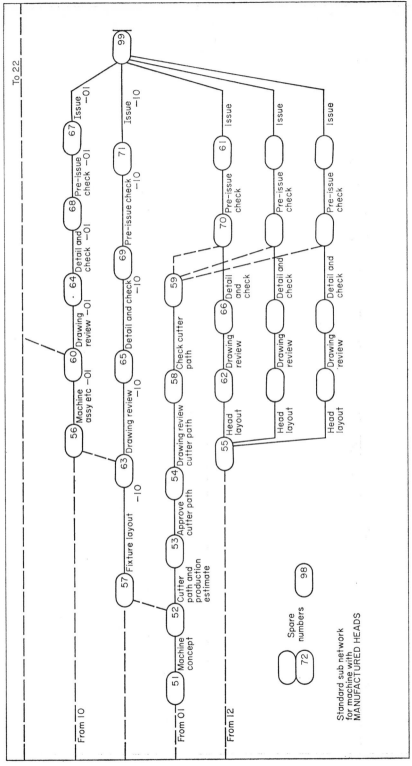

FIGURE 12:3 continued

Capacity — 22 — 23 — Foundations — 24 — Check — 25 — Issue — 26

Scheduled dates on file

Event number	Date	Event number	Date	Event number	Date	Event number	Date

27

Spare numbers

50

Standard network for process machine

Section end

FIGURE 12:3 continued

possible because every machine in a section is given a separate number. The two subnetworks for starting and finishing each section take their first pairs of event numbers from the works order number of the first machine in the section. If ever any subnetwork requires extending, in order to include additional activities, the new events will obviously not have pre-printed numbers. Some means for allocating the last two digits of each new number must be provided, in order to avoid the risk of duplicating an event number that has already been used somewhere else on the same network. This problem has been solved by printing the range of spare numbers available as a key on each subnetwork.

Now suppose that the company receives an order for a transfer line machine. The planning engineer will receive a copy of the machine specification, once the final configuration of the machine has been decided. From the specification, the engineer can determine the number of machines in the transfer section, the order in which they are to be placed along the transfer, the cutting operations and arrangement of heads and the works order number for every machine. Of course there will also be a wealth of detailed information to describe the operation, construction and performance requirements. But the planning engineer is basically concerned with the overall project content at this early planning stage.

Construction of the project network is very simple. The planner selects the appropriate number of subnetwork stick-ons and attaches them to a large sheet of tracing paper. The limited amount of space available on the page of a book does not allow sensible reproduction of a large network, and it has been necessary to choose a very small project as a demonstration. The example chosen is identical with that used as the first machine scheduled in Chapter 10. Direct comparison is therefore possible between the network drawn by conventional methods, in Figure 10:1, and that built up from the subnetworks.

In Figure 12:4 the results of the project planner's initial efforts are shown. Three standard subnetworks have been stuck onto one sheet of paper. The first subnetwork starts the section, the second represents the only machine required in the transfer section, and the final subnetwork ties up the ends for the section main design. One cylinder boring head has been specified for the machine. This will have to be specially designed and manufactured, so that the machine subnetwork which provides for manufactured heads has been used. If the section had contained more than one machine, additional subnetworks would have been positioned along the network, as indicated in Figure 12:6.

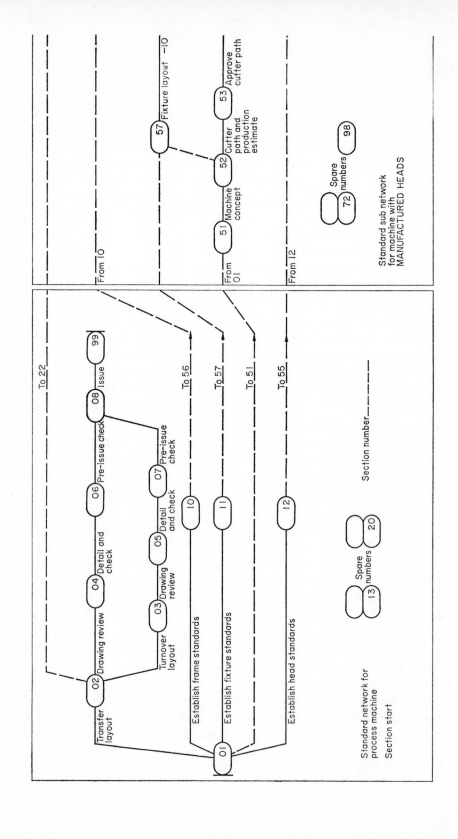

Standard network for
process machine

Standard sub network
for machine with
MANUFACTURED HEADS

Section start —⟨ ⟩— Section number

Spare
numbers {13 — 20}

Spare
numbers {72 — 98}

From 10 ... To 22

Transfer layout — 02 Drawing review — 04 Detail and check — 06 Pre-issue check — 08 Issue — 99

Turnover layout — 03 Drawing review — 05 Detail and check — 07 Pre-issue check

Establish frame standards — 10 ... To 56

Establish fixture standards — 11 ... To 57

Establish head standards — 12 ... To 55

To 51

01

From 01 — 51 Machine concept — 52 Cutter path and production estimate — 53 Approve cutter path

57 Fixture layout — 10

From 12

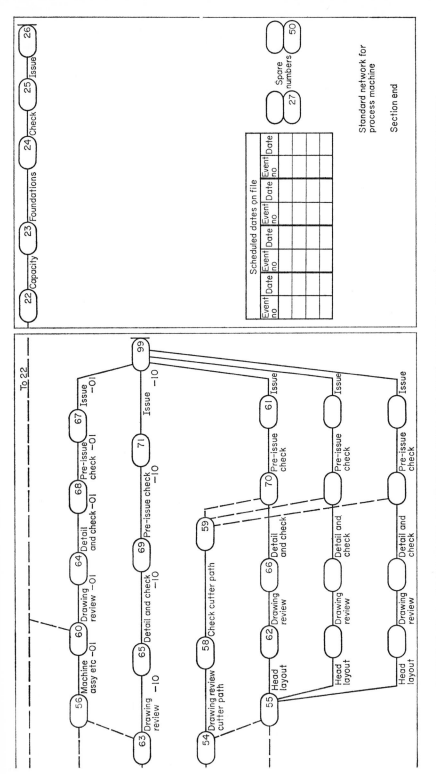

FIGURE 12:4 STANDARD NETWORK FOR MACHINE TOOL DESIGN—INITIAL PREPARATION

This diagram shows how subnetworks can be used to build up a complete arrow diagram simply by sticking them on to a sheet of tracing paper

Up to this point, technical management have not been involved at all in preparation of the project network. Much of their time has been saved. If this example had contained several machines, it is true to claim that the management time saved could amount to several hours. But the network must be shown to the project engineers in order to check that the logic is correct, and to obtain estimates for the durations and resource needs of every activity. Sometimes special constraints have to be shown, usually resulting in the addition of some strategically placed dummy activities. Suppose, for example, that a section contained four machines whose fixtures were all very similar. One machine would be chosen by the engineers for the basic design task on the fixture. All other fixtures in the section would then have their estimates made suitably short, because most of the design effort has been included in the time allowed for the first fixture. Once this planning decision has been made, however, the network logic must be amended in order to make certain that the fixtures are designed in sequence. This is achieved by leading a dummy from the finish event of the design activity for the first fixture into the start event of the next. All of the design activities for related fixtures can be linked together like a chain by this means. This technique is often followed to make certain that the final schedule will allow one single specialist engineer to carry out all tasks of one type in sequence.

No logic changes were necessary in this simple project network, other than some editing in order to remove two unwanted heads from the machine arrow diagram. The final result is shown in Figure 12:5. If the logic of this synthesised network is compared with that of the original diagram in Figure 10:1, it is seen that the two networks are substantially the same. The short-cut version is perfectly suitable for use with the computer, it is a faithful statement of the project plan, and yet it has only taken a fraction of the time needed to prepare a conventional network for the same contract.

The system which has just been described for the planning of machine tool design projects was used with considerable success in two different companies. Any project which did not fall into the transfer line category could not, obviously, be planned from the same set of standard subnetworks. This was overcome by the introduction of another range of standard networks to cover the other main machine types produced by the two companies. This enabled all the major projects to be incorporated in the multi-project resource allocation. Approximately three big projects would be in the design department at any one time, amounting to some 2500 activities. Considerable success was achieved in scheduling the work of some forty

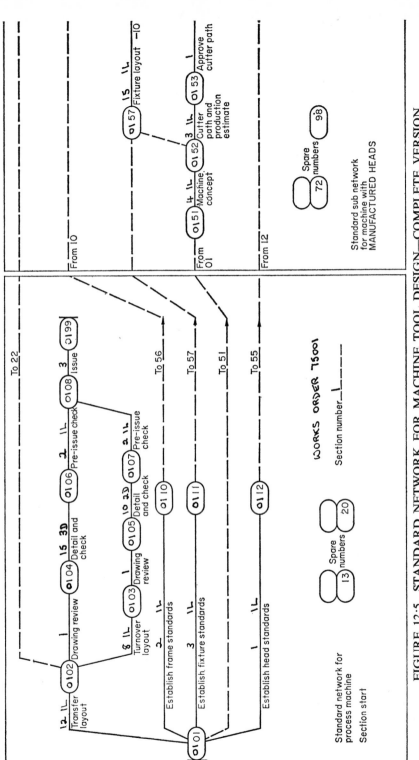

FIGURE 12:5 STANDARD NETWORK FOR MACHINE TOOL DESIGN—COMPLETE VERSION

After some editing, and the addition of event numbers and estimates, it is seen that the bones of the network shown in Figure 12:4 now carry sufficient meat to represent a working plan. In fact, this is the same project as that used for the case study in Chapter 10 (Figure 10:1). Notice that event numbers already printed on the network masters have been completed by the addition of the last two numbers from the company's works order number

continued on next page

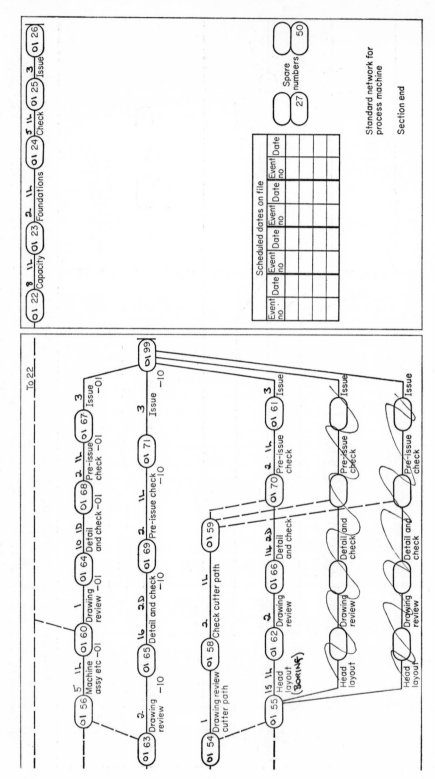

FIGURE 12:5 continued

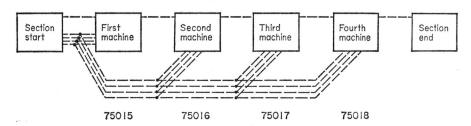

Event number prefixes					
15	15	16	17	18	15

FIGURE 12:6 BUILD UP TECHNIQUE FOR STANDARD
DESIGN NETWORKS

This diagram illustrates the way in which the four basic networks shown in Figure 12:3 can be assembled into a complete network for the design of transfer machinery containing more than one machining station. The semi-automatic system for writing in event numbers is explained here. For each event, the last two numbers are already printed onto the masters, whilst the first two are taken from the works order number for each machining station. This method rules out any risk of error through unwanted duplication

designers and a hundred draftsmen in each office. Monitoring each project on a day by day basis against the very detailed schedules produced by the computer enabled the identification of exceptions at an early stage. Corrective action by the design management was then made possible in time for the projects to be kept on their true course. As an additional bonus, it was found that progress meetings became unnecessary.

A COMPLETE MULTIPROJECT NETWORK SYSTEM USING STANDARD NETWORKS

Although the use of standard subnetworks led to a very effective short-cut method for scheduling design work, it was realised that project commitments were by no means discharged by the issue of sets of manufacturing drawings. Design costs accounted for less than 20 per cent of total project costs, leaving some 80 per cent of the total work value of each contract outside the network planning system. Once the drawings were handed over to the manufacturing departments, there was no effective method for planning production resources ahead on a true multiproject basis. This meant that the manufacture and procurement of components was not being organised in the sequence best suited to machine assembly and testing. Calculations of production manpower requirements had to be undertaken on a crude basis, with the use of graphs. Each graph took a considerable time to calculate and draw, but it quickly became outdated as one project after another started to slip behind its due date. It was therefore decided to attempt an extension of the methods proved successful for design scheduling into the larger area of manufacturing.

It is not practicable to give a completely detailed account here of the comprehensive multiproject scheduling system which resulted. In any case, many of its design features are specific to the machine tool companies themselves, and have no interest for most readers. An overall outline of the eventual solution will be given however. It is hoped that others will be able to derive encouragement from the powerful possibilities that can be opened up by the combination of network analysis, suitable computer facilities and a good deal of common sense. Many problems had to be overcome before a fully effective scheduling procedure could be claimed. Some of these problems occur whenever new planning techniques are being introduced, and the solutions presented in this chapter can probably be applied directly to a wide range of other industrial situations.

One difficulty lay in choosing the degree of detail to which networks should be drawn. At one extreme, it might have been possible to show every single component of every machine, and even to include all the machining operations. This level of detail is easily ruled out, however, when it is realised that the number of components required is not known at the planning stage of most projects. Preparation of parts lists or bills of material will determine the actual content of each machine, and that information will not be forthcoming until an advanced stage of design has been reached. Another reason for not wishing to plan into a level of detail which considers individual components is that the company's normal production control facility is better able to cope with the everyday loading of machines and allocation of priorities to individual parts and operations. The need, therefore, was to find a level of planning detail for the networking system from which production control routines could take over.

Most manufactured equipment, and many other industrial and construction projects can be split up into a series of subassemblies or major parts. It is customary for each of these subdivisions to be given its own bill of materials. Fortunately, the machine tool projects were no exception to this rule. It was therefore decided to use one standard subnetwork for the

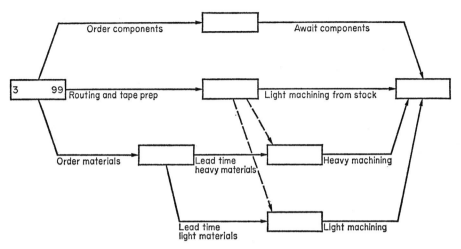

FIGURE 12:7 STANDARD MANUFACTURING NETWORK
MODULE
This module can be used for planning all activities necessary to transform
a set of manufacturing drawings and purchase specifications into a kit of
parts and components ready for an individual subassembly

provision of all the parts necessary to make up each subassembly. Activities within these subnetworks would each encompass the whole group of components required to build up the appropriate subassemblies. Much time and effort was spent in agreeing the final configuration of the basic subnetwork logic. Figure 12:7 shows the result.

Five-digit event numbering was chosen in order to avoid any danger of duplicating event numbers already allocated for the engineering design section of the same project network. Rectangles have been drawn to represent events, simply because they allow more space in which to write all five digits. All engineering events were given their fifth digit as a suffix "3." Thus an event which was previously numbered 3099 under the four-digit system became 33099 when the five-digit scheme was introduced. Figure "4" was used as the first digit for all the manufacturing events. It is seen that the first event on the subnetwork in Figure 12:7 has been given a number from the engineering series. This is easily explained. It is, in fact, *the same event* as the final event on the engineering design subnetwork for the same subassembly.

Events which are common to more than one network in this way really have the effect of combining the separate diagrams into one whole network.

And that, after all, was the aim of extending the study into the manufacturing area, namely to accomplish one comprehensive network for the whole of each project. These linking events are sometimes called *interface* events. Their use allows the production of clear arrow diagrams, uncluttered by criss-crossing dummies. Interface events can be placed anywhere on networks, and do not have to be restricted to start or finish events. The computer, because it identifies the network logic from event numbers, will not be aware of the physical distance between interface events on the separate network diagrams. It will simply recognise any two or more interface events which bear the same number as one event within a common network.

One subnetwork standard exists for each type of subassembly likely to be encountered in a process line project. All have the same logic arrangement. Only the pre-allocated event number digits differ. The arrangement is very similar to that already described for the design engineering networks. The first, fourth and fifth digits have been printed on the diagram for every event. Once again, the missing pair of digits is supplied by taking the last two digits from the relevant machine works order number. Some subassemblies, such as machining heads, can occur more than once on the same machine. A separate standard subnetwork had to be designed for each possibility, because otherwise all heads on the same machine would bear identical event numbers.

In Figure 12:8 a group of standard subnetwork stick-ons has been attached to a sheet of paper in order to constitute a complete, if simple, manufacturing network. This diagram contains all the logic necessary to plan the procurement and production of component parts required to assemble the single transfer machine used for the previous example in this chapter. At first sight the diagram appears to be not one whole network, but a series of separate small subnetworks. But extensive use of interface events will result in the eventual establishment of one complete diagram. Event numbers and estimates have been added in Figure 12:9, and when this diagram is compared with that of Figure 12:5 it is seen that all leading events on the manufacturing network interface with events that describe the issue of engineering drawings. The term "leading events" has been used here in preference to "start events" because, strictly speaking, only the engineering start events have no preceding activities. It is only the engineering start events, therefore, that the computer will identify as start events.

Every end event in Figure 12:9 represents the gathering together of a set

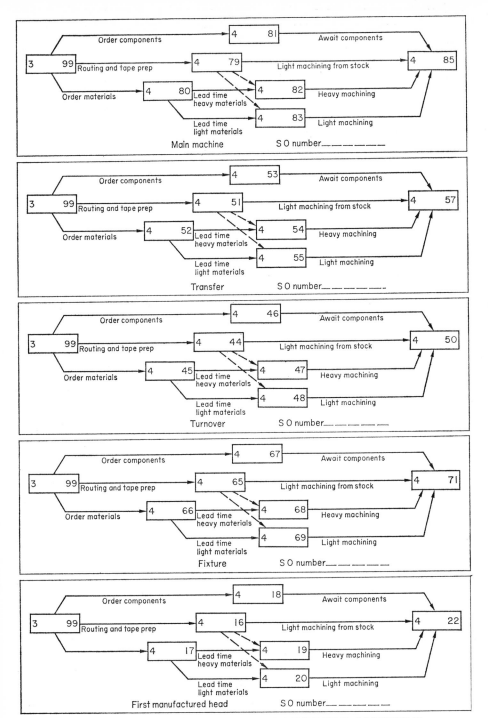

FIGURE 12:8 STANDARD MANUFACTURING NETWORK LOGIC

Here, a group of "stick-on" modules have been used to construct a simple manufacturing network. This example would be suitable for controlling the provision of all parts needed for the assembly of the project whose design activities were described by the network of Figure 12:5. The networks appear to be disconnected, but they are all associated directly with other subnetworks by the use of interface events. This process is explained in the text, in Figure 12:9

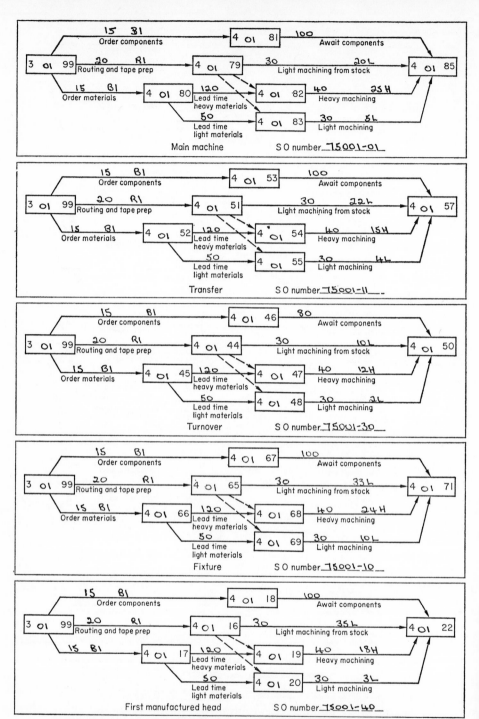

FIGURE 12:9 STANDARD MANUFACTURING NETWORK
This is the completed version of the manufacturing network first introduced in Figure 12:8. Estimates and event numbers have been added. All events which are either starts or finishes have been given event numbers which also appear on their corresponding interface events on other subnetworks. For example, it is seen that all the start events here have been given the same number, 30199. Thus, from the point of view of the computer, they become the *same* event. And on the engineering design network, the final event number was also 30199, so that this event represents not only the start of machining and procurement activities but also the completion of design

of component parts from which one subassembly can be constructed. This manufacturing network, therefore, will be followed by an assembly network which rounds off the project at the point where the machine is dispatched from the factory in fully tested condition. Every apparent end event on the manufacturing network has, therefore, a corresponding interface event on the assembly network. Compilation of the assembly networks will be described later in this chapter.

Treatment of the purchasing function

Many network analysts are content to include the procurement of raw materials and bought-out components on their networks as single activities. The descriptions "order materials" or "buy materials" are intended to cover the total time period from the decision to buy through to receipt of the goods. It may, therefore, seem surprising here that each procurement function has been allowed the apparent luxury of two activities within a standard subnetwork which purports to be cut to its barest essentials. It is seen that the preparation of purchase orders and the ensuing waiting periods for goods have been given separate activities.

The purchasing office is an indirect service function which would not normally be considered as a candidate for resource scheduling. However, it was found that there was a tendency for engineering drawing and bills of material to be scheduled for issue in small batches. Without any imposition of resource restrictions on the purchasing function the computer would proceed to schedule the preparation of purchase orders from these batches of bills of material at their earliest possible starting dates. Purchasing schedules would be produced showing large numbers of order activities starting on the same day, or at least in an impossible bunched arrangement. There was no need actually to perform these activities in this fashion because many of them possessed considerable float.

An artificial resource usage rate of "one buying unit" was applied to each order activity. This provided the computer with a basis for resource loading. The corresponding resource capacity which had to be declared in order to achieve a smooth load was found by trial and error. It could obviously not be based upon the manpower available in the buying office, because no single activity occupied a man full time. The initial level of purchasing capacity was therefore calculated in terms of buying units. An estimate was made of the total number of ordering activities that could be handled comfortably in the department simultaneously. The result was adjusted in subsequent computer runs until smooth scheduling resulted. This method of allocating purchasing resources led to some peculiar quantities in the resource tables printed out by the computer, but these were a useful barometer of the departmental workload.

When the departmental schedules were edited and sorted out from the total mass of multiproject data at the end of each computer run, it was found that the ordering activities and waiting activities for materials could be printed out on separate reports. This was made possible by the allocation of a different report code for each of the two activity types. One of the resulting schedules provided a very useful checklist for the buyers. All ordering activities were listed in priority sequence, and at a rate of working feasible to achieve within the capacity of the buying office. The other list included all the material waiting activities, listed in order of their scheduled completion dates. Once again a useful checklist resulted, this time having specific application to the role of expediting.

But the main reason for separating out the order preparation activities was linked to the cost scheduling potential of the complete multiproject system. Standard estimates for material costs were not available when the scheme was started, and these were to be a later development. However, if material costs were going to be scheduled, there had to be activities on which to hang the estimated costs. It is well known that budgetary control systems for materials should always rely on the collection of costs incurred at the time orders are written. These are the committed materials costs, and they are always available at an early stage in a project. Their build up can be monitored and checked against planned rates of expenditure. It is useless to wait until the invoices start to come in because by then it will be too late to apply any corrective actions to remedy overspending. Material costs are usually input to the computer as a complete cost estimate for an activity and not as a cost rate for a particular resource grade. The network of Figure 12:7 has been drawn to allow this method of cost input for materials.

Standard activity estimates for manufacturing subnetworks

Having achieved a scheme which allowed the construction of large manu-facturing networks in a matter of minutes, it seemed a pity that much of this advantage should be lost in the subsequent estimating process. If conventional methods were employed to gather estimates for the duration and resource needs of every activity, the lapse of several days could be expected before any network was ready for scheduling. If standard networks could be developed for the project control of non-standard projects, then why not a matching set of standard estimates? Standard estimates for some of the activities were relatively easy to establish. It was decided, for example, always to allow fifteen working days for the ordering of all the purchased components from any single bill of material. This period was considered sufficient for the purchasing department to obtain competitive quotations for some of the more expensive items.

Delivery times for purchased components, raw materials, heavy weldments, forgings and castings were at first estimated by the purchasing department. In all cases the item with the longest delivery time in the group of parts comprising one network activity must determine the overall activity duration. Until the last item has been received, there is an incomplete kit of parts from which to start assembly. However, some surprise was expressed at the lengthy periods demanded by the purchasing department. It was suspected that some inflation of delivery times had been introduced by the buyers in a ploy designed to give themselves more time for purchasing parts for future contracts. Since it was essential to work with estimates based on the true supply situation, and unclouded by prejudice or subjective influences, an independent statistical analysis of many hundreds of past orders was conducted.

Each order from the completed order files was examined by a clerk. Details of the type of material, supplier's name, weight of material, value of the order and the delivery time were noted, using short codes to save time. Entries were made directly onto computer punched card coding sheets, and a set of punched cards was then prepared. A simple program was written for the computer, enabling the data to be sorted, edited and printed out in a number of different reports. A few simple calculations were also arranged, so that the cost per pound weight of castings, for example, was calculated automatically by the computer and printed out. Although this exercise occupied some three clerks for a week, it generated results beyond those originally intended. Apart from providing valuable information on delivery times actually experienced for key items, it was also possible to build up comparative reports of suppliers' performances in respect of costs and deliveries.

To illustrate the method used to extract standard delivery estimates from the computer reports, consider one of the printed lists. This contained the data for every welded steel fabrication, printed out line by line, and arranged in ascending order of delivery time. Thus those items which were obtained within a few days appeared at the head of the list, whilst those which were received many months after being ordered were at the bottom of the list. Only one single item, right at the bottom of the list, took the length of time to procure that the purchasing department had specified as typical. The total list of weldments occupied several pages of print-out. Scanning these pages revealed that the number of items that exceeded a delivery time of thirty-five weeks to obtain was so small that they could be ignored. Those items were truly exceptions to any rule, amounting to only a handful from a total sample of over one thousand items.

Correlation between delivery time and the weight of any item was not apparent from the list. It was therefore deemed sensible to use the same delivery time estimate for weldments throughout the manufacturing networks, no matter for which subassembly they were intended. The actual delivery time chosen was some two weeks shorter than the maximum times in the list, after striking out those items at the foot of the list which were regarded as complete freaks. It was considered that any item actually arriving in the plant two weeks after the latest network date could still be accommodated in the programme. This reasoning was based on the knowiedge that the following activity, heavy machining, would have an estimated duration equal to the passage through the plant of all parts in the group. One individual part, such as a late arrival, could in fact be rushed through in a much shorter time.

Delivery times for weldments dominated the procurement time for all heavy materials, and the duration for awaiting heavy materials was therefore established. Times for machining each group of parts were found from past production records, and by consulting with the production control department. Detailed scheduling of machining, on a day by day loading basis, would be the prime concern of production control. Obviously the network scheduling system would have to allow sufficient time for every group of parts to be manufactured, but once this time had been agreed production control were bound by the scheduled dates calculated by the computer. Since these dates were to be based on a broad resource allocation of machine shop hours, the rate of working implied by the computer schedules should always enable production control to load the work within their total available capacity. The problem of individual machine bottlenecks would not, of course, be solved by the network scheduling system, but at least there would be no more unexpected total overload conditions.

Reference to the subnetwork in Figure 12:7 reveals the basis chosen for overall machine shop scheduling. Although the actual shops contained a wide variety of machines and operator skills, some fairly drastic simplification had to be accepted if the project networks were to be held within manageable proportions. Incredibly, it was found that an effective system could be built around a group of only three activities for each subassembly. These were light machining from stock raw materials, light machining from specially purchased raw materials and heavy machining from specially purchased materials. The purchased heavy materials normally consisted mainly of welded steel fabrications, castings and forgings. Man-hours, rather than machine hours were chosen for resource units. This decision was indicated because all contract cost estimates and actual cost accounting records used this basis. These machine shop man-hours were simply divided into two grades—light and heavy machining.

Nothing assists the task of project cost estimating better than the availability of comprehensive cost records containing details of actual performance achieved on previous contracts. In addition to actual costs, these records always need to show results in terms of man-hours, because labour times remain comparatively stable for similar jobs from one year to the next. Cost inflation, on the other hand, can ruin true comparison between job costs when their execution dates are separated by several years. Cost comparison is further complicated on a purely monetary basis when work is shared between factories in different countries, using currencies with fluctuating exchange rates. The people who designed the system now being described were fortunate in having access to a complete set of historical cost records for some ten years' previous work. More fortunately still, these records yielded the number of man-hours expended in both light and heavy machining for each of the subassemblies for which standard estimates had to be found.

Conversion of past cost records into usable standard resource estimating tables was a straightforward statistical process. But the short-cut method used, although by no means revolutionary, is described here because it is applicable to any company which needs to carry out a similar survey. The process, which is graphical, is best illustrated by consideration of one particular subassembly. For this purpose a single-spindle milling head has been selected. A start was made by scanning all the cost records in order to find the range of man-hours actually spent in both light and heavy machining of milling heads. From this initial search, maximum and minimum values were chosen for the graph scales.

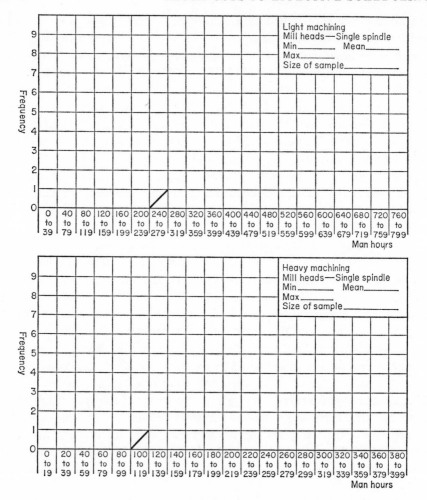

FIGURE 12:10   GRAPHICAL DERIVATION OF STANDARD
COST ESTIMATES

This diagram shows one possible method by which historical cost data
can be transformed statistically into standard tables from which resource
usages become predictable. At project level, rather than shop floor production control level, it is only necessary to consider these costs and
resources in fairly broad terms. This example has divided machining
resources into only two groups. These are heavy machining and light
machining. As with all basic estimating techniques, man-hours are used
in preference to the less stable monetary conversions. Two results have
been entered on these particular graphs to show how each past cost
record is considered and recorded as a stroke in its particular square.

Turn to Figure 12:11 to see how the patterns are evolved

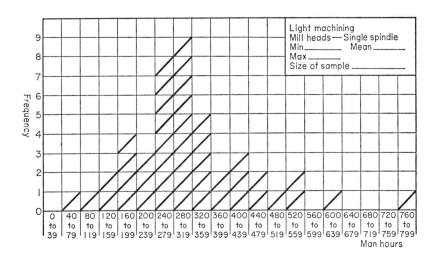

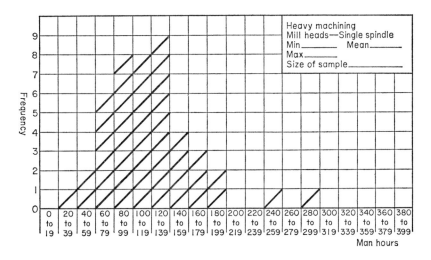

FIGURE 12:11 HISTORICAL COST HISTOGRAMS FOR MACHINE SHOP ESTIMATES

These two histograms show the man-hours that were expended on a number of past projects for single-spindle milling heads. Other histograms would be produced for all other subassemblies likely to need estimating. From the results, it is possible to estimate the number of predicted man-hours, and therefore the resource usage, for activities aimed at providing complete kits of machined parts for future mill heads

Subassembly	Number sampled	Resource category	Minimum actual hours	Maximum actual hours	Mean actual hours	Complexity	Standard estimate man-hours	Standard activity duration days	Associated usage rate per day
Standard estimates—Machine shop									
MACHINE BASES AND MAIN FRAME	156	LIGHT MACHINING	52	464	140	1 base + bedway	110	20	5·5 L
						compound slides	270	20	13·5 L
						multiple slides + wings	360	24	15·0 L
		HEAVY MACHINING	51	762	252	1 base + bedway	190	25	7·6 H
						compound slides	310	30	12·3 H
						multiple slides + wings	550	35	15·7 H
TRANSFER BASES AND MECHANISM	62	LIGHT MACHINING	182	1620	584	single machine + loading	400	25	16·0 L
						3 machines	800	30	26·4 L
						7 machines	1400	40	35·0 L
		HEAVY MACHINING	178	1322	305	single machine + loading	150	25	6·0 H
						3 machines	350	40	8·7 H
						7 machines	1000	40	25·0 H
MILLING HEAD WITH ONE OR TWO SPINDLES	147	LIGHT MACHINING	78	520	196	Small (0-5 HP)	130	25	5·2 L
						Medium 5-20 HP	210	28	7·5 L
						Large 20-100 HP	315	35	9·0 L
		HEAVY MACHINING	50	811	118	Small 0-5 HP	75	25	3·0 H
						Medium 5-20 HP	120	35	3·4 H
						Large 20-100 HP	235	45	5·2 H
		LIGHT				Small	100	20	5 L
						me		20	

FIGURE 12:12   STANDARD ESTIMATING TABLE FOR MACHINE SHOP ACTIVITIES

Here are the figures which result when the histograms of the type shown in Figure 12:11 are analysed and interpreted. Although these figures may be inaccurate for one particular assembly, they have been proved in practice to give consistent results for a complete project, lying within ±5 per cent of the most careful estimates made by a normal estimating department

The graphs themselves were produced in the form of frequency distribution histograms, but they involved no calculations. Once the scale range had been chosen, two sheets of graph paper were prepared for the milling heads; one for light and the other for heavy machining. The horizontal axis of each graph was divided into a series of grouped values which ranged from the minimum number of man-hours expected to the maximum. This had the effect of splitting the pages into columns. Figure 12:10 illustrates the arrangement.

With a pencil in one hand and a pile of cost records in the other, a clerk was then set to work. Every time a cost record for a single-spindle milling head was turned up, the clerk placed a diagonal stroke on the graph paper according to the number of light and heavy machining man-hours recorded.

Thus, for example, a head which previously took recorded times of 251 light machining hours and 119 heavy hours would have resulted in the entries marked in on Figure 12:10.

When the pile of cost records had been exhausted, several hundred milling heads had been found and their actual labour times entered on the graphs. Distribution curves were formed in this way, and a typical result is shown in Figure 12:11. From the patterns that were built up, it was possible to forecast, with a certain degree of courage, the number of man-hours necessary to assign for the light and heavy machining of future milling heads. This process was repeated for all subassemblies. For the expenditure of only one clerical man-week, a total range of estimating tables was evolved. The general content and arrangement of these standard estimating tables is displayed in Figure 12:12.

These simple techniques were extended to provide sets of standard estimating tables for all other types of machine tool project which were to be included in the total multiproject scheduling system. Application of standard estimating tables on such a broad basis places the method into a class of work that can be fairly described as crude but effective. Subsequent results from the computer schedules yielded total project labour estimates which consistently fell within 5 per cent of estimates obtained from more lengthy and conventional methods. When the results did not agree, it was often found that the original estimates were wrong, and the short-cut estimates nearer the mark.

Relationship between standard estimates for durations and resources

When an estimate is made for the resources needed to accomplish any activity, the result must be expressed on the network and in the computer input as a rate of usage per standard network unit of duration. Thus, if activity durations have been expressed in terms of working days, and a particular activity has a duration of five days, then a resource statement of two units means that two units will be needed for each of the five days. Or, in other words, an activity which has a total work content estimated at ten man-days and a duration of five days must have this estimate shown on the network as a resource rate of two men per day. The work content of any activity is equal to the product of the activity duration and the rate of resource usage. These conditions should, by now, be apparent from the number of case studies and examples already discussed.

The total multiproject scheduling system encompassed several departments however, and each of these applied its own working rules. The engineers and draftsmen worked for a nominal eight-hour day, whilst the machine shops operated one, two or even three shifts each day. Whereas the engineering department was staffed for five working days in each week, the machine shops were busy for six days each week. As an additional complication, the assembly department, the networks for which are described later in this chapter, worked a two-shift system. Engineering estimates and assembly estimates were made in man-days, whilst machining estimates were obtained in man-hours. From this complete hotch-potch of different units, some order had to be derived if the combined networks were to be scheduled together.

Duration estimates were standardised so that each unit of estimate referred to one complete calendar day, with five working days allowed in a full working week. An estimate of one for an engineering activity implied one eight-hour stint, but the same figure 1 applied for a machine shop activity must include all shifts worked within the calendar day. If two men were scheduled for an assembly activity, where two shifts were to be worked, this implied that two men would be employed during the twenty-four-hour period, or one on each shift. The extra weekday worked by the machine shop could have been allowed for by increasing the declared capacity on each of the five scheduled days by 20 per cent, but it was decided to ignore the existence of this extra day because some reserve capacity had to be left out of the schedule in order to cope with modifications and re-work. This ommission of weekend capacity, together with a general disregard for overtime capacity is a sensible rule that is usually applied to any scheduling process.

Now consider one activity for the machining of a group of components for a subassembly. Suppose that the estimated duration of this activity is eight weeks, shown on the network as forty working days. This is the time allowed for all of the parts needed for the subassembly to flow through the shop, from cut-off to final inspection. Some parts will only take a few days to make the journey, whilst others must be given a few weeks in order to accommodate lengthy operations such as heat treatment. Resource estimates will have to be made in man-hours, to accord with the units used in management systems and the standard estimating tables. If the total machining content of the work package for this subassembly needed eighty man-hours in the light machine shop, then a resource usage rate of $2L$ would give the necessary product of rate multiplied by duration. But what if the work content only amounted to sixty hours? Then the resource rate would have to be expressed as $1\frac{1}{2}L$ in order to achieve the correct duration/resource rate product. Transit times between different operations and queueing times at certain machines could even give rise to a total work content for a group of parts which represented a rate of working less than one man-hour per day. The computer program only allowed the input of whole resource units.

This problem was overcome quite simply by applying a common factor of ten to all machine shop resource units. Both the estimates and stated capacities were multiplied by ten, so that the units became, in effect, tenths of man-hours. The only drawback to this solution was that the computer reports for machine shop resources also came out ten times too big, and this had to be borne in mind when the reports were used. Application of this factor did not destroy the scheduling validity, however, because it was used to multiply both the estimates and the stated capacities.

Notice that a constant rate of resource usage has been specified for all activities in the system. But it is well known that if a group of parts is loaded onto a machine shop, the rate of working on that group of parts will be anything but constant. In fact, one can expect a slow start, with first one part and then another being picked up as machines become available from other work. After a few weeks, the working rate will reach a peak, after which there will be a gradual decline until the last parts have reached stores. It would have been possible to simulate this condition for every machining activity. Current computer programs for resource allocation from networks usually do allow for the input of resource usage rates that can be varied along the duration of any activity. But this multiproject system, in full operation, was going to contain some 10 000 activities. Any complication to the input data had to be avoided. In any case, it became apparent that the large number of activities involved would give rise to an integration process leading to a simulation of the true load curve shape for each major project. This argument is clarified in Figure 12:13.

Subnetworks for machine assembly

Once all the problems encountered in the search for engineering and manufacturing subnetworks had been overcome, attention was turned to the assembly department in order to complete the inclusion of all major departments within the multiproject system. No new difficulties were experienced, and the solution proved to be very similar to that found for engineering

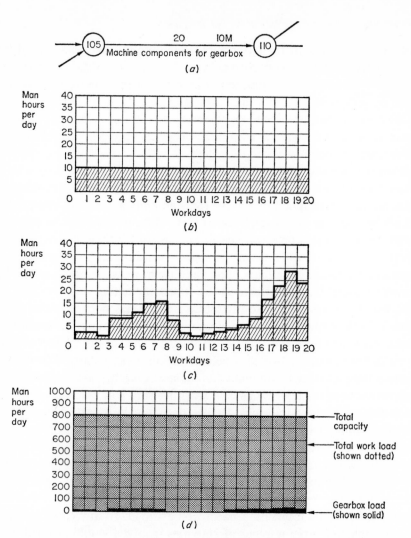

FIGURE 12:13 VALIDITY OF USING RATE CONSTANT
RESOURCE ESTIMATES

In (a) a small portion of a network is shown. The activity is seen to need
ten machine shop units for twenty days. This implies that, in this case,
ten man-hours will be spent each day for twenty days. In the actual
situation, it is most unlikely that such a constant rate of working could
be expected. Far from the pattern of rate constant usage shown in diagram (b), it would not be surprising to encounter a pattern more like that
of (c). But it is not necessary to attempt to plan for such daily variations
in work load on one particular activity. If this group of gearbox components is viewed in relation to the total number of parts being conducted
through the machine shop, then it can be appreciated (diagram (d))
that the many small activities will jostle with each other and produce a
smooth overall pattern. The responsibility for ensuring that a smooth
pattern is scheduled lies not with project control, but with the day to day
production control systems applied at shop floor level

design. Interface events were again used to improve network clarity. All assembly events were numbered within the common five-digit system but the figure "6" was used as the identifying first digit. The only new feature, not shared by networks for other departments, was that many assembly activities need more than one resource category at the same time. For example, certain activities demand the presence of mechanical fitters, pipefitters and wiremen simultaneously. This presented no problem, because the computer program was able to accept multiple resources for any activity.

Figure 12:14 shows the assembly network constructed for the project used as an example throughout the first parts of this chapter. It comprises a "backbone," which caters for the assembly of the transfer mechanism and machine bases. For every machining station along the transfer line there is a corresponding subnetwork which connects with the backbone by the use of common interface events. Other interface events are provided which link the entire assembly network with the manufacturing network, and so, indirectly, back to the engineering design network. Two versions of the subnetwork for a machining station were designed. One of these is shown in Figure 12:14. The other was almost identical, except that it was intended for use with machines that used purchased heads which did not need sub-assembly before fitting to the main machine. Networks for the assembly of machines outside the transfer line category were drawn as a separate range of standards. These completed the subnetwork design study, and resulted in a set of standards from which any company project could be included in the multiproject schedules.

Summary of multiproject scheduling from standard network modules
Perhaps the best way to appreciate the advantages of using standard subnetworks and standard estimates is to imagine the situation in the company when an order is received for a new large transfer machine project. On the day when work is authorised to start, a standard preliminary design network is printed from the existing master drawing and handed to the newly appointed project manager. This preliminary network serves as a useful checklist and work schedule for approximately the first three weeks of the new project. A point of interest here is that the work represented by all the activities on the preliminary network does not incur heavy costs and yet it can make a significant contribution to the duration of the critical path of the entire project. This work comprises all the start-up activities which must be cleared out of the way before main design forces can be assigned to

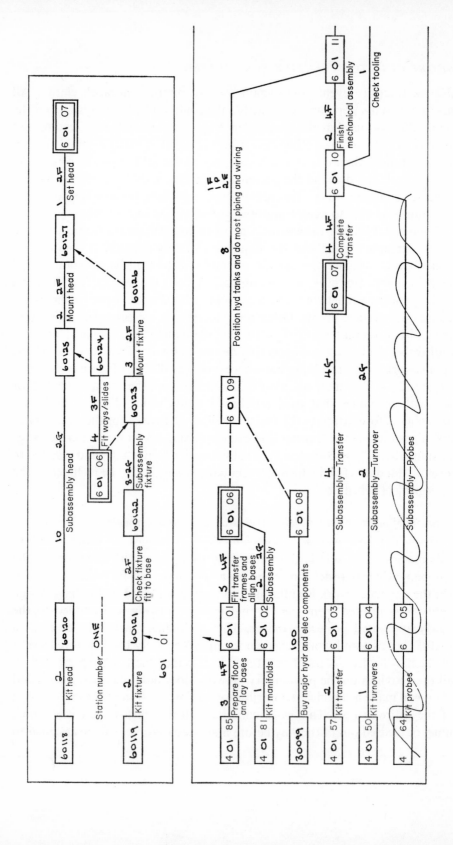

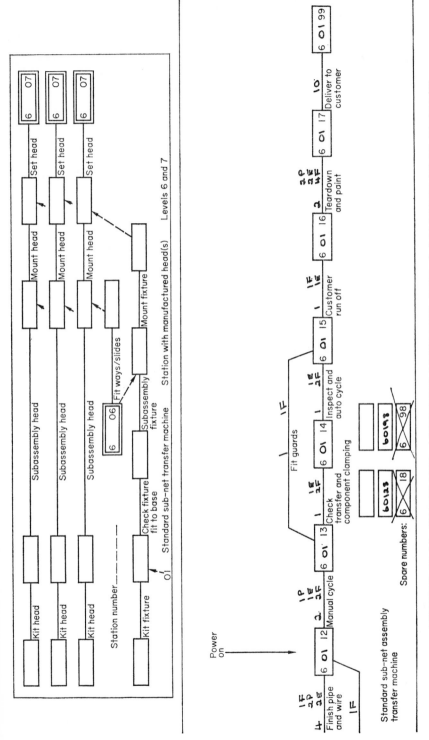

FIGURE 12:14 STANDARD ASSEMBLY NETWORK FOR A MACHINE TOOL PROJECT

This standard network shows all assembly activities needed to complete the last stage of the machine tool example that provided all the other standard network diagrams in this chapter. Once again, it is composed from a series of stick-on modules. The inset shows the standard module for a machine station, before editing

the project against a secure foundation for effective technical and commercial management. When market competition has forced the company into promising project completion at a very optimistic time, there is an understandable temptation to circumvent these early tasks and rush straight on into main design without adequate preparation. This approach can result in time and money lost later in scrapped drawings. In fact, it is sometimes justifiable, against all normal conventions, to accept risk by carrying out most of the preparatory work before a formal contract is made. The risk may be very small, amounting to only a few man-weeks cost. The reward may be a saving of three weeks total project time on a contract valued in millions of pounds.

Towards the end of the preliminary design period a finalised version of the machine specification will emerge, together with a plan showing the general disposition of individual machines and cutting heads along each section of the transfer line. From the information provided by these documents the network analyst is able to synthesise a network diagram for the complete project, using the range of standard network modules available to him. Estimates for the resource needs and durations of most activities can be derived from standard estimates. The entire network for main design, manufacture and assembly might contain some 2500 activities, but its initial preparation needs no special drawing or tracing effort. Within a day or so of the specification issue, a complete network diagram can be put before the project manager for his approval. Instead of a lengthy planning meeting lasting several days and involving many senior men, engineering involvement can be limited to a few hours' scrutiny and direction from the project manager.

Data coding is helped considerably by recourse to coding sheets in which much of the data is pre-printed. This is made possible because of the large degree of standardisation of activity descriptions and other data. In fact, for every standard subnetwork there is a corresponding standard coding sheet. Coding and card punching might take two days. As soon as the cards have been punched and verified they are run through a local computer where a simple program is used to arrange the automatic preparation of a set of report cards for the project. One card is produced for every activity being input, with the exception of dummies. These report cards are filed away until they are needed to report the completion of activities later in the project. It is convenient to have both decks of cards sorted into sequence of preceding event numbers, in order that individual cards can be found quickly.

By carrying out a strict routine of regular progress monitoring on all other projects, the completion of activities is picked up on a continuous basis. When any activity is finished, it is crossed out on a master control print of the appropriate network diagram. At the same time, the report card for that activity is found in the project report card file, and transferred to the computer input card file. Thus the update file is not left for preparation until the actual time when the computer run becomes due, but is instead assembled gradually as progress information is gathered. This procedure greatly reduces the amount of work necessary when each set of data is prepared for an update. When all the cards have been punched for the new project, therefore, most of the update cards for existing projects are already available. It is only necessary to choose a time-now date, and prepare a small number of punched cards for every project to report activities that are actually in progress, estimating their remaining duration from time-now.

The total combination of short-cut methods has included the use of standard subnetwork modules, standard data coding sheets, standard estimating tables and a complete set of pre-punched cards for reporting activities completed. These techniques have reduced the overall project planning effort to a level which can be accommodated within a department comprising only two permanent members. Equally important, the time needed for preparation of an updated schedule is reduced to a matter of a few days. None of the powerful benefits of multiproject scheduling is lost. Within approximately one week of the appearance of a full specification for the new project, management is provided with a comprehensive set of schedules. Each report can be used as a basis for management decision or executive action with a degree of confidence impossible to achieve by manual methods of calculation.

Although many thousands of network activities have been considered by the computer in arriving at the printed results, flexibility for rescheduling has been maintained at a very high level. In fact, the computer file can be regarded as a "model" of the company's total project fulfilment capacity. This model can be used for testing the probable effects of management decisions on future project achievement. Decisions to change manpower levels can, for example, be tested. If the marketing department has to choose between two or more possible orders, it is possible to prepare very simple networks to represent each order and then introduce them into the computer one at a time in order to test their interaction with the existing planned program. In order to safeguard the current working schedule files, all of these tests would normally be conducted on a specially prepared copy of the original file, made on request by the computer department or bureau.

Typical list of reports resulting from a schedule update

The total range of reports possible from a multiproject schedule update is enormous because of the number of permutations and combinations of data that the computer can produce. Obviously it is important to limit the amount of printed output to manageable proportions. There is no universal solution that can be used to specify a list of reports which could serve every company and all project situations. As an example, however, consider the machine tool company once again. Their new project has been input to the computer along with update information for all other current projects. In return, the following series of reports was generated.

1   A list of all unfinished activities, for all projects, scheduled according to available resources, but time limited within the scheduled target completion dates assigned. This list was divided up into separate projects by the computer, using the subproject codes for sorting.

Since the total list contained many thousands of activities, it was too big for general distribution. It was therefore further subdivided, so that each department received only the activities for which it was directly responsible. In this case the computer used the report codes assigned to each activity for sorting.

Thus each department received a separate list of activities for each project. These project lists only contained a few activities each, and were very convenient to use. In order to make them as useful as possible, the activities on each list were printed out in order of their shop order numbers.

As an example, one such list is shown in Figure 12:15. This is the schedule for the assembly shop foreman for subproject 15, corrected at an update referenced to a time-now of 29 October 1969. The assembly foreman would have a similar schedule for every other current project, and he knows that the schedule has been prepared with due regard to all other project priorities and his own department's resources. Although some twelve months elapsed between the time-now date and planned working dates, when the time arrived for the project to start it was found that this early schedule was still valid. The main benefit from planning so far ahead, however, is not so much in the preparation of detailed activity lists that might be rendered invalid by later schedule updates. Indeed, the assembly foreman will be far more concerned with activity schedules for projects actually undergoing assembly, or due for

- OVERALL PROJECT SCHEDULE

RUN 1   TIME NOW IS 29OCT69

ALL ACTIVITIES EXCLUDING DUMMIES   SHOP ORDER NO./REPORT CODE

S/P	PREC EVENT	SUCC EVENT	REPORT CODE	SHOP ORDER NO.	TASK DESCRIPTION	REM FLOAT	DUR	SCHED START	SCHED FINISH	EARLIEST START	LATEST FINISH
15	30142	40017	ASSY	69200-00	PREPARE ASSEMBLY AREA	1	2	23OCT70	26OCT70	23OCT70	27OCT70
15	40038	60013	ASSY	69200-00	S/A SPDL+QUILLS VERT	15	5	27OCT70	02NOV70	27OCT70	23NOV70
15	40071	60013	ASSY	69200-00	CMPLETE ALL MECH WORK		8	04JAN71	13JAN71	04JAN71	13JAN71
15	60001	30142	ASSY	69200-00	CLEAR ASSEMBLY SPACE	1	2	21OCT70	22OCT70	21OCT70	23OCT70
15	60006	60013	ASSY	69200-00	CMPLETE MACHINE FRAME	1	2	13NOV70	16NOV70	13NOV70	17NOV70
15	60009	60010	ASSY	69200-00	SCRAPE IN RAIL SLIDES		6	03DEC70	10DEC70	02DEC70	1CDEC70
15	60016	60017	ASSY	69200-00	INSPECTION-CHECK LIST	5	1	17FEB71	23FEB71	17FEB71	23FEB71
15	60017	60018	ASSY	69200-00	CUSTOMERDEMONSTRATION	1	1	24FEB71	24FEB71	24FEB71	24FEB71
15	60018	60019	ASSY	69200-00	DOWEL DISMANTLE+PAINT		1	25FEB71	04MAR71	25FEB71	04MAR71
15	60019	60020	ASSY	69200-00	TRANSPORT TO CUSTOMER	1	1	05MAR71	05MAR71	05MAR71	05MAR71
15	40071	60012	ASSY	69200-02	POSITION CONTROL GEAR	37	10	10NOV70	11NOV70	10NOV70	07JAN71
15	60012	60014	ASSY	69200-02	CARRY CUT MOST WIRING	37	10	12NOV70	25NOV70	12NOV70	21JAN71
15	60014	60015	ASSY	69200-02	COMPLETE ELECT WIRING	6		22JAN71	29JAN71	22JAN71	29JAN71
15	60015	60016	ASSY	69200-02	CHECKOUT ALL CONTROLS		12	01FEB71	16FEB71	01FEB71	16FEB71
15	40069	60013	ASSY	69200-03	FIT HYDRAULICS + LUBE	37	6	10NOV70	17NOV70	10NOV70	13JAN71
15	60013	60014	ASSY	69200-03	FINISH HYDRAULIC+LUBE		5	14JAN71	21JAN71	14JAN71	21JAN71
15	40070	60013	ASSY	69200-05	FIT COOLANT SYSTEM	38	5	16NOV70	19NOV70	10NOV70	13JAN71
15	40076	40079	ASSY	69200-10	SUB ASSEMBLY FIXTURE	27	12	04NOV70	19NOV70	27OCT70	31DEC70
15	40079	60014	ASSY	69200-17	ATTACH SUPPLY CARRIER	12	2	04JAN71	05JAN71	04JAN71	21JAN71
15	40082	40079	ASSY	69200-17	S/ASSY SUPPLY CARRIER	28	4	13NOV70	18NOV70	27OCT70	31DEC70
15	40002	60008	ASSY	69200-20	FIT TABLES TO MACHINE	1	2	17NOV70	19NOV70	17NOV70	20NOV70
15	40017	40089	ASSY	69200-20	LAY DOWN MACHINE BEDS	1	7	27OCT70	04NOV70	27OCT70	05NOV70
15	40086	40002	ASSY	69200-20	SUB ASSEMBLY - TABLES	5	8	30OCT70	10NOV70	20OCT70	17NOV70
15	40089	60003	ASSY	69200-20	SETUP MACHINE COLUMNS	1	1	05NOV70	09NOV70	05NOV70	10NOV70
15	40013	60002	ASSY	69200-21	S/ASSEMBLY JOHNSON DR	7	6	27OCT70	03NOV70	27OCT70	12NOV70
15	60002	40002	ASSY	69200-21	FINAL ASSY JOHNSON DR	3	3	10NOV70	12NOV70	05NOV70	17NOV70
15	40005	40002	ASSY	69200-24	S/ASSY TABLE FEED BOX	8	8	27OCT70	05NOV70	27OCT70	17NOV70
15	40005	40046	ASSY	69200-30	S/ASSEMBLY-CORNER BKT	9	8	02NOV70	11NOV70	27OCT70	24NOV70
15	40003	40002	ASSY	69200-30	S/ASSEMBLY-CROSSBRACE	1	6	02NOV70	09NOV70	27OCT70	10NOV70
15	40044	60008	ASSY	69200-30	S/ASSEMBLY CROSS RAIL		10	09NOV70	20NOV70	27OCT70	20NOV70
15	40046	40009	ASSY	69200-30	C/BKT C/SHAFT+R/LEVEL			24NOV70	02DEC70	24NOV70	02DEC70
15	50055	60003	ASSY	69200-30	SUB ASSEMBLY DIST BOX	3	8	27OCT70	05NOV70	27OCT70	10NOV70
15	50003	60006	ASSY	69200-30	FIT CROSSBRACE TO M/C	1	3	10NOV70	12NOV70	10NOV70	13NOV70
15	60008	40046	ASSY	69200-30	MOUNT RAIL ON MACHINE		3	23NOV70	24NOV70	20NOV70	24NOV70
15	40051	60003	ASSY	69200-34	S/A RAIL+HD FEEDBOXES	28	8	27OCT70	05NOV70	27OCT70	1CNOV70
15	40058	40079	ASSY	69200-40	SUB ASSEMBLY PENDANT		3	13NOV70	18NOV70	13NOV70	13NOV70
15	40036	50005	ASSY	69200-43	S/A POWER QU ADJ VERT	10	5	03NOV70	09NOV70	27OCT70	23NOV70
15	60005	60010	ASSY	69200-50	S/ASSEMBLY VERT HEADS	13		24NOV70	10DEC70	24NOV70	1CDEC70
15	60010	60011	ASSY	69200-50	MOUNT VERTICAL HEADS		8	11DEC70	16DEC70	11DEC70	16DEC70
15	60011	40079	ASSY	69200-50	SCRAPE IN VERT HEADS	8	7	17DEC70	31DEC70	17DEC70	31DEC70
15	40061	60013	ASSY	69200-67	SUB ASSY RT ANGLE ATT	35	10	06NOV70	19NOV70	27OCT70	13JAN71
15	40029	40079	ASSY	69200-68	S/A OFFSET SLOTTG ATT	33	4	04NOV70	11NOV70	27OCT70	31DEC70
15	40033	40079	ASSY	69200-69	S/ASSY ARBCR SUPPORTS	31	6	06NOV70	13NOV70	27OCT70	31DEC70
15	40055	40079	ASSY	69200-72	SUB ASSY END MILL ATT	31		06NOV70	13NOV70	27OCT70	31DEC70

FIGURE 12:15 EXAMPLE OF A COMPUTER REPORT FROM STANDARD NETWORK MULTIPROJECT RESOURCE ALLOCATION

The report shown here is one from a series of reports produced on an IBM/360/40 computer, using the K and H Business Consultants' CPM/RPSM program. It is an extract from one project, showing only those activities needed for assembly. Twenty other projects were scheduled simultaneously, all of them planned from standard networks

assembly within a few weeks. But this particular example does serve to illustrate the degree of care which is possible in planning future resource needs. It is comforting to know that the resource tables associated with this report have been based on such a careful examination of data. Plans for departmental expansion or contraction can be put in hand with confidence, and without last-minute haste.

2   A list of all unfinished activities, similar in most respects to that described for report 1. The only difference was that the report given to each department for every project was arranged with the activities listed in order of their scheduled start dates instead of shop order numbers. These reports were therefore complementary to report 1, providing each departmental foreman or manager with a cross-indexed list of activities for each project.
3   A separate resource usage table for each project. The day by day number of men needed from each resource category was printed out against calendar dates. Daily and cumulative costs of the scheduled resources were also included on the tables, calculated by the computer from a specified cost rate for each type of resource. The cumulative cost shown on the last working day of each project provided an estimate of the total labour cost. By plotting the daily cost totals on graphs, predictions were obtained of the rate of expenditure that should be maintained in order to secure the planned rate of progress. Actual costs were monitored and compared with these curves.
4   A total company resource table. Here, the available level declared for each type of resource was printed out against calendar dates. Also shown, side by side with the available levels, was the combined number of resources necessary to meet the total company project commitments.

By scanning down each column of resource usage it was possible to see forthcoming periods of overload or underload in any department. The trends displayed on these tables allowed management to take decisions in time for resulting actions to be effective. Subcontract facilities could be alerted in time for them to be reserved in order to cope during overload periods. Any fall-off in total labour requirements indicated not only the need for new orders but also the best practical time for fitting them in.

Any one from a number of available computer programs could have been chosen to carry out the data processing for this system. In fact, the CPM/RPSM program of *K* and *H* Business Consultants was adopted, with great success, on a bureau basis. With the exception of Figure 12:15, illustrations of the actual reports are not included in this chapter because the examples provided in Chapter 10 were also derived from the *K* and *H* program and they are very similar in general format.

COMPUTER-ASSISTED PREPARATION OF NETWORKS

Library subnetworks

Data can be stored as a series of visual images on sheets of paper in a filing cabinet. It can also be stored as a series of magnetic or other physical quantities within the file or "memory" of a computer. Just as the standard subnetworks for a multiproject system can be stored as drawings on sheets of paper, so they can be held instead within the computer file. The techniques are somewhat advanced, and definitely not recommended for beginners. They also carry certain disadvantages. Chief among these is the difficulty of making changes to any of the standard information held on file. If it is necessary, for example, to input the duration of most activities or to carry out extensive editing, the amount of data which has to be written onto coding sheets and punched onto cards in order to effect the changes may be just as great as if the networks were input afresh, and there might also exist a higher risk of error.

One example of a library subnetwork application is shown in Figure 12:16. It is based upon techniques employed in the project planning department of Industrial Development and Construction Limited, who make use of the bureau service offered by BARIC from Kidsgrove in Staffordshire. Resource scheduling is not used, but the computer facilities at Kidsgrove are fully capable of carrying out resource planning, if required, along the lines of the other systems demonstrated in Chapters 9 and 10. An ICL KDF9 computer is used.

In Figure 12:16(*a*), part of a network for a construction project is shown. Many of the activities in a construction network are predictable in the sense that similar activities can be expected to occur on networks for other construction projects. This is true, for instance, of activity 140,150. It is quite usual to have an activity labelled "Brickwork to damp proof course." But whenever this activity does crop up it is also customary to consider some of the associated tasks, such as the procurement and delivery of materials. Indeed, whenever the bricklaying activity is needed it can always be assumed that it must form part of a small subnetwork of activities necessary to provide direct support to the bricklaying operation. One interpretation of this subnetwork is shown in Figure 12:16(*b*).

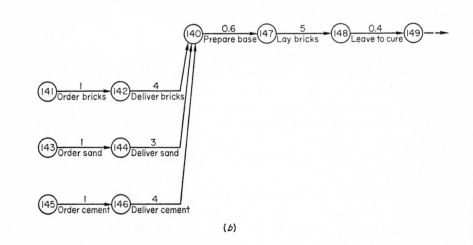

(a)

(b)

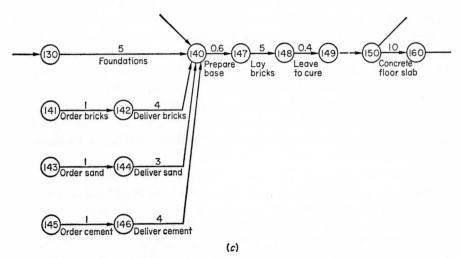

(c)

FIGURE 12:16 LIBRARY SUBNETWORKS

Just as standard subnetworks can be carried on paper stick-ons, so they can be stored within the computer itself, by means of magnetic tape or some other device. The method shown here is used by Industrial Development and Construction Limited (IDC) at Stratford-on-Avon, using the BARIC bureau's KDF9 computer. The network portion at (a) shows the network as it would be drawn by the planner. Within the computer, the subnetwork of (b) is already stored, and the use of the event number 140 automatically causes the computer to convert the simple diagram of (a) into the more detailed version shown at (c)

In the subnetwork version, the original activity 140,150 has been expanded into three activities 140,147; 147,148; and 148,149. In addition, six activities have been appended at the front end to cover the supply of materials. These six leading activities do not enter the logic of the larger network, but stem from the three start events 141; 143; and 145. The relationship between the subnetwork and the main network is shown in Figure 12:16(*c*), where it is seen that the subnetwork has been fitted into the main diagram.

Predictability of the subnetwork pattern is sufficiently assured to warrant its treatment as standard. It follows that the planner will seek some method for avoiding the need to redraw this pattern every time a new project network is produced. One method open to him is to use pre-printed adhesive network modules, similar to those described earlier in this chapter. However, the problem was solved at IDC by actually storing the patterns within the computer files. For every suitable type of construction activity likely to be needed on future projects a corresponding subnetwork was designed. Each subnetwork was stored in the computer, complete with its standard event numbers, duration estimates, descriptions and departmental reporting codes. The computer was programmed to recognise any subnetwork from specific event numbers. In the example given, for instance, the occurrence of event number 140 in the network input automatically caused the computer to change the network as shown in Figure 12:16(*a*) to that shown in Figure 12:16(*c*).

The segment of main network shown in Figure 12:16(*a*), therefore, represents several library subnetworks comprising altogether many more activities than it is necessary to draw. Event 150, for example, would cause another library to be extracted by the computer from its file and added into the basic network for the project. Since the leading event numbers of activities on the main network are in general associated with particular library subnetworks, one has to be careful in numbering the network and make use of dummies in order to ensure that the correct numbers can be used. This explains the existence of a dummy 149,150. The number 150 has been reserved for the start of the subnetwork needed for concreting the floor slab. It could not, therefore, be used as the last event number of the subnetwork for laying bricks up to damp proof course height.

This account describes only the bare outline of the use that IDC make of library subnetworks. By using this technique each new project can be planned with a network diagram that only need contain a small fraction of the total number of activities actually considered by the computer during time analysis. Output reports are fully detailed, with comprehensive schedules for every department. Several other companies use the concept of library networks, and all of the computer systems mentioned in this book that are capable of resource allocation can also accept library networks. Any reader who wishes to explore the use of library techniques is advised to become familiar first with the straightforward use of input techniques. Once full proficiency has been achieved, an approach can be made to a suitable bureau for guidance. But it is always wise to consider the use of paper stick-on subnetworks as an alternative, especially when the subnetworks are not perfectly standard and need frequent editing or data changes.

Digital plotters

It would be very pleasant indeed if the last section of this chapter could be devoted to a description of a computer facility capable of taking over the complete role of network preparation. Unfortunately this state of technology is not yet reality, and unlikely to become so for a considerable time. One really has got to start any network planning exercise by picking up a sheet of paper and producing some sort of arrow diagram. Only by this means can the planner evolve his logic and ensure that the network is a faithful representation of the intended plan of campaign.

Mention should be made here, however, of the use to which digital plotting machines can be put in this connection. These machines are capable of plotting a series of points on paper to produce graphs or diagrams from the results of computer calculations. Each point on the curve, or each element of a diagram is made by a stylus. The stylus is positioned on the paper according to a pair of co-ordinates which dictate its location with respect to X and Y axes. It is possible to arrange for such machines to plot out the results of a network time analysis in the form of an arrow diagram, complete with all activity descriptions. Earliest and latest event times can be included on the diagrams, making them very useful schedule documents.

Before any automatic network drafting can take place, however, it is necessary to input the network diagram to the computer in the form of punched cards or tape. The best starting point for preparing coding sheets for punching instructions is a network diagram. It follows that any diagram that the plotter can produce can only take place practicably after the network has been drawn by hand in the first place. It is also unfortunately true that the conversion of network data into co-ordinates from which the

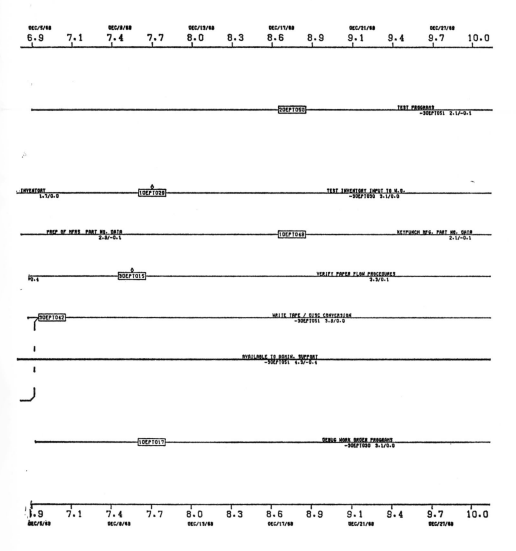

FIGURE 12:17 PLOTTED NETWORK DIAGRAM
Here is a fragment of a network that shows the possibilities that can be
obtained by harnessing a digital plotter to the computer used for network
analysis (*CalComp Limited*)

continued on next page

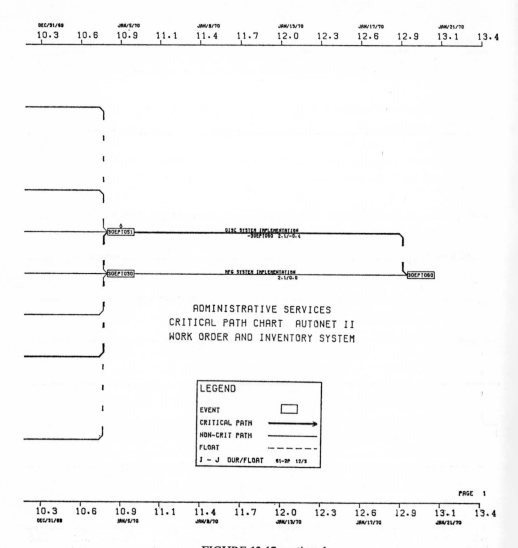

FIGURE 12:17 continued

plotter can work demands a most complicated piece of computer programming. The program occupies so much of the computer's storage capacity that the amount of storage remaining for network processing is greatly reduced. It follows that only relatively small networks can be drawn by this method, and the process is expensive. The facts are that:

1 It is almost essential to start with a hand-drawn network
2 Networks over about 400 activities become impracticable
3 Costs are very high
4 Only a limited number of plotters exist in combination with suitable computers and programs

It would seem, therefore, that the use of a digital plotter should never be considered. However, there is one particularly irksome chore that the automatic plotting system can take over, provided that the networks are not too big. Every time that a project schedule is updated, the results can be plotted out as a revised network diagram. This removes the need to update the original drawing in order to keep the logic up to date with any changes that have been made, or to record progress. The output from the plotter should be an accurate record of the true state of the network data as it actually exists on the computer file. Drafting time is saved, and there is also a reduced risk of any input error on subsequent update runs.

A small section of a plotted network diagram is shown in Figure 12:17. This was produced by a CalComp plotter, and it will be noticed that the computer has not only reproduced the network logic, but it has also converted each activity into an arrow whose length is proportional to its duration. Thus the network diagram has been drawn to a timescale. This type of presentation can be very useful, but imagine the effort that would be needed to update such a diagram without the aid of a computer and a digital plotter.

13 INTRODUCTION OF SCHEDULING TECHNIQUES

The evolution of network analysis, the development within the United Kingdom of several resource allocation programs and the availability of spare computer capacity at many bureaux have, together, provided planning engineers and project managers with the most effective combination of planning tools ever known in our industrial experience. Full multiproject resource allocation from networks can produce valid schedules from which projects can be controlled with uncanny precision. These techniques, once learned are in fact easier to use than the older graphical or manual methods, at least when the levels of detail being considered are comparable.

It is therefore very surprising to learn that the experience of some of the larger computing houses points to the fact that although time analysis of networks is fairly generally used, resource allocation still accounts only for a very small proportion of the total computing time expended on project planning. A schedule that does not take resources into account is not a complete plan. One wonders, therefore, how those companies who do not consider their resource needs at the planning stage manage to complete their projects on time and within budget. Perhaps the answer is that they do not. One interesting indication of the value of resource allocation by the computer is that it has been found that project plans produced from time analysis alone need frequent updating, to take account of activity slippages, whereas those which have been prepared from a resource levelling program tend to remain valid for the duration of a project, or at least until another project comes along to compete for the same resources.

Of course, many companies are well aware of these problems. They are not so naïve as to ignore their resource restrictions altogether. And indeed several companies have tried to implement resource scheduling from networks, but they have failed. Any reader who has attended a large conference on project planning will know that although the theoretical aspects of planning techniques are apparently well understood and accepted, their practical application is another story. Many individuals faced with the possibility of adopting a planning system that has already been proved by one company will reach the conclusion that their own company has such a completely different set of circumstances that they must either abandon any attempt at the use of a computer, or develop their own tailor-made techniques. In consequence one can identify, on the one hand, a group of planners who avoid the application of computer-based resource scheduling because they cannot personally appreciate how to operate the methods successully in their own industrial environment. At the other extreme one has seen the emergence of a number of variations on the original network theme, so that there is now a wide range of network notations from which a newcomer can choose to start his experience.

Development of new planning systems can be very expensive. This is especially true when they are associated with the writing and testing of new computer programs. It is never possible to predict accurately just how successful an entirely new planning system will prove in practice, and it must usually be accepted as a venture that will cost money and carry some element of risk. Any company who does wish to adopt the use of a computer for planning and scheduling project resources would be well advised to start from some well tried system that uses a proven program. When the planning team has gained one or two years' experience in the practical application of those established techniques it will be possible for them to make an evaluation of any shortcomings. They will then be able to make a considered decision on whether to change to another available system, develop their own methods or stay with the original system and accept any shortcomings. Very often a computer company will be willing to assist a user by modifying an existing program to provide additional facilities, but the user must first be very clear in his mind that he is asking for something that really reflects his needs accurately.

CHOOSING A SYSTEM

Before any company can make a choice between the multiplicity of techniques and systems that exist, it must carry out some sort of survey to decide which methods are most likely to serve its own particular requirements. This means that some individual within the company has got to be charged with the responsibility for making the survey, and this in turn implies that the company has got to find a person who has sufficient training and experience to enable him to make the right decision. It is logical to suppose that the individual who carries out the first study should at least be allowed to remain with the implementation stages of the operation until successful schedules are being produced. To this end, he can either be regarded as the potential manager of the routine scheduling operations, or he can be a consultant who moves on to some other assignment on the successful conclusion of his task.

An external consultancy organisation might be employed during the implementation stages in order to evaluate all possible courses of action, train permanent staff and then implement their proposals to the company's satisfaction. In general, however, the employment of external consultants is to be avoided if a person of suitable calibre can be found from within the company itself. It is relatively easy to take a man experienced in the standards and practices of his company and then train him in the use of networks and computer scheduling. It may be less desirable to rely on the services of an external expert who has no previous knowledge of the company whatsoever, and then expect him to come up with an accurate definition of the company's needs.

Choice of techniques will be influenced by personal preference to some degree. For example, in the construction industry many site teams prefer to see their schedules represented as bar charts. Even when computers are used to plan resources from networks, the foreman on the site likes to have his bar chart on his hut wall. Sometimes one has to live with this situation. There would be little point in giving a site foreman a tabulation from the computer if it is going to be rejected. Certainly efforts must be made to educate all levels of management to accept the most effective tools available, but if these tools are not accepted, then they cannot be expected to work. And one cannot force any individual to accept a system that he does not want in these enlightened days. Success in this direction can only come from persuasion and demonstration.

Assuming that a company does want to take advantage of the most effective techniques available for planning its project resources, it may have some difficulty in knowing exactly where to start, and which systems to use. As a starting point, refer to Figure 13:1. This is a chart which shows, step by step, the sequence of stages through which any project must be taken in order to arrive at an effective resource schedule. Alongside each step, possible methods are indicated. These, at least, should serve as a useful guide to companies without previous project scheduling experience.

PLANNING STEP	METHOD FOR LARGE PROJECTS	METHOD FOR VERY SIMPLE PROJECTS
1 Define the project (a) Performance (b) Cost (c) Timescale	Specification Estimates Bar chart or simple network diagram	Specification Estimates Bar chart or simple network diagram
2 Prepare work breakdown	Family tree	Family tree
3 Place all jobs in a feasible working sequence	Network diagram	Network diagram or bar chart
4 Make estimates for the duration and resource needs of each activity	By judgement, or using standard estimates. Add the results to the network diagram	By judgement. Use the estimates to decide the bar chart scale, or add them to the activities if a network is used
5 Carry out time analysis to find expected the earliest possible completion date and the float for every activity. Find the critical path	Use the network to predict completion date. Then rearrange logic if necessary to reconcile this prediction with program needs. Use remote computer terminal if available to assist. Then calculate float using a computer	By mental arithmetic from the bar chart or network
6 Resource allocation to departmental level	Use a computer. If possible, include all other projects in one multiproject calculation. This step would follow step 5 immediately, during the same computer run	Convert the network into a bar chart and arrange the activities to provide smooth usage rates for resources
7 Assign tasks to individuals	This is the job of supervision. It can be arranged from a Gantt chart (see Figure 4:9(a)).	This is the job of supervision. It can be arranged from a Gantt chart

FIGURE 13:1   THE SEVEN STEPS OF SCHEDULING

Effective schedules can only be reached after consideration of many variable factors. Each variable must be eliminated in turn, according to mathematical rather than intuitive principles. The sequence of seven steps shown here is the logical way to carry out this process. Against each step is shown the techniques most likely to produce a sound solution

Indeed, many companies who do have extensive planning experience may not appreciate the significance of the need to carry out the planning stages in their correct sequence, as shown.

The total scheduling process, which converts a project specification into detailed working plans, has to consider a large number of factors. Many of these factors are variable, and conflict one with another. For this reason, planning used to be regarded as something of an intuitive art. But intuition can be wrong. It is true that one or two individuals exist who seem to be gifted in this direction, and they may get results from their unique capabilities. However, no company wants to rely entirely upon the peculiar abilities of one mortal man. It is far better to rely on sound mathematical principles that can be understood and applied by people of average intelligence, without supernatural powers. That is what the sequence of planning steps is all about. By pursuing this careful path, each set of variables is considered separately, and they can be eliminated one at a time. Planning and scheduling have been transformed from an intuitive art into a simpler, and more definable routine.

INTEGRATED PROJECT CONTROL

Scheduling is only one stage in the total process of project control. It establishes a base from which control of progress and costs can be launched and carried through until all work has been successfully completed. The sequence of seven steps shown in Figure 13:1 is necessary, not only to eliminate unknown variables one at a time to derive a total schedule solution. These steps are also deliberately contrived to provide the most accurate basis for cost control that can be devised. In Figure 13:2 the relationship between the seven scheduling steps, project budgets and control is displayed. Together, all these considerations constitute an integrated system, where the total range of techniques employed are brought together to help ensure the successful management of the project.

It has to be recognised that the situation depicted in Figure 13:2 represents an ideal that cannot always be realised in practice. The weakest link can certainly be identified right at the start. It is often extremely difficult to uncover all the technical problems likely to be encountered in meeting the performance specification set. This can be especially true of large construction and civil engineering projects, where geological or other site conditions may provide unwelcome surprises. Of course, careful feasibility studies will

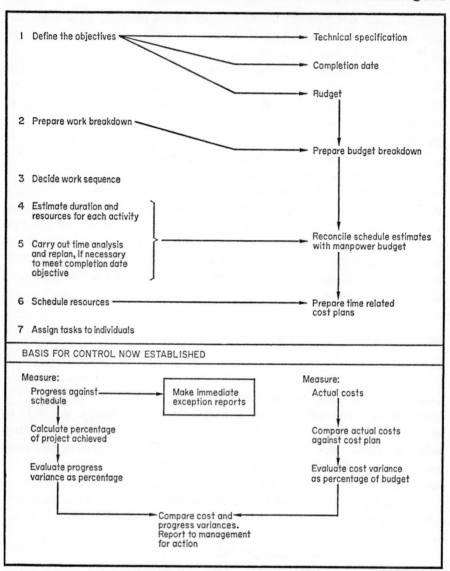

FIGURE 13:2   THE TOTAL SYSTEM OF PROJECT CONTROL
Here are the seven planning steps again, but this time they are shown in
relation to the total system of project planning and control

be made for every significant project, and these should reveal most of the major snags. But even so one hears of nightmare situations which do arise, such as the company who made a series of careful borehole explorations on a construction site, only to find subsequently that one vital hole had by chance penetrated the only boulder available for some distance around. When foundation excavations started, firm rock was limited to the boulder with the hole in it, and all around was wet running sand. Nevertheless, sceptics who criticise attempts to introduce advanced planning methods on the grounds that too many variables must intervene to wreck their implementation must admit, in general, that most breakdowns in planning occur because one or more of the seven steps was ignored or given insufficient attention.

CHOICE OF COMPUTER AND PROGRAM

Large companies may already have their own computer. This can sometimes be less of an advantage than it first appears, because management will want the computer used to its fullest extent, and the program chosen must, therefore, be one that is suitable for the computer. It may not be the best program for the job. Unfortunately, the supplier of one of the most universally used computers also supplies programs that are complicated to use and do not always give the practical results needed. Small companies, who do not own a computer, may be better placed. They can approach any bureau without restriction. Their only problem lies in making the right choice.

A word of encouragement can be given here to the small companies. No firm can be considered to be deprived of the opportunity to use a computer for project scheduling. Small projects are cheap to schedule, and the computer can be paid for on a "pay as you schedule" basis. There is no risk, and no capital investment. It is not necessary to employ programmers, or punch operators. All of these services can be provided by a bureau. As an approximate guide, scheduling of resources may add one quarter per cent to the gross factory cost of a small project, and a far smaller proportion to a large project. The returns should easily recover this investment, in terms of smoother working and fewer late deliveries.

Before the optimum computer and program can be chosen, the company has to learn the basic techniques, using whichever facilities they care to choose at first. But when experience has been gained, it is possible to write a detailed specification of the planning system needed. This might, for example, specify the maximum number of activities to be scheduled simultaneously, the number of different resource categories, types of output report and so on. Then, all available computer programs are compared by listing their characteristics in a tabulation. This tabulation forms a sort of "consumer report" along the lines of *Which* magazine. The planner uses the tabulation to highlight the system that contains most of his requirements. Any deficiencies can often be rectified by consultation with the computer company or software house, who might even alter their program free of charge.

For any company in doubt as to which computer company should be approached in the first instance, both of the organisations who processed the larger case studies for this book can be given unhesitating recommendation. BARIC Computing Services Limited operate several bureaux, and have two major resource allocation programs. One of these uses the KDF9 computer, and has some limitations in its scope. The other program is the very powerful ICL 1900 PERT package, which can carry out complex multiproject resource scheduling. *K* and *H* Business Consultants Limited are a software house who specialise in project scheduling. They offer a range of programs which can operate from CPM or precedence diagrams. Perhaps the outstanding feature of the *K* and *H* facilities is that they are cheap and easy to use as a bureau, and yet they can deal with very large projects indeed. Neither of these companies is guilty of "high pressure" salesmanship, which can be a condemning feature of some other large computer organisations.

PROVISION OF STAFF

Obviously, if a company wants to schedule its projects, then someone has to be appointed to carry out the task. Often, the man or woman chosen will be called something like "project co-ordinator" and the duties will include complete administrative responsibility for project planning and control. A planning team does not have to be large. Adoption of short-cut methods, such as those described in Chapter 12, can remove most of the drudgery and make the effort of planning a slick operation in itself. By these means, a whole company's projects can be planned by a department that comprises one supervisor and one or two assistants. Of course, bigger companies will need more people. It is not always possible to know the correct number in advance, and the installation process when scheduling is being introduced as a technique will need more effort than the routine operation. One United Kingdom company scheduled a £4 million turnover with a department of one man and one girl. Their annual scheduling budget was £10 000, which included computer charges.

The individual chosen to spearhead the introduction of the new planning systems must, obviously, be selected with some due care. It is probably going to be necessary to give special training before any degree of proficiency results. This training can either be to give the theory and practice of scheduling to a person with a good working knowledge of the industry, or it can be aimed at providing a professional planner with an adequate degree of background knowledge for the type of project being undertaken. It would be unwise to choose an individual who does not possess experience in one of these areas. Whilst it may be entirely feasible to provide training along one of the paths mentioned, one should avoid the necessity to train the newcomer in both planning techniques and industrial practice.

TRAINING

Some form of training in network analysis and project control techniques must obviously be provided for the man or woman chosen to lead the project planning function. Several professional and academic institutions arrange short seminars from time to time where the basic bones of networking can be learned. Proficiency, as in so many other pursuits, can only be acquired through practice. Certainly several projects should be scheduled from simple hand-calculated networks before more advanced techniques are used. When the planner feels sufficiently confident to attempt the use of a computer, an approach to the computer organisation chosen will almost certainly result in the provision of patient guidance and explanation in the use of their program.

Training in scheduling techniques must also be given to other project participants. Those who will be expected to contribute to the preparation of network diagrams should at least be aware of the significance of the notation. Department managers and foremen who are going to be given the resulting schedules as their control documents must have an appreciation of the difference between critical and non-critical jobs, including familiarity with the concept of float. This kind of training can be arranged within the company itself, and it should give the appointed project planner an opportunity to generate, if not enthusiasm, at least general acceptance of the principles and projected objectives.

This book has concentrated on a collection of techniques and systems that set up initial plans. But any plan must form the basis for subsequent project control. There is no point in producing a beautifully smooth resource schedule, for example, if it is not going to be transferred effectively into practice. Just as there exist methods for setting up schedules, so there are other sets of procedures that allow close monitoring and control of the resulting work. Control of modifications or variation orders is one particularly important aspect of these follow up routines (see Lock, *Project Management*, Gower Press, 1970). It was seen earlier, in Chapter 10, that the use of a computer demands special preparation of input when a schedule is updated. Staff training, therefore, has to be conducted within a syllabus which ensures that each relevant man is able to operate his own segment of the control function, including the preparation of progress reports that can be directly translated into computer input when needed.

OUTPUT REPORTS

Any project management system depends upon the existence of good lines of communication. For every command given, a feedback report should be expected. Exception reporting must also be arranged. When scheduling is performed by a computer the planner has to distribute the resulting print-outs among various individuals throughout the project. These printed reports are the control documents for scheduling. If they are not used, for any reason, communications can be said to have broken down. But they may run the risk of being ignored if too much irrelevant detail is printed out, or if the reports are badly arranged and inadequately explained.

The capacity of the computer to edit and sort data into convenient reports has been discussed in earlier chapters. This facility can be harnessed to arrange reports which carry different levels of detail according to the needs of their respective recipients. The general manager, for example, should not be forced to read long lists containing every activity in every project. His reaction on receiving a print-out several inches thick is likely to be either apathetic or openly hostile. At his level of seniority, the general manager need only be supplied with heavily edited reports that contain perhaps 1 per cent of all activities. Those activities or events chosen will usually be selected because they herald the completion or start of key activities in the company's work. At junior levels, more detailed activity lists will be needed, but these must still be very carefully edited and sorted, so that each man is given the data that he needs, and no more.

It is possible to specify certain selected events in any network diagram as "key events" or "milestones." These are chosen by the planner as points in the network which signify fairly major stages in the progress of the project. The computer is able to print reports that contain only these key events or milestones. The actual mechanics of the method depend upon the program being used, but the idea is the same in all cases. This arrangement for looking only at selected activities or events can be taken a stage further. The IBM network analysis programs which are collectively known as PMS (Project Management System) can accept milestone events at no less than nine different priority reporting levels. This means that reports could be produced for nine different levels of supervision and management, with the top management receiving only milestone events at the highest priority reporting level, whilst those on the shop floor supervision, or on a construction site, would get the greatest level of detail provided by the ninth priority milestone events. Incidentally, it is difficult to imagine a situation where such a large number of distinctions would ever become necessary. This is one symptom of computer packages that try to cater for every eventuality, and become complicated to understand in the process. The IBM PMS programs are extremely powerful, can handle very large projects, have cost and resource control facilities, and can be arranged to provide comprehensive graphical and tabular print-outs. But the system is not an easy one to use, with complex input coding sheets. It is not a system that can readily be recommended for beginners. It is also expensive if used on a bureau basis, and is perhaps better suited for users with their own computer.

A technique that is somewhat related to the use of milestones is network skeletonisation. In this case the computer actually simplifies not only the output reports, but also the network itself. The process is primarily used as a device which allows computers with limited capacity to handle very large networks by taking them in a series of segments. The general idea is that the planner first specifies a number of milestone events. Some of these milestones are so significant that they can be used as separating points, enabling the large network to be divided up into two or more subnetworks. For every two subnetworks there will obviously be at least one common linking event, and these are specially designated as "interface events." The computer proceeds to calculate a time analysis result for each subnetwork, and then it summarises the results into a reduced number of activities that link all the milestones only. Thus the number of activities within each subnetwork is substantially reduced, although the time analysis condition at each interface event is accurately determined. Then, all the summarised, or "skeletonised" subnetworks can be processed together without exceeding the maximum number of activities that the computer can handle. Skeletonisation only becomes necessary for very large projects. It depends on the computer, the program and the number of activities in the network. It is not usually necessary to skeletonise networks with less than 6000 activities, and some computer installations can handle far larger networks directly.

MULTIPROJECT SCHEDULING
AS A CONTRIBUTION TO STRATEGIC DECISION-MAKING

In recent years the availability of computing facilities has led to the development of a branch of operational research that is concerned with the use of mathematical models in order to test the possible effects of management decisions upon a company's future fortunes. For example, a company might be able to evolve a mathematical formula relating its share of a market, the price of its products, the production cost related to volume of production, and gross profits. The effect of any policy decision which directly influenced one or more of these factors could be tried out by allowing the computer to make a series of changes, and then picking out the preferred solution. In effect, a model of the company has been made within the computer. Great skill is needed, obviously, in choosing the best formula.

This terminology of "model-making" stems from the scientific practice of making small-scale models to represent situations difficult to test on a life-sized scale because of the time and expense that would be involved. One obvious example is the use of wind tunnels in order to try out the aerodynamic properties of aircraft and other vehicles. In just the same way, model making within the computer enables management to try out the possible effects of strategical decisions, without the risk and expense that must be incurred if they were to be implemented directly in the real situation. By this means, the policies best calculated to succeed can be adopted. The results from the model also allow step by step progress of the effects resulting from decision implementation to be measured against a predicted plan. Any schedule represents a model, or simulation of the real situation. This is true even of a loading chart drawn on paper. In a Gantt chart, such as that shown in Figure 4:7, the chart represents a model of the company's capacity. An even simpler version of a model is seen in a theatre box office, where a book of tickets is, in fact, no more than a model of the seating capacity for part of the theatre on a particular occasion.

Resource allocation by computer is a form of model making, or simulation. Indeed the Operational Research Society embraces a section devoted to the application of computers to network analysis problems. In Chapter 10 it was seen how the results of test schedules, calculated according to different sets of policy decisions, can lead to the adoption of the most practicable solutions. Apart from the direct control of projects, the most obvious decision-making benefits to be derived from multiproject scheduling lie in the contribution that is made to manpower planning. The total usage tables printed out by the computer for each category of resource scheduled provide management with an excellent guide to the economic manpower levels that should be authorised in company budgets and administrative planning.

Now suppose that a company has the opportunity to go all out to get one or two orders from customers who have called for tenders for major project work. And imagine that the sales force is insufficient in size to do justice to all the potential order inquiries. The company decides that their best plan of campaign is to concentrate on one of the possibilities, to make it as near a certainty as possible by producing a very professional specification and tender. If this policy were not adopted, assume in this case that no order would be gained at all. The question must now be asked "Which order do we want most?" Many factors will intervene to influence such a decision. One of these must undoubtedly be the predicted results caused by the interaction of a new project with other projects that are already making demands upon the total company resources available. A company which is conducting multiproject scheduling has the power to run test schedules as an aid to their decision-making. It is only necessary to draw up a very simple network that represents each possible new project. These networks can be restricted in size to something under ten activities if necessary. Resources and durations can be estimated in bulk. Each network is then regarded as a new subproject, and added to the actual company multiproject schedules in the computer.

By substituting each new potential project in turn, the computer can calculate complete project schedules which would show the probable effects on workload and delivery resulting. Obviously the project which fits best into a company's working capacity must be considered as having something to commend it in preference to other possible orders that are otherwise on a par commercially. However, it is not difficult to realise that schedules containing many thousands of activities from current projects are likely to be expensive items to produce in terms of computer costs. Each test run could cost hundreds of pounds. Of course, there will be occasions when costs of such magnitude are justified. But there are ways and means for avoiding them.

One method for reducing the cost of testing with model schedules lies in the provision of hammock activites. As their name implies, hammock activities are simply activities which can be added to a network between any two milestones. The hammock activity can be imagined as being slung between the two milestone events like a hammock. Hammocks are artificial activities that are added specifically for the purpose of allowing network simplification. By arranging a series of milestones at suitable intervals throughout a network, and by linking them all with hammock activities, the planner can provide the computer with a basis for reducing the effective size of the network down to the number of hammock activities. This process is not unlike skeletonisation. The total costs and resources embraced by each hammock activity are loaded on to that hammock by the computer. Of course, the resource patterns for each hammock become complex, and are no longer rate constant. But the overall size of a network can be reduced to a handful of hammock activities. The computer itself takes care of the complication associated with calculation of complex resources, and the resulting summary networks are very cheap to run, and yet are sufficiently representative of their projects to provide a sensible model against which to test new order opportunities.

SEQUENCE OF IMPLEMENTATION

In any technique, practice makes perfect. This is especially true of project planning and scheduling by network analysis. In particular, the preparation and time analysis of networks by manual methods provides a sound training from which the bigger step into computer scheduling of resources can be taken. It is important to learn the notation and principles of network logic thoroughly before attempting the introduction of a computer. Otherwise a great deal of money is going to be wasted, and there is a strong possibility that everyone who matters in the company will become disillusioned with the whole concept. It is better to start by scheduling single projects by hand, and gradually build up the scope of the networks as confidence is gained.

When resource scheduling is undertaken, start by only considering one department or trade. Do not try to schedule all the jobs being undertaken in that department. Remember that even when full multiproject scheduling is under way, there will be many miscellaneous jobs on hand that cannot be sensibly included in the computer schedules. Simply choose resource levels that represent the number of people who can be made available to work on activities that are definable. Make allowance in these availability figures for those who are going to be away sick, on annual leave, on training courses, or working on *ad hoc* tasks. Do not try to schedule these complex items, but simply reduce the departmental strength declared to the computer. These questions were highlighted in the case study of Chapter 10.

As experience is gained, the planner will learn which types of output report are likely to prove most acceptable to their recipients. At all events these reports must be kept down to their simplest size, and each must be arranged in its most convenient form. Start by scheduling the newest projects received into the company. As more and more current projects are completed, the multiproject situation will eventually be reached. When that day comes, there will be surprise at just how easy the whole process has become. The advantages of effective multiproject scheduling outweigh many times the effort and expense of its introduction. Adequate warning of overloads, effective manpower planning, delivery of projects on time and within budgets, and the abolition of panic progress meetings are all real benefits that can be expected.

INDEX